BELLY LAUGHS FOR ALL!

Adult Version
Volume 2

ROBERTA CAVA

Copyright © 2013 by Roberta Cava

All rights reserved. No part of this work covered by the copyrights hereon may be reproduced or used in any form or by any means - graphic, electronic or mechanical, including photocopying, recording, taping or information storage and retrieval systems - without the prior written permission of the publisher.

Belly Laughs for All!
Adult Version
Volume 2
Roberta Cava

Published by Cava Consulting
105 / 3 Township Drive,
Burleigh Heads, 4220, Queensland, Australia
info@dealingwithdifficultpeople.info

Discover other titles by Roberta Cava at
www.dealingwithdifficultpeople.info

National Library of Australia
Cataloguing-in-publication data:

ISBN 978-0-9923402-9-2

BOOKS BY ROBERTA CAVA

Dealing with Difficult People

(22 publishers – in 16 languages)

Dealing with Difficult Situations – at Work and at Home

Dealing with Difficult Spouses and Children

Dealing with Difficult Relatives and In-Laws

Dealing with Domestic Violence and Child Abuse

Dealing with School Bullying

Dealing with Workplace Bullying

What am I going to do with the rest of my life?

Before tying the knot – Questions couples Must ask each other Before they marry!

How Women can advance in business

Survival Skills for Supervisors and Managers

Easy Come – Hard to go – The Art of Hiring, Disciplining and Firing Employees

Human Resources at its best!

Time and Stress – Today's silent killers

Take Command of your Future – Make things Happen

Human Resources Policies and Procedures

Employee Handbook

Belly laughs for All! - Volumes 1-4

Wisdom of the World! The happy, sad and wise things in life!

That Something Special

BELLY LAUGHS FOR ALL
Volume 2
Table of Contents

Introduction	7
Chapter 1 – Animals	9
Chapter 2 – Food	29
Chapter 3 – Religious	37
Chapter 4 - At Work	81
Chapter 5 – Genie	101
Chapter 6 - Is that right?	105
Chapter 7 – Miscellaneous	141
Chapter 8 – History	169
Chapter 9 – Letter	183
Chapter 10 – Bar	193
Chapter 11 - High technology	201
Chapter 12 - Rules for living	211
Chapter 13 - On the serious side	219
Conclusion	227

INTRODUCTION

This book is a continuation of Volume I and covers humour in different areas, so there's no repetition. These four volumes are unlike any others I have written. Most of my books relate to how to deal with difficult people and situations. I had been feeling very depressed after writing my last three books - which focused around bullying - at home, at school and at work. This was a lovely change from that disturbing and depressing research.

I had collected jokes for years and enjoyed reading them whenever I felt down-in-the-dumps. This is what stimulated me to write a book on humour. It was soon evident that I had too many jokes for just one volume, hence wrote Volume 1, 2, 3 and 4. These books were meant for adult audiences and **are not suitable for children.**

I hope you enjoy this volume enough to want to obtain Volume 1, 3 and 4.

CHAPTER 1

ANIMALS

Jesus:

Late one night, a burglar broke into a house that he thought was empty. He tiptoed through the living room but suddenly he froze in his tracks when he heard a loud voice say: *'Jesus is watching you!'*

Silence returned to the house, so the burglar crept forward again. *'Jesus is watching you!'* the voice boomed again. The burglar stopped dead again. He was frightened. Frantically, he looked all around. In a dark corner, he spotted a bird cage and in the cage was a parrot. He asked the parrot, *'Was that you who said Jesus is watching me?'*

'Yes,' said the parrot.

The burglar breathed a sigh of relief and then asked the parrot, *'What's your name?'*

'Clarence,' said the bird.

'That's a dumb name for a parrot,' sneered the burglar. *'What idiot named you Clarence?'*

The parrot replied, *'The same idiot who named the Rottweiler Jesus.'*

Garbage Disposal:

We've all had trouble with our animals, but I don't think anyone can top this one:

Calling in sick to work makes me uncomfortable. No matter how legitimate my excuse, I always get the feeling that my boss thinks I'm lying. On one recent occasion, I had a valid reason but lied anyway, because the truth was just too darned humiliating. I simply mentioned that I had sustained a head injury and I hoped I would feel up to coming in the next day. By then, I reasoned, I could think up a doozy to explain the bandage on the top of my head.

The accident occurred mainly because I had given in to my wife's wishes to adopt a cute little kitty. Initially, the new acquisition was no problem then one morning, I was taking my shower after breakfast when I heard my wife, Deb, call out to me from the kitchen. *'Honey! The garbage disposal is dead again. Please come reset it.'*

'You know where the button is,' I protested through the shower pitter-patter and steam. *'Reset it yourself!'*

'But I'm scared!' she persisted. *'What if it starts going and sucks me in?'* There was a meaningful pause and then, *'C'mon, it'll only take you a second.'*

So out I came, dripping wet and butt naked, hoping that my silent outraged nudity would make a statement about how I perceived her behaviour as extremely cowardly. Sighing loudly, I squatted down and stuck my head under the sink to find the button. It is the last action I remember performing.

It struck without warning and without any respect to my circum-stances. No, it wasn't the hexed disposal, drawing me into its gnashing metal teeth. It was our new kitty that discovered the fascinating dangling objects she spied hanging between my legs. She had been poised around the corner and stalked me as I reached under the sink. And, at the precise moment when I was most vulnerable, she leapt at the toys I unwittingly offered and snagged them with her needle-like claws. I lost all rational thought to control orderly bodily movements, blindly rising at a violent rate of speed, with the full weight of a kitten hanging from my masculine region.

Wild animals are sometimes faced with a 'fight or flight' syndrome. Men, in this predicament, choose only the 'flight' option. I know this from experience. I was fleeing straight up into the air when the sink and cabinet bluntly and forcefully impeded my ascent. The impact knocked me out cold.

When I awoke, my wife and the paramedics stood over me. Now there are not many things in this life worse than finding oneself lying on the kitchen floor butt naked in front of a group of 'been-there, done-that' paramedics. Even worse, having been fully briefed by my wife, the paramedics were all snorting loudly as they tried to conduct their work, all the while trying to suppress their hysterical laughter ... and not succeeding.

Somehow I lived through it all. A few days later I finally made it back in to the office, where colleagues tried to coax an explanation out of me about my head injury. I kept silent, claiming it was too painful to talk about, which it was.

'What's the matter?' They all asked, *'Cat got your tongue?'* If they only knew!

Why is it that only the women laugh at this?

The Parrot

David received a parrot for his birthday. The parrot was fully-grown with a bad attitude and worse vocabulary. Every other word was an expletive. Those that weren't expletives, were to say the least, rude. David tried hard to change the bird's attitude and was constantly saying polite words, playing soft music, anything he could think of the try to set a good example.

Nothing worked. He yelled at the bird and the bird yelled back. He shook the bird and the bird just got angrier and ruder. Finally, in a moment of desperation, David put the parrot in the freezer. For a few minutes he heard the bird squawk and kick and scream - then suddenly, there was quiet. Not a sound for half a minute.

David was frightened that he might have hurt the bird and quickly opened the freezer door. The parrot calmly stepped out onto David's extended arm and said, *'I believe I may have offended you with my rude language and actions. I will endeavour at once to correct my behaviour. I am truly sorry and beg your forgiveness.'*

David was astonished at the bird's change in attitude and was about to ask what had made such a dramatic change when the parrot continued, *'May I ask what the chicken did?'*

A magician was working on a cruise ship in the Caribbean. The audience would be different each week, so the magician allowed himself to do the same tricks over and over again. There was only one problem: the captain's parrot saw the shows each week and began to understand how the magician did every trick. Once he understood, he started shouting in the middle of the show:

'Look, it's not the same hat!'
'Look, he's hiding the flowers under the table.'
'Hey, why are all the cards the Ace of Spades?'

The magician was furious but couldn't do anything. It was, after all, the captain's parrot.

One day the ship had an accident and sank. The magician found himself in the middle of the ocean floating on a piece of wood with the parrot (of course). They stared at each other with hate, but did not utter a word. This went on for a day, then another and another. After a week the parrot finally said, *'Okay, I give up. Where's the boat?'*

A man is browsing in a pet shop and sees a parrot sitting on a little perch. It doesn't have any feet or legs. The man says aloud, *'Jeesh, I wonder what happened to this parrot?'*

The parrot says, *'I was born this way. I'm a defective parrot.'*

'Holy crap,' the guy replies. *'You actually understood and answered me!'*

'I got every word,' says the parrot. *'I happen to be a highly intelligent and thoroughly educated bird.'*

'Oh yeah?' the guy asks, *'Then answer this - how do you hang onto your perch without any feet?'*

'Well,' says the parrot, *'this is very embarrassing, but since you asked - I wrap my weenie around this wooden bar like a little hook. You can't see it because of my feathers.'*

'Wow,' says the guy, *'You really can understand and speak English can't you?'*

'Actually, I speak both Spanish and English and I can converse with reasonable competence on almost any topic - politics, religion, sports, physics and philosophy. I'm especially good at ornithology. You really ought to buy me. I'd be a great companion.'

The guy looks at the $20,000 price tag, *'Sorry, I just can't afford that.'*

'Pssssssssst,' says the parrot, *'I'm defective, so the truth is nobody wants me because I don't have any feet. You can probably get me for $20; why don't you make an offer?'*

The man offers $20 and walks out with the parrot. Weeks go by. The parrot is sensational. He has a great sense of humour; he's interesting, he's a great pal, he understands everything, he sympathises and he's insightful. The guy is delighted.

One day, the guy comes home from work and the parrot goes, *'Pssssssssst,'* and motions him over with one wing, *'I don't know if I should tell you this or not, but it's about your wife and the postman.'*

'What are you talking about?' asks the guy.

'When the postman delivered the mail today, your wife greeted him at the door in a sheer black nightie.'

'What???' the guy asks incredulously. *'Then what happened?'*

'Well, then the postman came into the house and lifted up her nightie and began petting her all over.' reported the parrot.

'*NO!*' he exclaimed. '*And she let him?*'

'*Yes. Then he continued taking off the nightie! He got down on his knees and began to kiss her all over.*'

Then the frantic guy demands, '*And then what happened?*'

'*Damned if I know. I got a hard on and fell off my perch!*'

A Canadian Hunter

An 86-year-old man went to his doctor for his quarterly check-up. The doctor asked him how he was feeling, and the 86-year-old said, '*Things are great and I've never felt better. I now have a 20 yr-old bride who is pregnant with my child. So what do you think about that Doc?*'

The doctor considered his question for a minute and then began to tell a story.

'*I have an older friend, much like you, who is an avid hunter and never misses a season. One day he was setting off to go hunting. In a bit of a hurry, he accidentally picked up his walking cane instead of his gun. As he neared a lake, he came across a very large male beaver sitting at the water's edge. He realised he'd left his gun at home and so he couldn't shoot the magnificent creature. Out of habit he raised his cane, aimed it at the animal as if it were his favourite hunting rifle and went 'bang, bang'.*

'*Miraculously, two shots rang out and the beaver fell over dead. Now, what do you think of that?*' asked the doctor.

The 86-year-old said, '*Logic would strongly suggest that somebody else pumped a couple of rounds into that beaver.*'

The doctor replied, '*My point exactly.*'

Zebra

There was this zebra that had lived her entire life in a zoo and was getting on a bit, so the zoo keeper decided as a treat that she could spend her final years in bliss on a farm. The zebra was so excited, she got to see this huge space with green grass, hills and trees and all those strange animals. She saw a big fat weird-looking brown thing and ran up to it all excited, '*Hi, I'm a zebra. What are you?*'

'*I'm a cow.*'

'*Right, right. What do you do?*'

'*I make milk for the farmer.*'

'*Cool.*' The zebra then saw this funny-looking white thing and ran over to it. '*Hi, I'm a zebra. What are you?*

'*I'm a chicken.*'

'*Oh right. What do you do?*'
'*I make eggs for the farmer.*'
'*Right, great, see ya around.*' Then the zebra saw this very handsome beast that looked almost exactly like her without the stripes. She ran over to it and said, '*Hi, I'm a zebra. What are you?*'
'*I'm a stallion,*' said the stallion.
'*Wow,*' said the zebra. '*What do you do?*'
'*Take off your pyjamas and I'll show you.*'

Animals are funny:

Did you ever notice that when you blow in a dog's face, he gets mad at you, but when you take him on a car ride he sticks his head out the window?

Did you ever walk into a room and forget why you walked in? I think that's how dogs spend their lives.

I ask people why they have deer heads on their walls. They always say because it's such a beautiful animal. There you go. I think my wife is attractive, but I have photographs of her.

A lady came up to me on the street and pointed at my suede jacket. '*You know a cow was murdered for that jacket.*' she sneered. I replied in a psychotic tone, '*I didn't know there were any witnesses. Now I'll have to kill you too.*'

Why does Sea World have a seafood restaurant? I was half way through my fish burger when I realised, '*Oh my God. I could be eating a slow learner.*'

What do you call a cow that lost its calf? Decaffeinated.
How can you tell when a moth farts? He flies in a straight line for a couple of seconds.

What has four legs and an arm? A happy pit-bull.

What's the difference between a porcupine and a BMW? A porcupine has the pricks on the outside.

Why don't bunnies make noise when they have sex? Because they have cotton balls.

What did one doe say to the other doe as they walked out of the woods? '*I'll never do that for two bucks again!*'

Why don't chickens wear knickers? Because their peckers are on their face!

What do you get when you have a cow and a duck? Milk and quackers.

Why does an elephant have four feet? Because it wouldn't work with 6 inches.

How many flies does it take to screw in a light bulb? Two, but how are you gonna get them in there?

Why do whales make such great lovers? Because they have a hole in the back of their head they can breathe out of.

What do you call a cow with three legs? Lean beef.

What do you call a cow with no legs? Ground beef.

What do elephants use for tampons? Sheep.

What did one Florida alligator say to another alligator? *'This airplane food isn't so bad.'*

A three-legged dog walks into a saloon in the Old West. He saddles up to the bar and announces, *'I'm looking for the man who shot my paw.'*

A mother mouse and a baby mouse were walking along when suddenly a cat attacks them. The mother mouse shouts, *'Bark!'* and the cat runs away. The mother mouse says to her baby, *'Now do you see why it's important to learn a foreign language?'*

The Bat:

A vampire bat came flapping in from the night covered in fresh blood and parked himself on the roof of the cave to get some sleep. Pretty soon, all the other bats smelled the blood and began hassling him about where he got it. He told them to knock it off and let him get some sleep - but they persisted in hassling him to no end until he finally gave in.

'Okay!' he said with exasperation, *'follow me,'* and flew out of the cave with hundreds bats following close behind him. Down through the valley they went, across the river and into the deep forest. Finally he slowed down and all the other bats excitedly gathered around him.

'Do you see that tree over there?' he asked.

'Yes, yes, yes!' screamed the bats in unison.

'Good,' said the first bat, *'because I didn't!'*

How to wash a cat:

1. Thoroughly clean the toilet.
2. Add the required amount of shampoo to the toilet water and have both lids lifted.
3. Obtain the cat and soothe it while you carry it towards the bathroom. In one smooth movement, put the cat in the toilet and close both lids. (You might have to sit or stand on the lid).

4. Caution: Do not let any part of your body get too close to the edge as its paws will be reaching out for any purchase they can find. The cat will self-agitate and make suds. Never mind the noise coming from your toilet - the cat is actually enjoying this.
5. Flush the toilet three or four times. This will provide a 'power-wash and rinse' which has been found to be quite effective.
6. Have someone open the door to the outside and ensure there are no people between the toilet and the outside.
7. Stand behind the toilet as far as you can and quickly lift both lids.
8. The now clean cat will rocket out of the toilet and run outside where it will dry itself.

What is a Cat?

Cats do what they want, when they want. They rarely listen to you. They're totally unpredictable. They whine when they're not happy. When you want to play, they want to be left alone. When you want to be alone, they want to play. They expect you to cater to their very whim. They're moody. They leave their hair everywhere. They drive you nuts.

Conclusion: Cats are little, tiny women in cheap fur coats!

What is a Dog?

Dogs lie around all day, sprawled on the most comfortable piece of furniture in the house. They can hear a package of food opening half a block away, but they can't hear you when you're in the same room. They growl when they are not happy. When you want to play, they want to play. When you want to be alone, they want to play. They are great at begging. They will love you forever if you rub their tummies. They leave their toys everywhere. They do disgusting things with their mouths and then try to give you a kiss.

Conclusion: They are little men in fur coats.

Beware of Dog:

Upon entering the little country store, the stranger noticed a sign saying Danger! Beware of Dog! posted on the glass door. Inside he noticed a harmless old dog asleep on the floor beside the cash register.

He asked the store manager, *'Is that the dog folks are supposed to beware of?'*

'Yep, that's him,' he replied.

The stranger couldn't help but be amused. *'That certainly doesn't look like a dangerous dog to me. Why in the world would you post that sign?'*

'Because,' the owner replied, *'before I posted that sign, people kept tripping over him.'*

A Dog called Sex:

Everybody I know who has a dog usually calls him 'Rover' or 'Spot.' I called mine Sex. Now, Sex has been very embarrassing to me. When I went to the City Hall to renew the dog's license, I told the clerk that I would like a license for Sex. He said, *'I would like to have one too!'* Then I said, *'But she is a dog!'* He said he didn't care what she looked like. I said, *'You don't understand. I've had sex since I was nine years old.'* He replied, *'You must have been a strong boy.'*

When I decided to get married, I told the minister that I would like to have Sex at the wedding. He told me to wait until after the wedding was over. I said, *'But, Sex has played a big part of my life and my whole world revolves around Sex.'* He said he didn't want to hear about my personal life and would not marry us in his church. I told him everyone would enjoy having Sex at the wedding. The next day we were married at the Justice of the Peace. My family was barred from that church from then on.

When my wife and I went on our honeymoon, I took the dog with me. When we checked into the motel, I told the clerk that I wanted a room for my wife and me and a special room for Sex. He said that every room in the motel is a place for sex. I said, *'You don't understand. Sex keeps me awake at night.'* The clerk replied, *'Me too!'*

One day I entered Sex in a contest, but before the competition began, the dog ran away. Another contestant asked me why I was just looking around. I told him that I was going to have Sex in a contest. He said that I should have sold my own tickets. *'You don't understand,'* I said, *'I hoped to have Sex on TV.'* He called me a show off.

When my wife and I separated, we went to court to fight for custody of the dog. I said, *'Your honour, I had Sex before I was married, but Sex left me after I was married.'* The Judge said, *'Me too!'*

Last night Sex ran off again. I spent hours looking all over for her. A cop came over and asked me what I was doing in the alley at 4:00 am. I said, *'I'm looking for Sex.'*

My case comes up next Thursday. Well, now I've been thrown in jail, been divorced and had more troubles with that dog than I ever foresaw. Why just the other day when I went for my first session with the psychiatrist, she asked me, *'What seems to be the trouble?'* I replied, *'Sex has been my best friend all my life, but now it has left me forever. I couldn't live any longer I'm so lonely.'* And the doctor said, *'Look, mister, you should understand that sex isn't a man's best friend. Go get yourself a dog.'*

Smart Dogs

Four men were bragging about how smart their dogs were. One was an engineer, the second man was an accountant, the third man was a chemist and the fourth was a government worker.

To show off, the engineer called to his dog. *'T-Square, do your stuff.'* T-Square trotted over to a desk, took out some paper and a pen and promptly drew a circle, a square and a triangle. Everyone agreed that was pretty smart.

But the accountant said his dog could do better. He called to his dog and said, *'Spreadsheet, do your stuff.'* Spreadsheet went out to the kitchen and returned with a dozen cookies. He divided them into four equal piles of three cookies each. Everyone agreed that was pretty good.

But the chemist said his dog could do better. He called to his dog and said, *'Measure, do your stuff.'* Measure got up, walked over to the fridge, took out a quart of milk, got a ten ounce glass from the cupboard and poured exactly eight ounces without spilling a drop. Everyone agreed that was pretty impressive.

Then government worker called to his dog and said, *'Coffee Break, do your stuff.'* Coffee Break jumped to his feet, ate the cookies, drank the milk, had a shit on the paper, sexually assaulted the other three dogs, claimed he injured his back while doing so, filed a grievance report for unsafe working conditions, put in for workers compensation and went home for the rest of the day on sick leave. They all agreed that was brilliant.

Turtles:

Three turtles, Joe, Steve and Poncho decided to go on a picnic, so Joe packed the picnic basket with cookies, bottled sodas and sandwiches. The trouble was the picnic site was ten miles away, so the turtles took ten days to get there. By the time they arrived, everyone was exhausted. Joe took out the sodas and said, *'All right, Steve, gimme the bottle opener.'*

'I didn't bring the bottle opener,' Steve says. *'I thought you packed it.'*

So the turtles are stuck ten miles away from home without soda.

Joe and Steve beg Poncho to turn back home and retrieve it, but Poncho flatly refuses, knowing that they'll eat everything by the time he gets back. Somehow, after about two hours, the turtles manage to convince Poncho to go, swearing on their great-grand turtles' graves that they won't touch the food.

So Poncho set off down the road, slowly and steadily. Twenty days pass, but no Poncho. Joe and Steve were very hungry and puzzled, but a promise was a promise. Another day passed and still no Poncho, but a promise was a promise. After three more days pass without Poncho in sight, Steve starts getting restless. 'I need food!' he exclaimed with a hint of dementia in his voice.

'No!' Joe retorts. *'We promised.'*

Five more days pass. Joe realised that Poncho probably skipped out to the Burger King down the road, so the two turtles weakly lift the lid, get a sandwich and open their mouths to eat. But then, right at that instant, Poncho popped out behind a rock and said, *'Just for that, I'm not going!'*

Randy:

A farmer has about 200 hens, but no rooster and he wants chicks. So he goes down the road to the next farmer and asks if he has a rooster. The other farmer says, *'Yeah, I've got a great rooster, named Randy; he'll service every chicken you've got - no problem.'*

Well, Randy the rooster cost a lot of money, but the farmer decides he'd be worth it. So he buys Randy and takes him home. He set him down in the barnyard and gave the rooster a pep talk, *'Randy, I want you to pace yourself now. You've got a lot of chickens to service here and you cost me a lot of money so I'll need you to do a good job. So, take your time and have some fun,'* said the farmer with a chuckle.

He pointed towards the hen house and Randy took off like a shot. Wham! He nailed every hen in there three or four times and the farmer is just shocked! He then ran out of the hen house and saw a flock of geese down by the lake. Wham! He got all the geese as well.

Randy's up in the pigpen. He's in with the cows. Randy is jumping every animal the farmer owns. The farmer is distraught, worried that his expensive rooster won't even last the day.

Sure enough, the farmer goes to bed and wakes up the next day to find Randy lying in the middle of the yard on his back with his feet in the air. Buzzards are circling overhead. The farmer, saddened by the loss of such an animal, shakes his head and says, *'Oh Randy, I told you to pace yourself. I tried to get you to slow down. Now look what you've done to yourself.'*

Randy opens one eye, nods towards the sky and says, *'Shhh, they're getting closer ...'*

A farmer went out one day and bought a brand new stud rooster for his chicken coop. The new rooster struts over to the old rooster and says, *'Okay old fart, time for you to retire.'*

The old rooster replies, *'Come on, surely you can't handle all of these chickens. Look what it's done to me. Can't you just let me have the two old hens over there in the corner?'*

The young rooster replies, *'Beat it. You're washed up and I'm taking over.'*

The old rooster says, *'I'll tell you what, young stud. I will race you around the farmhouse. Whoever wins gets the exclusive domain over the entire chicken coop.'*

The young rooster laughs, *'You know you don't stand a chance, old man. So just to be fair, I'll give you a head start.'*

The old rooster takes off running. About fifteen seconds later the young rooster takes off running after him. They round the front porch of the farmhouse and the young rooster has closed the gap. He's only about five feet behind the old rooster and gaining fast. The farmer, meanwhile, is sitting in his usual spot on the front porch when he sees the roosters running by. He grabs his shotgun and - Boom - he blows the young rooster to bits. The farmer sadly shakes his head and says, *'Darned - that's the third gay rooster I've bought this month.'*

The moral of this story is: *'Don't mess with the old farts - age, skill and treachery will always overcome youth and arrogance!'*

The Monkey:

A police officer came upon a terrible wreck where the driver and passenger had been killed. As he looked upon the wreckage, a little monkey came out of the bush and hopped around the crashed car. The officer looked at the monkey and said, *'I wish you could talk.'*

The monkey looked up at him and shook his head up and down. *'You can understand what I'm saying?'* asked the officer.

Again, the monkey shook his head up and down.

'Well, did you see this?'

'Yes,' motioned the monkey.

'What happened?'

The monkey pretended to have a can in his hand and turned it up by his mouth. *'They were drinking?'* asked the officer.

'Yes.' The monkey motioned.

'What else?'

The monkey pinched his fingers together and held them to his mouth. *'They were smoking marijuana?'*

'Yes.' The monkey confirmed.

'What else?'

The monkey motioned, *'Screwing.'* as he gyrated his hips.

'They were screwing, too?' asked the astounded officer.

'Yes.'

'Now wait, you're saying your owners were drinking, smoking and screwing before they wrecked the car?'

'Yes.'

'What were you doing during all of this?'

'Driving,' motioned the monkey.

The Woodpeckers:

An Alaskan woodpecker and a Texas woodpecker were in Alaska arguing about which state had the toughest trees to peck. The Alaskan woodpecker said that they had a tree that no woodpecker could peck.

The Texas woodpecker challenged him and was able to peck a hole in the tree with no problem. The Alaskan woodpecker was in awe.

The Texas woodpecker challenged the Alaskan woodpecker to peck a tree in Texas that no woodpecker had been able to peck successfully. The Alaskan wood-pecker expressed confidence that he could do it.

After flying to Texas and successfully pecking the tree in Texas, the two woodpeckers couldn't figure out why the Texas woodpecker was able to peck the Alaskan tree and the Alaskan woodpecker was able to peck the Texan tree when neither was able to peck the tree in their own state.

After thinking for some time, they both came to the same conclusion that ... *'Your pecker is always harder when you're away from home.'*

Garden snakes can be dangerous...

Green Tree Snakes (Dendrolaphis punctulata) can be dangerous.

Yes, tree snakes or grass snakes, not brown snakes or taipans. Here's why:

A couple in Townsville, Australia had a lot of potted plants. During a recent cold winter (for Townsville that is!) the wife was bringing some of the valued tender ones indoors to protect them from the cold night.

It turned out that a little green tree snake was hidden in one of the plants. When it had warmed up, it slithered out and the wife saw it go under the lounge. She let out a very loud scream.
The husband (who was taking a shower) ran out into the living room naked to see what the problem was. She told him there was a snake under the lounge. He got down on the floor on his hands and knees to look for it.

About that time the family dog came and cold-nosed him on the behind. He thought the snake had bitten him, so he screamed and fell over on the floor.

His wife thought he had had a heart attack, so she covered him up, told him to lie still and called an ambulance. The paramedics rushed in, would not listen to his protests, loaded him on the stretcher and started carrying him out.

About that time, the snake came out from under the lounge and the paramedic saw it and dropped his end of the stretcher. That's when the man broke his leg and why he was in the hospital.

The wife still had the problem of the snake in the house, so she called on a neighbour who volunteered to capture the snake. He armed himself with a rolled-up newspaper and began poking under the lounge. Soon he decided it was gone and told the woman, who sat down on the lounge in relief. But while relaxing, her hand dangled in between the cushions, where she felt the snake wriggling around. She screamed and fainted, the snake rushed back under the lounge.

The neighbour, seeing her lying there passed out, tried to use CPR to revive her. The neighbour's wife, who had just returned from shopping at Woolies, saw her husband's mouth on the woman's mouth and slammed her husband in the back of the head with a bag of canned goods, knocking him out and cutting his scalp to a point where it needed stitches.

The noise woke the woman from her dead faint and she saw her neighbour lying on the floor with his wife bending over him, so she assumed that the snake had bitten him. She went to the kitchen and got a small bottle of whiskey and began pouring it down the man's throat.

By now, the police had arrived. They saw the unconscious man, smelled the whiskey and assumed that a drunken fight had occurred. They were about to arrest them all, when the women tried to explain how it all happened over a little garden snake!
The police called another ambulance, which took away the neighbour and his sobbing wife.

Now, the little snake again crawled out from under the lounge and one of the policemen drew his gun and fired at it. He missed the snake and hit the leg of the end table. The table fell over, the lamp on it shattered and as the bulb broke, it started a fire in the curtains.

The other policeman tried to beat out the flames and fell through the window into the yard on top of the family dog that, startled, jumped out and raced into the street, where an oncoming car swerved to avoid it and smashed into the parked police car.
Meanwhile, neighbours saw the burning curtains and called in the fire brigade. The firemen had started raising the fire ladder when they were halfway down the street. The rising ladder tore out the overhead wires, put out the power and disconnected the telephones in a ten-square city block area (but they did get the house fire out).

Time passed! The snake was caught and both men were discharged from the hospital, the house was repaired, the dog came home, the police acquired a new car and all was right with their world.

A while later they were watching TV and the weatherman announced a cold snap for that night. The wife asked her husband if he thought they should bring in their plants for the night. And that's when he shot her.

Bear Warning:

The Department of Fish and Wildlife is advising hikers, hunters and fishermen to take extra precautions and keep alert of bears while in the field. We advise that people wear noisy little bells on their clothing so as not to startle bears that aren't expecting them. We also advise outdoorsmen to carry pepper spray with them in case of an encounter with a bear.

It's also a good idea to watch out for fresh signs of bear activity. People should recognise the difference between black bear and grizzly bear droppings. Black bear droppings are smaller and contain lots of berries and squirrel fur. Grizzly bear droppings have little bells in them and smell like pepper spray.

Giraffe Test

There are 4 questions. Don't miss one.

1. How do you put a giraffe into a refrigerator?
   Stop and think about it and decide on your answer before reading more.
   The correct answer is: Open the refrigerator; put in the giraffe and close the door. This question tests whether you tend to do simple things in an overly complicated way.
2. How do you put an elephant into a refrigerator?
   Did you say, *'Open the refrigerator, put in the elephant and close the refrigerator?'*
   Wrong answer.
   Correct Answer: Open the refrigerator, take out the giraffe, put in the elephant and close the door. This tests your ability to think through the repercussions of your previous actions.
3. The Lion King is hosting an animal conference. All the animals attend except one. Which animal does not attend?
   Correct Answer: The Elephant. The elephant is in the refrigerator. You just put him in there. This tests your memory. Okay, even if you did not answer the first three questions correctly, you still have one more chance to show your true abilities.
4. There is a river you must cross but it is used by crocodiles and you do not have a boat. How do you manage it?
   Correct Answer? You jump into the river and swim across. Have you not been listening? All the crocodiles are attending the Animal Meeting. This tests whether you learn quickly from your mistakes.

According to Anderson Consulting Worldwide, around 90% of the Professionals they tested got all questions wrong, but many preschoolers got several correct answers. Anderson Consulting says this conclusively proves the theory that most professionals do not have the brains of a four-year-old.

The Frog:

A frog goes into a bank and approaches the teller. He can see from her nameplate that her name is Patricia Whack.

'*Miss Whack, I'd like to get a $30,000 loan to take a holiday.*'

Patty looks at the frog in disbelief and asks his name.

The frog says his name is Kermit Jagger, his dad is Mick Jagger and that it's okay, he knows the bank manager. Patty explains that he will need to secure the loan with some collateral.

The frog says, '*Sure. I have this,*' and produces a tiny porcelain elephant, about an inch tall, bright pink and perfectly formed.

Very confused, Patty explains that she'll have to consult with the bank manager and disappears into a back office. She finds the manager and says, '*There's a frog called Kermit Jagger out there who claims to know you and wants to borrow $30,000 and he wants to use this as collateral.*'

She holds up the tiny pink elephant. '*I mean, what in the world is this?*' (Wait for it)

The bank manager looks back at her and says, '*It's a knickknack, Patty Whack. Give the frog a loan. His old man's a Rolling Stone.*'

You're singing it, aren't you? Yeah, I know you are ...

Never take life too seriously! Come on now, you grinned, I know you did!!!

The Cow, the Ant and the Old Fart

A cow, an ant and an old fart are debating on who is the greatest of the three of them.

The cow said, '*I give 20 quarts of milk every day and that's why I am the greatest!*'

The ant said, '*I work day and night, summer and winter, I can carry 52 times my own weight and that's why I am the greatest!*'

Why are you scrolling down? It's your turn to say something.

The Engineer and the Frog

An engineer finds a frog that calls out to him, *'If you kiss me, I'll turn into a beautiful princess.'*

He picks up the frog and puts it in his pocket. The frog speaks up again and says, *'If you kiss me and turn me back into a beautiful princess, I will stay with you for one week.'*

The engineer takes the frog out of his pocket, smiles at it and returns it to his pocket. The frog then cries out, *'If you kiss me and turn me back, I'll stay with you for a month and do whatever you say!'*

Again the engineer takes the frog out, smiles and puts it back into his pocket. Finally, the frog asks, *'What's the matter? I've told you I'm a beautiful princess; I'll stay with you for a month and do whatever you say. What more do you want?'*

The engineer says, *'Look, I'm an engineer. I don't have time for a girlfriend, but a talking frog – now that's cool!'*

The old snake

An old snake goes to see his optometrist. *'I need something for my eyes,'* he hisses. *'I can't see very well these days.'*

The optometrist fixes him up with a pair of glasses and tells him to come back in two weeks to see how they went. After two weeks and he returns to say he's very depressed.

'What's the problem? Didn't the glasses help you?' asks the optometrist.

'The glasses are fine,' the snake replies. *'But I just discovered I've been living with a water hose for two years!'*

Is she in the mood?

Alpacas have a unique system in that a week after mating you can bring the male back to the female. If she sits (alpacas mate sitting) she's not pregnant. But if she *spits* in the first week, she's ovulated and if she spits in the second week, she's pregnant.

It's called a spit-off and it's as reliable as an ultrasound.

Stuttering

A teacher is explaining biology to her fourth grade students. *'Human beings are the only animals that stutter,'* she said.

A little girl raises her hand. *'I had a kitty-cat who stuttered.'*

The teacher, knowing how precious some of these stories could become, asked the girl to describe the situation.

'Well,' she began, 'I was in the back yard with my kitty and the Rottweiler that lives next door got a running start and before we knew it, he jumped over the fence into our yard!'

'That must've been scary,' said the teacher.

'It sure was,' said the little girl.

'My kitty raised her back, went 'Fffff! Fffff! Fffff! but before she could say 'F**k-off! the Rottweiler ate her!

The teacher had to leave the room.

The penguins

A man was driving down the road with twenty penguins in the back seat. The police stopped him and said that he can't drive around with the penguins in the car and should take them to the zoo. The man agreed and drove off.

The next day the same man is driving down the road with twenty penguins in the back seat again. He is again stopped by the same police officer who says, 'Hey! I thought I told you to take those penguins to the zoo.'

The man replied, 'I did. Today, I'm taking them to the movies.'

Locked in love

An elderly spinster who was a dog lover agreed to look after and house her neighbour's dog while they went on their holidays. The only problem was that the spinsters own dog was a bitch that was 'in heat' and the neighbour's dog was a male. Nevertheless she had a large house and she was able to keep the two dogs apart.

As she lay in her bed drifting off to sleep, the spinster was suddenly awakened by an awful howling and moaning sound from downstairs. She rushed downstairs to find the dogs locked together - mating. The dogs were in obvious pain howling but unable to disengage. Try as she might she could not part them and she was perplexed as what to do next.

Though it was late she reluctantly phoned the Vet and after a few rings a rather grumpy voice of the Vet answered the phone. The spinster explained the problem.

The Vet said. 'I want you to take the phone to the dogs and place it down alongside them. I will then phone your number back and the noise of the telephone ringing should make the male dog lose his erection and be able to withdraw from the bitch.'

'Oh,' said the spinster ... 'Do you think that will work?'

'*Well,*' the Vet replied, *'IT JUST WORKED ON ME !!!!!!'*

CHAPTER 2
FOOD JOKES

Rules for eating chocolate:

1. If you've got melted chocolate all over your hands, you're eating too slowly.
2. Chocolate covered raisins, cherries orange slices and strawberries all count as fruit, so eat as many as you want.
3. The problem: how to get one kilo of chocolate home from the store in a hot car. The solution: Eat it in the parking lot.
4. Diet tip: Eat a chocolate bar before each meal. It'll take the edge off your appetite and you'll eat less.
5. A nice box of chocolates can provide your total daily intake of calories in one place. Isn't that handy?
6. If you can't eat all your chocolate, it will keep in the freezer. But if you can't eat all your chocolate, what's wrong with you?
7. All calories are an issue; store your chocolate on top of the fridge. Calories are afraid of heights and they will jump out of the chocolate to protect themselves.
8. If I eat equal amounts of dark chocolate and white chocolate, is that a balanced diet? Don't they actually counteract each other?
9. Money talks. Chocolate sings.
10. Chocolate has many preservatives. Preservatives make you look younger.
11. Why is there no such organisation as Chocoholics Anonymous - Because no one wants to quit.
12. If not for chocolate there would be no need for control top pantyhose. An entire garment industry would be devastated.
13. Put 'eat chocolate' at the top of your list of things to do today. That way, at least you'll get one thing done!

Chilli Cook-off

Recently, I was honoured to be selected to be a judge at a chilli cook-off (because no one else wanted to do it.) Also the original person called in sick at the last moment and I happened to be standing at the judge's table asking for directions to the beer wagon when the call came. The other two judges assured me that the chilli wouldn't be all that spicy and besides they told me I could have free beer during the tasting. So I accepted this as being one of those burdens people have to endure. Here are the scorecards from the event:

Chilli #1: Mike's Maniac Mobster Monster Chilli
Judge One: A little too heavy on tomato. An amusing kick.
Judge Two: Nice, smooth tomato flavour. Very mild.
Me: Holy smokes - what is this stuff? You could remove dried paint from your driveway with it. It took me two beers to put the flames out. Hope that's the worst one. These people are crazy.

Chilli #2: Arthur's Afterburner Chilli
Judge One: Smoky (barbecue?) with a hint of pork. Slight Jalapeno tang.
Judge Two: Exciting BBQ flavour needs more peppers to be taken seriously.
Me: Keep this out of children's reach! I'm not sure what I'm supposed to taste besides pain. I had to wave off two people who wanted to give me the Heimlich manoeuvre. I shoved my way to the front of the beer line. The barmaid looks like a professional wrestler after a bad night. She was so irritated over my gagging sounds that the snake tattoo under her eye started to twitch. She has arms like Popeye and a face like Winston Churchill. I will not pick a fight with her. Downed two more beers.

Chilli #3: Fred's Famous Burn Down the Barn Chilli
Judge One: Excellent firehouse chilli! Great kick. Needs more beans.
Judge Two: A bean-less chilli, a bit salty, good use of red peppers.
Me: This has got to be a joke. Call the EPA; I've located a uranium spill. My nose feels like I have been sneezing Drano. Everyone knows the routine by now and got out of my way so I could make it to the beer wagon. Barmaid pounded me on the back. Now my backbone is in the front part of my chest. She said her friends called her, 'Sally.' Probably behind her back they call her 'Forklift.'

Chilli #4: Bubba's Black Magic:
Judge one: Black bean chilli with almost no spice. Disappointing.
Judge Two: A hint of lime in the black beans. Good side dish for fish or other mild foods. Not much of a chilli.
Me: I felt something scraping across my tongue but was unable to taste it. Sally was standing behind me with fresh refills so I

wouldn't have to dash over to see her. When she winked at me her snake sort of coiled and uncoiled - it's kinda cute.

Chilli #5: Linda's Legal Lip Remover:
Judge One: Meaty, strong chilli. Cayenne peppers freshly ground adding considerable kick. Very impressive.
Judge Two: Chilli using shredded beef; could use more tomato. Must admit the cayenne peppers make a strong statement.
Me: My ears are ringing and I can no longer focus my eyes. I belched and four people in front of me needed paramedics. The contestant seemed hurt when I told her that her chilli had given me brain damage. Sally saved my tongue by pouring beer directly on it from a pitcher. Sort of irritates me that one of the other judges asked me to stop screaming.

Chilli #6: Vera's Very Vegetarian Variety
Judge One: Thin yet bold vegetarian variety chilli. Good balance of spice and peppers.
Judge Two: The best yet. Aggressive use of peppers, onions and garlic. Superb.
Me: My intestines are now a straight pipe filled with gaseous flames. No one seems inclined to stand behind me except Sally. I asked if she wants to go dancing later.

Chilli #7: Susan's Screaming Sensation Chilli
Judge One: A mediocre chilli with too much reliance on canned peppers.
Judge Two: Ho Hum, tastes as if the chef threw in canned chilli peppers at the last moment. I should note that I'm worried about Judge Number 3. He appears to be in a bit of distress.
Me: You could put a hand grenade in my mouth and pull the pin and I wouldn't feel it. I've lost sight in one eye and the world sounds like it is made of rushing water. My clothes are covered with chilli, which slid unnoticed out of my mouth at some point. At my autopsy they'll know what killed me. Go Sally, save yourself before it's too late. I've decided to stop breathing, it's too painful and I'm not getting any oxygen anyway. If I need air, I'll just let it in through the hole in my stomach.

Chilli #8: Helen's Mount Saint Chilli
Judge One: This final entry is a good, balanced chilli, neither mild nor hot. Sorry to see that most of it was lost when Judge Number 3 fell and pulled the chilli pot on top of himself.

Judge Two: A perfect ending. This is a nice blend of chilli, safe for all. Not too bold, but spicy enough to declare its existence.
Me: The paramedics said I was babbling like a lunatic when they hauled me off to the emergency department.

Biblical Nutrition

In the beginning, God created the Heavens and the earth and populated the Earth with broccoli, cauliflower and spinach, green and yellow and red vegetables of all kinds, so Man and Woman would live long and healthy lives.

Then using God's great gifts, Satan created Ben and Jerry's Ice Cream and Krispy Creme Donuts. And Satan said, *'You want chocolate with that?'* And Man said, *'Yes!'* and Woman said, *'and as long as you're at it, add some sprinkles.'* And they gained 10 kilos. And Satan smiled.

And God created the healthful yogurt that Woman might keep the figure that Man found so fair. And Satan brought forth white flour from the wheat and sugar from the cane and combined them. And Woman went from size 12 to size 18.

So God said, *'Try my fresh green salad.'* And Satan presented Thousand-Island Dressing, buttery croutons and garlic toast on the side. And Man and Woman unfastened their belts following the repast.

God then said, *'I have sent your heart healthy vegetables and olive oil in which to cook them.'* And Satan brought forth deep fried fish and chicken-fried steak so big it needed its own platter. And Man gained more weight and his cholesterol went through the roof.

God then created a light, fluffy white cake, named it *'Angel Food Cake,'* and said, *'It is good.'* Satan then created chocolate cake and named it *'Devil's Food Cake.'*

God then brought forth running shoes so that His children might lose those extra pounds. And Satan gave cable TV with a remote control so Man would not have to toil changing the channels. And Man and Woman laughed and cried before the flickering blue light and gained kilos.

Then God brought forth the potato, naturally low in fat and brimming with nutrition. And Satan peeled off the healthful skin and sliced the starchy centre into chips and deep-fried them. And Man gained more kilos.

God then gave lean beef so that Man might consume fewer calories and still satisfy his appetite. And Satan created

McDonald's and its 99-cent double cheeseburger. Then said, *'You want fries with that?'* And Man replied, *'Yes! And super size them!'* And Satan said, *'It is good.'* And Man went into cardiac arrest.

God sighed and created quadruple bypass surgery. Then Satan created Private Health Care and Men have been broke ever since.

Five food funnies

Little Johnny and his family lived in the country and as a result seldom had guests. He was eager to help his mother after his father appeared with two dinner guests from the office. When the dinner was nearly over, Little Johnny went to the kitchen and proudly carried in the first piece of apple pie, giving it to his father who passed it to a guest. Little Johnny came in with a second piece of pie and gave it to his father, who again gave it to a guest. This was too much for Little Johnny, who said, *'It's no use, Dad. The pieces are all the same size.'*

A man was on a walking holiday in Ireland. He became thirsty so decided to ask at a home for something to drink. The lady of the house invited him in and served him a bowl of soup by the fire. There was a wee pig running around the kitchen, running up to the visitor and giving him a great deal of attention. The visitor commented that he had never seen a pig this friendly. The housewife replied: *'Ah, he's not that friendly. That's his bowl you're using.'*

The Japanese eat very little fat and suffer fewer heart attacks than the British or Americans. On the other hand, the French eat a lot of fat and also suffer fewer heart attacks than the British or Americans.

The Japanese drink very little red wine and suffer fewer heart attacks than the British or Americans. The Italians drink excessive amounts of red wine and also suffer fewer heart attacks than the British or Americans. Conclusion: Eat and drink what you like. It's speaking English that kills you.

The four food groups: Fast, Frozen, Instant and Chocolate

A dietician was once addressing a large audience in Sydney. *'The material we put into our stomachs is enough to have killed most of us sitting here, years ago. Red meat is awful. Vegetables can be disastrous and none of us realises the germs in our drinking* water. *But there is one thing that is the most dangerous of all and we all of us eat it. Can anyone here tell me what lethal product I'm referring to? You, sir, in the first row, please give us your idea.'* The man lowered his head and said, *'Wedding cake.'*

Vegetarians

The leader of the vegetarian organisation just couldn't control himself any more. He needed to try some pork, just to see what it tasted like. So one summer day, he told his members he was going on a holiday, drove out of the city and headed to the nearest restaurant, where he ordered a roast port meal.

After just a few minutes, he heard someone call his name and to his great chagrin, saw one of his fellow members walking towards him, just as the waiter walked over with a huge platter holding a full roasted pig with an apple in its mouth.

'Isn't that something?' said the man, *'all I do is order an apple and look what it comes with?'*

Chicken preparation

A waitress at a busy city restaurant asked a diner if he was ready to order.

'Yes,' the bloke replied, *'but first I'd like to know how you prepare the chicken.'*

'Well,' replied the waitress casually, *'Firstly, we just tell them straight out they are gonna die.'*

Easy Chicken Recipe

Here is a chicken recipe that also includes the use of popcorn as a stuffing - imagine that. When I found this recipe, I thought it was perfect for people like me, who just are not sure how to tell when poultry is thoroughly cooked, but not dried out. Give this a try.

    1 Chicken
    1 cup melted butter
    1 cup stuffing
    1 cup uncooked popcorn
    Salt/pepper to taste

Preheat oven to 200 degrees. Brush chicken well with melted butter salt and pepper. Fill cavity with stuffing mixed and popcorn. Place in baking pan with the neck end toward the back of the oven. Listen for the popping sounds.

When the chicken's arse blows the oven door open and the chicken flies across the room and lands on the table, it's done and ready to eat.

And, you thought I couldn't cook ...!

A Trip to Aldi

Yesterday I was at my local Aldi buying a large bag of Purina dog chow for my loyal pet Dog, and was in the checkout line when a woman behind me asked if I had a dog.

What did she think I had; an elephant? So since I'm retired and have little to do, on impulse I told her that no, I didn't have a dog, I was starting the Purina Diet again. I added that I probably shouldn't, because I ended up in the hospital last time, but that I'd lost 50 pounds before I awakened in an intensive care ward with tubes coming out of most of my orifices and IVs in both arms.

I told her that it was essentially a perfect diet and that the way that it works is to load your pants pockets with Purina nuggets and simply eat one or two every time you feel hungry. The food is nutritionally complete so it works well and I was going to try it again. (I have to mention here that practically everyone in line was now enthralled with my story.) Horrified, she asked if I ended up in intensive care because the dog food poisoned me. I told her no, I stepped off a curb to sniff an Irish Setter's ass and a car hit us both.

I thought the guy behind her was going to have a heart attack he was laughing so hard. Aldi won't let me shop there any more.

Better watch what you ask retired people. They have all the time in the world to think of crazy things to say. Forward this (especially) to all your retired friends ... it will be their laugh for the day.

Rules for eating chocolate:

- If you've got melted chocolate all over your hands, you're eating it too slowly.
- Chocolate covered raisins, cherries orange slices and strawberries all count as fruit, so eat as many as you want.
- The problem: How to get 1 kilo of chocolate home from the store in a hot car. The solution: Eat it in the parking lot.
- Diet tip: Eat a chocolate bar before each meal. It'll take the edge off your appetite and you'll eat less.
- If you can't eat all your chocolate, what's wrong with you?

- A nice box of chocolates can provide your total daily intake of calories in one place. Isn't that handy?
- If calories are an issue, store your chocolate on top of the fridge. Calories are afraid of heights and they will jump out of the chocolate to protect themselves.
- If I eat equal amounts of dark and white chocolate, is that a balanced diet? Don't they actually counteract each other?
- Money talks. Chocolate sings.
- Chocolate has many preservatives. Preservatives make you look younger.
- Question: Why is there no such organisation as Chocoholics Anonymous? Answer: Because no one wants to quit!
- If not for chocolate, there would be no need for control top pantyhose. An entire garment industry would be devastated.
- Put 'eat chocolate' at the top of your list of things to do today. That way, at least you'll get one thing done.

Food Rules:

If no one sees you eat it, it has no calories.

If you drink a diet soda with a candy bar, they cancel each other out.

If you eat standing up, it doesn't count!

'Stressed' is just 'Desserts' spelled backwards.

If you eat the food off someone else's plate, it doesn't count.

Cookie pieces contain no calories because the process of breakage causes calorie leakage.

Food used for medicinal purposes have no calories. This includes: any chocolate used for energy, brandy, cheesecake and Haagen-Dazs Ice Cream.

When eating with someone else, calories don't count if you both eat the same amount.

Movie-related foods are much lower in calories simply because they are a part of the entertainment experience and not part of one's personal fuel. This includes: Milk Duds, popcorn with butter, Junior Mints, Snickers and Gummi Bears.

CHAPTER 3

RELIGIOUS JOKES

The Pearly Gates:

A woman died and found herself standing outside the Pearly Gates being greeted by St. Peter. She asked him, *'Oh, is this the place what I think it is? It's so beautiful. Did I really make it to Heaven?'* To which St. Peter replied, *'Yes my dear, these are the Gates to Heaven. But you must do one more thing before you can enter.'*

The woman was very excited and asked of St. Peter what she must do to pass through the gates. *'Spell a word,'* St. Peter replied. *'What word?'* she asked. *'Any word,'* answered St. Peter, *'It's your choice.'*

The woman replied, *'Then the word I will spell is love. L-O-V-E.'*

St. Peter congratulated her on her good fortune to have made it to Heaven and asked her if she would mind taking his place at the gates for a few minutes while he completed a chore.
'I'd be honoured,' she replied, *'but what should I do if someone comes while you're gone?'*

St. Peter reassured her and instructed the woman to simply have any newcomers to the Pearly Gates spell a word as she had done. So the woman is left sitting in St. Peter's chair and watching the beautiful angels soaring around her. Then lo and behold, a man approaches the gates and she realises it is her husband.

'What happened?' she cried, *'Why are you here?'*
Her husband stared at her for a moment and then said, *'I was so upset when I left for your funeral, I was in an accident - and now I'm here. Did I really make it to Heaven?'* To which the woman replied, *'Not yet. You must spell a word first.'*

'What word?' he asked. The woman responded, *'Czechoslovakia.'*

Two priests died at the same time and met Saint Peter at the Pearly Gates. St. Peter said, *'I'd like to let you guys in now, but our computer is down. You'll have to go back to Earth for about a week, but you can't go back as priests. What'll it be?'*

The first priest says, *'I've always wanted to be an eagle, soaring above the Rocky Mountains.'*

'So be it,' says St. Peter and off flies the first priest.

The second priest mulls this over for a moment and asks, *'Will any of this week 'count' St. Peter?'*

'No, I told you the computer's down. There's no way we can keep track of what you're doing.'

'In that case,' says the second priest, *'I've always wanted to be a stud.'*

'So be it.' Says St. Peter and the second priest disappears.

A week goes by, the computer is fixed and the Lord tells St. Peter to recall the two priests. *'Will you have any trouble locating them?'* He asks.

'The first one should be easy,' says St. Peter. *'He's somewhere over the Rocky Mountains, flying with the eagles. But the second one could prove to be more difficult.'*

'Why?' asked the the Lord.

'He's on a snow tire, somewhere in North Dakota.'

Arthur Davidson of the Harley Davidson Motorcycle Corporation dies and goes to heaven. At the gates, an angel tells Davidson, *'Well, you've been such a good guy and your motorcycles have changed the world. As a reward, you can hang out with anyone you want to in Heaven.'*

Davidson thinks about it and says, *'I want to hang out with God, Himself.'*

A be-feathered fellow at the gates takes Arthur to the Throne Room and introduces him to God. Arthur asks God, *'Hey, aren't you the inventor of woman?'*

God replies, *'Ah, yes.'*

'Well,' says Davidson, *'you have some major design flaws in your invention:*

1. There's too much front end protrusion,
2. It chatters at high speeds,
3. The rear end wobbles too much and
4. The intake is placed too close to the exhaust.

'Hmmmm...' replies God, *'Hold on.'*

God goes to the celestial supercomputer, types in a few keystrokes and waits for the result. The computer prints out a slip of paper and God reads it. *'It may be that my invention is flawed,'* God replies to Arthur Davidson, *'but according to the computer, more people are riding my invention than yours.'*

A Lutheran minister has died and is at the gates of Heaven. St. Peter arrives and tells him he will now be shown around and then escorted to the room where the Lutherans stay.

Passing the first room, St. Peter explains that this is where the Baptists live. The next room they pass is the Presbyterians, then Jews. As they approach the next room, St. Peter puts his finger to his lips in request for total silence. They creep past the room and the minister notices that the door is closed and there is no window.

Safely past, he inquires about the room. *'It's the Catholics,'* says St. Peter. *'They think they're the only ones here.'*

A cab driver reaches the Pearly Gates and announces his presence to St. Peter, who looks him up in his Big Book. Upon reading the entry for the cabby, St. Peter invites him to grab a silk robe and golden staff and to proceed into heaven.

A preacher is next in line behind the cabby and has been watching these proceedings with interest. He announces himself to St. Peter. Upon scanning the preacher's entry in the Big Book, St. Peter furrows his brow and says, *'Okay, we'll let you in, but take that cloth robe and wooden staff.'*

The preacher is astonished and replies, *'But I'm a man of the cloth. You gave that cab driver a gold staff and a silk robe. Surely I rate higher than a cabby!'*

St. Peter responded matter-of-factly: *'Here we are interested in results. When you preached, people slept. When the cabby drove his taxi, people prayed.'*

Three buddies die in a car crash and they find themselves at an orientation to enter Heaven. They are all asked, *'When you are in your casket and friends and family are mourning you, what would you like to hear them say about you?'*

The first guy says, *'I would like to hear them say that I was a great doctor of my time and a great family man.'*

The second guy says, *'I would like to hear that I was a wonderful husband and school teacher who made a huge difference in the children of tomorrow.'*

The last guy replies, *'I would like to hear them say ...'* Look!!! He's moving!!!'

Two guys were walking home from a pub. On their way, they walked through a cemetery. The first guy happened to glance at a gravestone. It read, *'Here lies Tom, a lawyer and an honest man.'* The first guy said to the second guy, *'Hey John, there's three people in this grave.'*

A divorce lawyer died and arrived at the pearly gates. St. Peter asks him, *'What have you done to merit entrance into Heaven?'*
The lawyer thought a moment, then said, *'A week ago, I gave a quarter to a homeless person on the street.'*

St. Peter said, *'Well, that's fine, but it's not really quite enough to get you into Heaven.'*

The lawyer said, *'Wait! Wait! There's more! Three years ago, I also gave a homeless person a quarter.'*

St. Peter whispers to Gabriel, *'What do you suggest we do with this fellow?'*

Gabriel gave the lawyer a sidelong glance and then said to St. Peter, *'Let's give him back his 50 cents and tell him to go to Hell!'*

Did you hear about the dyslexic Rabbi? He walks around saying *'Yo.'*

How do you get holy water? Boil the Hell out of it.

Hugh and only Hugh can prevent florist friars.

The Bicycle

In a small town, there were only two churches - one at each end of town. Nearly everyone in town attended one or the other every Sunday. The respective pastors got by without cars and either walked or bicycled when getting around town.

One Saturday they happened to meet, one on his bike, the other on foot. *'Brother, where's your bicycle?'* asked the first one.

'Well,' replied the other one, *'I'm not sure. Either it's been stolen or I rode it somewhere and forgot and walked back home.'*

'Here's what we can do,' said the first preacher. *'In our sermons tomorrow we will preach on the Ten Commandments and we will emphasise 'thou shalt not steal.' That way, if someone has taken it or has found it, he will perhaps be moved to return it.'*

They agreed to do that and went on their way. Two days later they met again; the second preacher was on his bike again. *'Say, brother,'* said the first, *'I see that one of our sermons did the trick.'*

'Well yes,' the second responded, *'It was mine, but not in the way we intended. When I got to 'thou shalt not commit adultery,' I remembered where I had left it.'*

Two nuns were riding their bikes down the back streets of Rome. One leaned over to the other and said, *'You know, I've never come this way before.'*

The other nun replies, *'It's the cobblestones.'*

Missionary

A missionary who had spent years showing a tribe of natives how to farm and build things so they would be self-sufficient, gets word that he is to return home. He thinks that the one thing he never did was to teach these natives how to speak English, so he takes the chief and starts walking in the forest.

He points to a tree and tells the chief, *'This is a tree.'*

The chief looks at the tree and grunts, *'Tree.'*

The missionary is pleased with the response. They walk a little farther and the padre points to a rock and says, *'This is a rock'* at which the chief looks and grunts, *'Rock.'*

The padre is really getting enthusiastic about the results when he hears a rustling in the business. As he peeks over the top he sees a couple in the midst of heavy romantic activity. The padre is really flustered and quickly responds, *'Riding a bike.'*

The chief looks at the couple briefly, pulls out his blowgun and kills them. The padre goes ballistic and yells at the chief that he has spent years teaching how to be civilised and kind - so how could he kill these people?

The chief replied, *'My bike.'*

What religion are we?

Three little boys were concerned because they couldn't get anyone to play with them. They decided it was because they had not been baptized and didn't go to Sunday school.

So they went to the nearest church. But, only the janitor was there.

One little boy said, *'We need to be baptized because no one will come out and play with us. Will you baptize us?'*

'Sure,' said the janitor with a smile.

He took them into the bathroom and dunked their little heads in the toilet bowl, one at a time. Then he said, *'You are now baptized!'*

When they got outside, one of them asked, *'What religion do you think we are?'*

The oldest one said, '*We're not Kathlick, because they pour the water on you.*'

'*We're not Babtis, because they dunk all of you in the water.*'

'*We're not Methdiss, because they just sprinkle water on you.*'

The littlest one said, '*Didn't you smell that water?*'

They all joined in asking, '*Yeah! What do you think that means?*'

'*I think it means we're Pisskopailians!*'

The Chauffeur

After getting all of Pope Benedict's luggage loaded into the limo, (and he doesn't travel light), the driver notices the Pope is still standing on the curb.

'*Excuse me, Your Holiness,*' says the driver, '*Would you please take your seat so we can leave?*'

'*Well, to tell you the truth,*' says the Pope, '*they never let me drive at the Vatican when I was a cardinal and I'd really like to drive today.*'

'*I'm sorry, Your Holiness, but I cannot let you do that. I'd lose my job! What if something should happen*' protests the driver, wishing he'd never gone to work that morning.

'*Who's going to tell*' says the Pope with a smile.

Reluctantly, the driver gets in the back as the Pope climbs in behind the wheel. The driver quickly regrets his decision when, after exiting the airport, the Pontiff floors it, accelerating the limo to 205 kph. (Remember, the Pope is German.)

'*Please slow down, Your Holiness*' pleads the worried driver, but the Pope keeps the pedal to the metal until they hear sirens.

'*Oh, dear God, I'm going to lose my license -- and my job!*' moans the driver.

The Pope pulls over and rolls down the window as the cop approaches, but the cop takes one look at him, goes back to his motorcycle and gets on the radio.

'*I need to talk to the Chief,*' he says to the dispatcher.

The Chief gets on the radio and the cop tells him that he's stopped a limo going 205 kph.

'*So bust him,*' says the Chief.

'*I don't think we want to do that, he's really important,*' said the cop.

The Chief exclaimed, '*All the more reason!*'

'No, I mean really important,' said the cop with a bit of persistence ...

The Chief then asked, *'Who do you have there, the mayor?'*
Cop: *'Bigger.'*
Chief: *'A senator?'*
Cop: *'Bigger.'*
Chief: *'The Prime Minister?'*
Cop: *'Bigger.'*
'Well,' said the Chief, *'who is it?'*
Cop: *'I think it's God!'*
The Chief is even more puzzled and curious, *'What makes you think it's God?'*
Cop: *'His chauffeur is the Pope!'*

Having faith

A couple of nuns, who worked as nurses, had gone out to the country to minister to an outpatient. On the way back home they ran out of petrol. They were standing beside their car on the shoulder when a truck approached. Seeing ladies of the cloth in distress, the driver stopped to offer his help.

The nuns explained they needed some petrol. The driver of the truck said he would gladly drain some from his tank but he didn't have a bucket or can.

One of the nuns dug out a clean bedpan and asked the driver if he could use it. He said, *'Yes,'* and proceeded to drain a couple of litres of petrol into the pan. He waved goodbye to the nuns and left.

The nuns were carefully pouring the precious fluid into their gas tank when a highway patrol officer arrived. The trooper stopped and watched for a moment, then stated, *'Sisters, I don't think it will work, but I sure do admire your faith!'*

The Pastor's False Teeth

A Pastor goes to the dentist for a set of false teeth. The first Sunday After he gets his new teeth, he talks for only eight minutes. The second Sunday, he talks for only ten minutes. The following Sunday, he talks for 2 hours and 48 minutes.

The congregation had to mob him to get him down from the pulpit and they asked him what happened.

The Pastor explains the first Sunday his gums hurt so bad he couldn't talk for more than 8 minutes. The second Sunday his gums hurt too much to talk for more than 10 minutes. But, the third Sunday, he put his Wife's' teeth in by mistake and he couldn't shut up ...

(I love it when I make you smile ... and I KNOW you are smiling.)

Bible talk

A little boy opened the big old family Bible with fascination and looked at the old pages as he turned them. Suddenly, something fell out of the Bible. He picked it up and looked at it closely. It was an old leaf from a tree that had been pressed between the pages. *'Momma, look what I found,'* the boy called out, then added with astonishment, *'I think it's Adam's suit!'*

The preacher was wired for sound with a lapel mike and as he preached, he moved briskly about the platform, jerking the microphone cord as he went. Then he moved to one side, got wound up in the cord and nearly tripped before jerking it again. After several circles and jerks, a little girl in the third pew leaned towards her mother and whispered, *'If he gets loose, will he hurt us?'*

Six-year-old Angie and her four-year-old brother Joel were sitting together in church. Joel giggled, sang and talked out loud. Finally his big sister had had enough. *'You're not supposed to talk out loud in church.'*

'Why? Who's going to stop me?' Joel asked. Angie pointed to the back of the church and said, *'See those two men standing by the door? They're hushers.'*

A ten-year-old, under the tutelage of her grandmother, was becoming quite knowledgeable about the Bible. Then one day she floored her grandmother by asking, *'Which Virgin was the mother of Jesus: the Virgin Mary or the King James Virgin?'*

An exasperated mother, whose son was always getting into mischief, finally asked him, *'How do you expect to get into Heaven?'*

The boy thought it over and said, *'Well, I'll run in and out and in and out and keep slamming the door until St. Peter says, 'For Heaven's sake, Dylan, come in or stay out!'"*

It was that time during the Sunday morning service, for the children's sermon. All the children were invited to come forward. One little girl was wearing a particularly pretty dress and, as she sat down, the pastor leaned over and said, *'That is a very pretty dress. Is it your Easter Dress?'*

The little girl replied, directly into the pastor's clip-on microphone, *'Yes and my Mom says it's a bitch to iron.'*

A Sunday school class was studying the Ten Commandments. They were ready to discuss the last one. The teacher asked if anyone could tell her what it was. Susie raised her hand, stood tall and quoted, *'Thou shall not take the covers off your neighbour's wife.'*

My grandson was visiting one day when he asked, *'Grandma, do you know how you and God are alike?'*

I mentally polished my halo while I asked, *'No, how are we alike?'*

'You're both old,' he replied.

Who was Jesus really?

Three proofs that Jesus was Jewish:
1. He went into his father's business.
2. He lived at home until the age of 33.
3. He thought his mother was a virgin and his mother thought he was God.

Three proofs that Jesus was Irish:
1. He never got married.
2. He never held a steady job.
3. His last request was a drink.

Three proofs that Jesus was Puerto Rican:
1. His first name was Jesus.
2. He was always in trouble with the law.
3. His mother did not know who his real father was.

Three proofs that Jesus was Italian:
1. He talked with his hands.
2. He had wine with every meal.
3. He worked in the building trade.

Three proofs that Jesus was Black:
1. He called everybody 'brother.'
2. He had no permanent address.
3. Nobody would hire him.

Three proofs that Jesus was Californian:
1. He never cut his hair.
2. He walked around barefoot.
3. He invented a new religion

Bill Gates:

Bill Gates dies in a car accident and finds himself being sized up by God.

'Well, Bill, I'm really confused on this call; I'm not sure whether to send you to Heaven or Hell. After all, you enormously helped society by putting a computer in almost every home, yet you also created that ghastly Windows program. I'm going to do something I've never done before. I'm going to let you decide where you want to go.'

Bill replied, *'Well, what's the difference between the two?'*

God replied, *'I'm willing to let you visit both places briefly to see if it will help your decision.'*

'Fine, but where should I go first?'

'I'll leave that up to you.'

'Okay then,' said Bill, *'let's try Hell first.'* So Bill went to Hell.

It was a beautiful, clean, sandy beach with clear waters and lots of beautiful women running around, playing in the water, laughing and frolicking about. The sun was shining; the temperature perfect. He was very pleased. *'This is great!'* he told God, but if this is Hell, I really want to see Heaven.

'Fine,' said God and off they went.

Heaven was a place high in the clouds, with angels drifting about, playing harps and singing. It was nice, but not as enticing as Hell. Bill thought for a quick minute and rendered his decision. *'Hmmm. I think I'd prefer Hell,'* he told God.

'Fine,' retorted God, *'as you desire.'* So Bill went to Hell. Two weeks later, God decided to check on the late billionaire to see how he was doing in Hell. When he got there, he found Bill shackled to a wall screaming amongst hot flames in dark caves, being burned and tortured by demons. *'How's everything going,'* he asked Bill.

Bill responded with his voice filled with anguish and disappointment. *'This is awful. This is nothing like the Hell I visited two weeks ago. I can't believe this is happening. What happened to the other place, with the beaches and the beautiful women playing in the water??'*

'Oh,' God said, *'that was Hell XP, this is Hell Windows 7.'*

Religious Bras:

A man walked into the ladies department of one of the largest department store chains. He shyly walked up to the woman behind the counter and said, *'I'd like to buy a bra for my wife?'*

'What type of bra?' asked the clerk.

'Type?' inquired the man, *'There's more than one type?'*

'Look around,' said the saleslady as she showed a sea of bras in every shape, size, colour and material. *'Actually, even with all of this variety, there are really only three types of bras,'* she added.

Confused, the man asked what were the types. The saleslady replied, *'The Catholic type, the Salvation Army type and the Baptist type. Which one do you need?'*

Still confused, the man asked, *'What's the difference between them?'*

The lady responded, *'It's really quite simple. The Catholic type supports the masses, the Salvation Army type lifts up the fallen and the Baptist type makes mountains out of mole hills.'*

Have you ever wondered why A, B, C, D, DD, E, F, G and H are the letters used to define bra sizes (or as others call them - flopper-stoppers)? If you have wondered why, but couldn't figure out what the letters stood for, it's about time you became informed!

- Almost boobs.
- Barely there.
- Can't complain!
- Dang!
- Double Dang!
- Enormous!
- Fake.
- Get a reduction
- Help me. I've fallen and can't get up!

And don't forget the German bra. Holtzemfromfloppen.

Life in Hell:

One day a guy dies and finds himself in Hell. As he is wallowing in despair, he has his first meeting with a demon.

Demon: *'Why so glum, chum?'*

Guy: *'What do you think? I'm in Hell!'*

Demon: *'Hell's not so bad. We actually have a lot of fun down here. Are you a drinkin' man?'*
Guy: *'Sure, I love to drink.'*
Demon: *'Well, you're gonna love Mondays then. On Mondays that's all we do is drink. Whiskey, tequila, Guinness, wine coolers, even Fresca. We drink till we throw up and then we drink some more! It doesn't matter, it can't kill you ... you're already dead!'*
Guy: *'Gee that sounds great.'*
Demon: *'Are you a smoker?'*
Guy: *'You'd better believe it!'*
Demon: *'All right! You're gonna love Tuesdays. We get the finest cigars from all over the world and smoke our lungs out! If you get cancer - no biggie ... you're already dead, remember?'*
Guy: *'Wow. That's awesome!'*
Demon: *'Wednesday you can gamble all you want. Craps, Blackjack, Roulette, Poker, Slots, whatever. If you go bankrupt ... well you're dead anyhow. Are you into drugs?'*
Guy: *'Are you kidding? You don't mean ...?'*
Demon: *'That's right! Thursday is drug day. Help yourself to a great big bowl of crack or smack. Smoke a doobie the size of a submarine. You can do all the drugs you want and if ya overdose - that's right you're dead - who cares! O.D.!!'*
Guy: *'Holy moly! I never realised Hell was such a swingin' place!!*
Demon: *'You gay?'*
Guy: *'No ...'*
Demon: *'You're gonna hate Fridays ...'*

Adam:

One day, the Lord decided to make a companion for Adam. He summoned St. Peter and told him of his decision. He told St. Peter that he wanted to make a being that was similar to man, yet was different and could offer him comfort, companionship and sex. The Lord said he would call this being a woman.

So St. Peter went about creating this being that was similar to man, yet was different in ways that would be appealing and could provide physical comfort to man. When St. Peter was finished creating this being that could now be called woman, he summoned The Lord.

'Ah, St. Peter, once again you have done an excellent job,' said the Lord.

'Thank you, Great One,' replied St. Peter. 'I am now ready to provide the brain, nerve endings and senses to the being, this ... woman. I require your assistance on this matter, Lord.'

'You shall make her brain, slightly smaller, yet more intuitive, more feeling, more compassionate and more adaptable than man's.' said The Lord.

'The nerve endings,' said St. Peter. 'How many will I put in her hands?'

'How many did we put in Adam?' Asked The Lord.

'Two hundred, my Lord,' replied St. Peter.

'Then we shall do the same for this woman,' said The Lord.

'And how many nerve endings shall we put in her feet?' Inquired St. Peter.

'How many did we put in Adam?' asked The Lord.

'Seventy-five, my Lord,' replied St. Peter.

'A yes, these beings are constantly on their feet, so they benefit from having less nerve endings there. Do the same for woman,' said The Lord.

'How many nerve endings should we put in woman's genitals?' inquired St. Peter.

'How many did we put in Adam?' asked The Lord.

'Four hundred and twenty, my Lord,' replied St. Peter.

'Of course, we did want Adam to have a means of receiving extra in his life didn't we? Do the same for woman,' said The Lord.

'Yes my Lord,' said St. Peter.

'No, wait,' said The Lord. 'Give her ten thousand! I want her to scream my name!'

One day God came to Adam to pass on some news. 'I have some good news and some bad news,' the Lord said.

Adam looked at him and said, 'Well, give me the good news first.'

Smiling, God explained, 'I've got two new organs for you. One is called a brain. It will allow you to be very intelligent, create new things and have decent conversations with Eve. The other organ I have for you is called a penis. It will allow you to reproduce your now-intelligent life form and populate this planet. Eve will be very happy that you now have this organ to give her children.'

Adam, very excited, exclaimed, *'These are great gifts you have given me. What could possibly be bad news, after such great tidings?'*

The Lord looked upon Adam and said with great sorrow, *'The bad news is that when I created you, I only gave you enough blood to operate one of these organs at a time.'*

One day in the Garden of Eden, Eve called out to God. *'Lord, I have a problem!'*

'What's the problem Eve?'

'Lord, I know you created me and provided this beautiful garden and all of these wonderful animals and that hilarious comedic snake, but I'm just not happy.'

'Why is that, Eve?' Came the reply from above.

'Lord, I am lonely and I'm sick to death of apples.'

'Well Eve, in that case. I have a solution. I shall create a man for you.'

'What is a man, Lord?'

'This man will be a flawed creature, with many bad traits. He'll lie, cheat and be vainglorious; all in all, he'll give you a hard time. But, he'll be bigger, faster and will like to hunt and kill things. He will look silly when he's aroused, but since you've been complaining, I'll create him in such a way that he will satisfy your physical needs. He will be witless and will revel in childish things like fighting and kicking a ball about. He won't be too smart, so he'll also need your advice to think properly.'

'Sounds great.' 'What's the catch, Lord?'

'Well. You can have him on one condition.'

'What's that, Lord?'

'As I said, he'll be proud, arrogant and self-admiring. So you'll have to let him believe that I made him first. Just remember, it's our little secret - you know - woman to woman.'

Bible Belt

Way down in the Deep South of USA, in an area known as the 'Bible Belt,' there lived a Baptist minister with a very large congregation. One morning after a particularly moving sermon, he announced, *'Friends, I have been hearing very nasty rumours!'*

The crowd fell into an expectant silence. The minister continued, *'One of you here among us has been reporting that I am a member of the dreaded 'Klu Klux Klan.' This, of course, is* not true! I am asking that the guilty party confess and apologise now - right here - before my flock of loyal followers.'

Sister Margaret quickly stood up and pleaded, *'Preacher, please, I don't know how this all came to be. I just mentioned to one of my close friends that you were a wizard under the sheets.'*

Amen!

This fellow comes to confession. *'Father,'* he said, *'forgive me for I have sinned.'*

'What did you do, my son?' replied the priest.

'I lusted,' the young man replied.

'Tell me about it,' the priest said.

The fellow then related his story. *'Father, I am a deliveryman for UPS. Yesterday I was making a delivery in the affluent section of the city. When I rang the bell, the door opened and there stood the most beautiful woman I have ever seen. She had long blonde hair and eyes like emeralds. She was dressed in a sheer dressing gown that showed her perfect figure and she asked if I would like to come in.'*

'And, what did you do, my son?' asked the priest.

'Father, I did not go in the house, but I lusted. Oh, how I lusted,' replied the man.

'Your sin has been forgiven,' replied the priest. *'You will get your reward in Heaven, my son.'*

'A reward, Father? What do you think my reward might be?' the guy asked.

The priest replied, *'I think a bale of hay would be appropriate, you jackass.'*

Temperance Sermon

A preacher was completing a temperance sermon. With great expression, he said, *'If I had all the beer in the world, I'd take it and throw it into the river.'*

With even greater emphasis, he said, *'And if I had all the whiskey in the world, I'd take it and throw it into the river.'* He sat down.

The song leader then stood very cautiously and announced with a smile, *'For our closing song, let us sing Hymn #365: 'Shall we gather at the river?'*

Church Bulletin Announcements:

Don't let worry kill you; let the church help.

Thursday night, potluck supper. Prayer and medication to follow.

Remember in prayer the many who are sick of our church and community.

For those of you who have children and don't know it, we have a nursery downstairs.

The rosebud on the altar this morning is to announce the birth of David Alan Belzer, the sin of Rev. and Mrs. Julius Belzer.

This afternoon there will be a meeting in the south and north ends of the church. Children will be baptised at both ends.

Tuesday at 4:00 pm there will be an ice cream social. All ladies giving milk will please come early.

Wednesday, the ladies Liturgy Society will meet. Mrs. Jones will sing *'Put me in my little bed,'* accompanied by the pastor.

Thursday at 5:00 pm there will be a meeting of the 'Little Mothers Club.' All wishing to become little mothers please see the minister in his study.

This being Easter Sunday, we will ask Mrs. Lewis to come forward and lay an egg on the altar.

The service will close with 'Little Drops of Water.' One of the ladies will start and the rest of the congregation will join in.

Next Sunday, a special collection will be taken to defray the cost of the new carpet. All those wishing to do something on the new carpet will come forward and do so.

The ladies of the church have cast off clothing of every kind and they may be seen in the church basement on Friday.

A bean supper will be held on Tuesday evening in the church hall. Music will follow.

At the evening service tonight, the topic will be *'What is Hell?'* Come early and listen to our choir practice.

The Pastor and Minister of Music

There was a church where the preacher and the song leader were not getting along. This began to spill over into the worship service. One week the preacher preached on commitment and how we should dedicate ourselves to service. The song leader led the song, *'I Shall Not Be Moved.'*

The next Sunday, the preacher preached on gossiping and how we should watch our tongues. The song leader led the song, *'I Love To Tell The Story.'*

The preacher became very disgusted over the situation and the next Sunday he told the congregation he was considering resigning. The song leader then led the song *'Oh, Why Not Tonight.'*

As it came to pass, the preacher resigned and the next week informed the church that it was Jesus that led him there and it was Jesus that was taking him away. The song leader then led the song, *'What A Friend We Have in Jesus.'*

Pastor calling

A new pastor was visiting in the homes of his parishioners. At one house it seemed obvious that someone was at home, but no answer came to his repeated knocks at the door. Therefore, he took out a business card and wrote, *'Revelation 3:20'* on the back of it and stuck it in the door.

When the offering was processed the following Sunday, he found that his card had been returned. Added to it was this cryptic message,

'Genesis 3:10.' Reaching for his Bible to check out the citation, he broke up in gales of laughter. Revelation 3:20 begins *'Behold, I stand at the door and knock.'* Genesis 3:10 reads, *'I heard your voice in the garden and I was afraid for I was naked.'*

Why did you die?

A man placed some flowers on the grave of his dearly departed mother and started back toward his car when his attention was diverted to another man kneeling at a grave.

The man seemed to be praying with profound intensity and kept repeating, *'Why did you have to die? Why did you have to die? Why did you have to die?'*

The first man approached him and said, *'Sir, I don't wish to interfere with your private grief, but this demonstration of pain is more than I've ever seen before. For whom do you mourn so deeply? A child? A parent?'*

The mourner took a moment to collect himself and then replied, *'My wife's first husband.'*

Driver's Permit

A young man had just obtained his driver's permit and inquired of his father (an Evangelist) if they could discuss the use of the car. His father took him to the study and said to the boy, *'I'll make a deal with you, son. You bring your grades up from a C to* a B- average, study your Bible a little and get a haircut and we'll talk about the car.'

Well, the boy thought about that for a moment and decided he'd best settle for the offer and they agreed.

After about six weeks, the boy came back and again asked his father about the car. Again they went to the study where his father said, *'Son, I've been real proud of you. You've brought your grades up and I've observed that you've been studying your Bible and participating a lot more in Bible study class on Sunday morning. But I'm real disappointed seeing you haven't got your hair cut.'*

The young man paused a moment and then said, *'You know, Dad, I've been thinking about that and I've noticed in my studies of the Bible that Sampson had long hair, Moses had long hair, John the Baptist had long hair and there's even strong argument that Jesus Himself had long hair.'*

To which his father replied, *'Perhaps, but they walked everywhere they went.'*

The Old Priest

An old priest invited a young priest over for dinner. During the meal, the young priest couldn't help noticing how attractive and shapely the housekeeper was. Over the course of the evening he started to wonder if there was more between the old priest and the housekeeper than met the eye. Reading the young priest's thoughts, the old priest volunteered, *'I know what you must be thinking, but I assure you, my relationship with my housekeeper is purely professional.'*

About a week later, the housekeeper came to the old priest and said, *'Father, ever since the young Father came to dinner, I've been unable to find the beautiful silver gravy ladle. You don't suppose he took it do you?'*

The old priest said, *'Well, I doubt it, but I'll write him a letter just to be sure.'* He sat down and wrote: *'Dear Father, I'm not saying that you 'did' take the gravy ladle, but the fact remains that one has been missing ever since you were here for dinner.'*

Several days later the old priest received a letter from the young priest which read: *'Dear Father, I'm not saying that you 'do' sleep with your housekeeper, but the fact remains that if you were sleeping in your own bed, you would have found the gravy ladle by now.'*

The Golfers:

The Pope met with his cardinals to discuss a proposal from Benjamin Netanyahu, the leader of Israel. *'Your Holiness,'* said one of the cardinals, *'Mr. Netanyahu wants to challenge you to a game of golf to show the friendship and ecumenical spirit shared by the Jewish and Catholic faiths.'*

The Pope thought it was a good idea, but he had never held a golf club in his hand. *'Don't we have a Cardinal who can represent me?'*

'None that plays golf very well,' a Cardinal replied. *'But,'* he added, *'There is a man called Jack Nicklaus, an American golfer who is a devout Catholic. We can offer to make him a Cardinal; then ask him to play Benjamin Netanyahu as your personal representative. In addition to showing our spirit of cooperation, we'll also win the match.'*

Everyone agreed it was a good idea. The call was made. Of course, Nicklaus was honoured and agreed to play. The day after the match, Nicklaus reported to the Vatican to inform the Pope of the result.

'I have some good news and some bad news, Your Holiness,' said the golfer.

'Tell me the good news first, Cardinal Nicklaus,' said the Pope.

'Well, your Holiness, I don't like to brag, but even though I've played some pretty terrific rounds of golf in my life, this was the best I have ever played, by far. I must have been inspired from above. My drives were long and true, my irons were accurate and purposeful and my putting was perfect. With all due respect, my play was truly miraculous.'

'There's bad news? The Pope asked.

'Yes,' Nicklaus sighed, *'I lost to Rabbi Tiger Woods by three strokes.'*

A man who was an avid golfer finally got a once-in-a-lifetime chance for an audience with the Pope. After standing in line for hours, he got to the Pope and said, *'Your Holiness, I have a question that only you can answer. You see, I love golf and I feel a real need to know if there is a golf course in Heaven. Can you tell me if there is?'*

The Pope considered for a moment and replied, *'I do not know the answer to your question, my son, but I will talk to God and get back with you.'*

The next day, the man is called for another audience with the Pope to receive the answer to his question. He stood before the Pope, who said, *'My son, I have some good news and some bad news in relation to your question. The good news is that Heaven has a most fabulous golf course that you could imagine and is in eternally perfect shape. It puts all courses on earth to shame ... The bad news is that you have a tee time for tomorrow morning.'*

A golfer is in a competitive match with a friend, who is ahead by a couple of strokes. The golfer says to himself, *'I'd give anything to sink this next putt.'*

A stranger walks up to him and whispers, *'Would you give up a fourth of your sex life?'*

The golfer thinks the man is crazy and that his answer will be meaningless. At the same time he thinks this might be a good omen, so he says, *'Okay,'* and sinks the putt. Two holes later, he mumbles to himself, *'Boy, if I could only get an eagle on this hole.'*

The same stranger moves to his side and says, *'Would it be worth another fourth of your sex life?'*

The golfer shrugs and says, *'Sure.'* He makes an eagle.

On the final hole, the golfer needs yet another eagle to win. Although he says nothing, the stranger moves to his side and says, *'Would you be willing to give up the rest of your sex life to win this match?'*

The golfer says, *'Certainly!'* He makes the eagle.

As the golfer walks to the clubhouse, the stranger walks alongside and says, *'You know, I've really not been fair with you because you don't know who I am. I'm the Devil and from now on you will have no sex life.'*

'Nice to meet you,' says the golfer. *'My name's Father O'Malley.'*

Thank God for Children Saying Grace

Last week I took my children to a restaurant. My six-year-old son asked if he could say grace. As we bowed our heads he said, *'God is good. God is great. Thank you for the food and I would even thank you more if Mom gets us ice cream for dessert. And Liberty and justice for all! Amen!'*

Along with the laughter from the other customers nearby I heard a woman's loud remark, *'That's what's wrong with this* country. Kids today don't even know how to pray. Asking God for ice cream! Why, I never!'

Hearing this, my son burst into tears and asked me, *'Did I do it wrong? Is God mad at me?'*

As I held him and assured him that he had done a terrific job and God was certainly not mad at him, an elderly gentleman approached the table. He winked at my son and said, *'I happen to know that God thought that was a great prayer.'*

'Really?' my son asked.

'Cross my heart,' the man replied. Then in a theatrical whisper he added (indicating the woman whose remark had started this whole thing), *'Too bad she never asks God for ice cream. A little ice cream is good for the soul sometimes.'*

Naturally, I bought my kids ice cream at the end of the meal. My son stared at his for a moment and then did something I will remember the rest of my life. He picked up his sundae and without a word, walked over and placed it in front of the woman. With a big smile he told her, *'Here, this is for you. Ice cream is good for the soul sometimes; and my soul is good already.'*

I love this story. Sometimes we all need some ice cream. I hope God sends you some Ice Cream today.

Satan:

One bright, beautiful Sunday morning, everyone in the tiny town got up early and went to church. Before the service started, the townspeople were sitting in their pews and talking about their relatives, their families, etc. Suddenly, Satan appeared at the front of the church. Everyone started screaming and running for the entrance, trampling each other in a frantic effort to get away from evil incarnate. Soon everyone was evacuated from the church, except for one elderly gentleman who sat calmly in his pew, not moving and seemingly oblivious to the fact that God's ultimate enemy was in his presence.

This confused Satan a bit, so he walked up to the man and said, *'Don't you know who I am?'*

The man replied, *'Yep, sure do.'*

Satan asked, *'Aren't you afraid of me?'*

'Nope, sure ain't,' says the man.

Satan was a little perturbed at this and queried, *'Why aren't you afraid of me?'*

The man calmly replied, *'Been married to your sister for over 48 years.'*

Celibacy Test:

The Monsignor told three young candidates for the priesthood they have to pass one more test: The Celibacy Test. The Monsignor led them into a room, told them to undress and a small bell is tied to each man's penis.

In came a beautiful woman, wearing a sexy belly-dancer costume. She began to dance sensually around the first candidate. *Ting-al-ling* went the bell ...

'Oh Patrick,' said the monsignor, 'I'm so disappointed in your lack of control. Go take a long, cold shower and pray about your carnal weakness.' Patrick left.

The dancer continued, slowly dancing around the second candidate and peeling off her layers of veils. As the last veil drops: *Ting-al-ling* went the bell ...

'Joseph, Joseph,' Sighed the Monsignor. 'You too are unable to withstand your carnal desires. Go take a long, cold shower and pray for forgiveness.'

The dancer then proceeded to dance her sensuous dance around the third candidate. Slowly around him she dances, now devoid of all her veils, but the third candidate remains unmoved.

'James, my son, I'm truly proud of you,' says the Monsignor. 'Only you have the true strength of character needed to become a great priest. Now go and join your weaker brethren in the shower.' *Ting-al-ling* went the bell ...

The Painters:

Two nuns are ordered to paint a room in the convent and the last instruction of the Mother Superior is that they must not get even a drop of paint on their habits.

After conferring about this for a while, the two nuns decide to lock the door of the room, strip off their habits and paint in the nude. In the middle of the project, they heard a knock at the door.

'Who is it?' calls one of the nuns.

'The blind man,' replies a voice from the other side of the door.

The two nuns look at each other and shrug, deciding that no harm can come from letting a blind man into the room, so they open the door.

'Nice boobs,' says the man, 'Where do you want these blinds?'

The Emergency:

A priest was called away for an emergency. Not wanting to leave the confessional unattended, he called his rabbi friend from across the street and asked him to cover for him. The rabbi told him he wouldn't know what to say, but the priest told him to come on over and he'd stay with him for a little bit to show him what to do. The rabbi came and he and the priest entered the confessional.

In a few minutes, a woman came in and said, *'Father, forgive me for I have sinned.'*

The Priest asks, *'What did you do?'*

The woman replies, *'I committed adultery.'*

Priest: *'How many times?'*

Woman: *'Three times.'*

Priest: *'Say two Hail Marys, put $5 in the box and go and sin no more.'*

A few minutes later a man enters the confessional. He says, *'Father, forgive me for I have sinned.'* The Priest asks, *'What did you do?'*

The man replies, *'I committed adultery.'*

Priest: *'How many times?'*

Man: *'Three times.'*

Priest: *'Say two Hail Marys, put $5 in the box and go and sin no more.'*

The rabbi told the priest that he thought he had it, so the priest left. A few minutes later, a woman entered and said, *'Father, forgive me for I have sinned.'*

The Rabbi asks, *'What did you do?'*

The woman replies, *'I committed adultery.'*

Rabbi: *'How many times?'*

Woman: *'Once.'*

Rabbi: *'Go do it two more times. We have a special this week, three for $5.'*

Two Beggars:

Two beggars are sitting on a park bench in Mexico City. One is holding a cross and one a Star of David. Both are holding hats to collect contributions. People walk by, lift their noses at the man with the Star of David and drop money into the hat held by the man with the cross. Soon the hat of the man with the cross is filled and the hat of the man with the Star of David is empty.

A priest watches and then approaches the men. He turns to the man with the Star of David and says: *'Young man. Don't you realise that this is a Catholic country? You'll never get any contributions in this country holding a Star of David.'*

The man with the Star of David turns to the man with the cross and says, *'Moishe, can you imagine, this guy is trying to tell us how to run our business?'*

Nervous Priest:

A new priest at his first mass was so nervous he could hardly speak. After mass, he asked the monsignor how he had done. The monsignor replied, *'When I am worried about getting nervous on the pulpit, I put a glass of vodka next to the water glass. If I start to get nervous, I take a sip.'*

So the next Sunday, he took the monsignor's advice. At the beginning of the sermon, he got nervous so took several sips. He proceeded to talk up a storm. Upon his return to his office after mass, he found the following note on the door:

1. Sip the Vodka - don't gulp.
2. There are 10 commandments - not 12.
3. Jesus was consecrated, not constipated.
4. Jacob wagered his donkey, he did not bet his ass.
5. We do not refer to Jesus Christ as the late J.C.
6. The Father, Son and Holy Ghost are NOT referred to as Daddy, Junior and the Spook.
7. David slew Goliath; he did not kick the shit out of him.
8. When David was hit by a rock and knocked off his donkey, don't say, *'He was stoned off his ass.'*
9. We do not refer to the cross as the 'Big T.'
10. When Jesus broke bread at the Last Supper, he said, *'Take this and eat it, for it is my body.'* He did not say, *'Eat me.'*
11. The Virgin Mary is not called, *'Mary with the Cherry.'*
12. The recommended grace before a meal is not: *'Rub-a-dub-dub thanks for the grub, yeah God.'*
13. Next Sunday there will be a taffy-pulling contest at St. Peter's - not a peter-pulling contest at St. Taffy's.

The Donkey:

The pastor entered his donkey in a race and it won. The pastor was so pleased with the donkey that he entered it in another race and it won again. The local paper read: PASTOR'S ASS OUT IN FRONT.

The Bishop was so upset with this kind of publicity that he ordered the pastor not to enter the donkey in any more races. The next day, the local paper headline read: BISHOP SCRATCHES PASTOR'S ASS.

This was too much for the Bishop, so he ordered the pastor to get rid of the donkey. The pastor decided to give it to a nun in a nearby convent.

The local paper, hearing of the news, posted the following headline the next day: NUN HAS THE BEST ASS IN TOWN.
The Bishop fainted. He informed the nun that she would have to get rid of the donkey, so she sold it to a farmer for $10.

The next day the paper read: NUN SELLS ASS FOR $10.

This was too much for the Bishop, so he ordered the nun to buy back the donkey and lead it to the high plains where it could run wild.

The next day the headlines read: NUN ANNOUNCES HER ASS IS WILD AND FREE.

Alas; the Bishop was buried the next day.

Moral of the story? Being concerned about public opinion can bring you much grief and misery and even shorten your life. So, be yourself and enjoy life ... stop worrying about everyone else's ass and you'll live longer and be a lot happier

The Jewish Samurai:

Back in the time of the Samurai, there was a powerful emperor. This emperor needed a new head Samurai so he sent a message to one and all that he was searching for one. A year passes and only three people show up: A Japanese Samurai, a Chinese Samurai and a Jewish Samurai.

The emperor asks the Japanese Samurai to come in and demonstrate why he should be Head Samurai. The Samurai opens a matchbox and out pops a little fly. Whoosh! Goes the sword and the fly drops dead on the ground in two pieces.

The emperor says, *'That is very impressive!'* Then he asks the Chinese Samurai to come in and demonstrate. The Samurai opens a box and out pops a fly. Whoosh! Whoosh! The fly drops dead on the ground in four pieces.

'That was really impressive,' says the emperor and asks the Jewish Samurai to demonstrate why he should be the Head Samurai.

The Jewish Samurai thinks, *'If it works for the other two, why not try?'*

Whoooooosh! A gust of wind fills the room, but the fly is still alive and buzzing around.

The emperor asks in disappointment, *'Why is the fly not dead?'*

The Jewish Samurai replies, *'If you look very closely, you will see that the fly has been circumcised!'*

The Sons:

Four old college friends were having coffee. The first, a Catholic woman tells her friends, *'My son is now a Priest. When he walks into a room, everyone calls him 'Father.''*

The second Catholic woman chirps, *'My son is a Bishop. Whenever he walks into a room, people call him 'Your Grace.''*

The third Catholic crone says, *'My son is a Cardinal. Whenever he walks into a room, he's called, 'Your Eminence.''*

Since the fourth woman, a Jewish lady, simply sipped her coffee in silence, the first three women give her this subtle, *'Well ...?'*

So she replies, *'My son is 6'6. He dresses very well; has a tight muscular body; tight hard buns; and a very nice bulge; and whenever he walks into a room women gasp, 'Oh my God!''*

The Dog:

A farmer named Muldoon lived alone in the Irish countryside except for a pet dog he doted on. The dog finally died and Muldoon went to the parish priest, saying, *'Father, my dog is dead. Could you possibly be saying a mass for the poor creature?'*

Father Patrick told the farmer, *'No, we can't have services for an animal in the church, but I'll tell you what, there's a new denomination down the road apiece and no telling what they believe in, but maybe they'll do something for the animal.'*

Muldoon said, *'I'll go right now. By the way, do you think $50,000 is enough to donate for the service?'*

Father Patrick replied, *'Why didn't you tell me the dog was Catholic?'*

Army of the Lord:

A friend was in front of me coming out of church one day and the preacher was standing at the door, as he always was to shake hands. He grabbed my friend by the hand and pulled him aside. The preacher said to him, *'You need to join the Army of the lord!'*

My friend replied, *'I'm already in the Army of the lord, Pastor.'*

The Pastor questioned, *'How come I don't see you except at Christmas and Easter?'*

He whispered back, *'I'm in the secret service.'*

Joining the Church:

Three couples, an elderly couple, a middle-aged couple and a young newlywed couple wanted to join a church. The pastor said, *'We have a special requirement for new parishioners. You must abstain from having sex for two weeks.'* The couples agreed and came back at the end of two weeks.

The pastor went to the elderly couple and asked, *'Were you able to abstain from sex for the two weeks?'*

The old man replied, *'No problem at all, Pastor.'*

'Congratulations! Welcome to the church,' said the pastor. The pastor then went to the middle-aged couple and asked, *'Well, were you able to abstain from sex for the two weeks?'*

The man replied, *'The first week was not too bad. The second week I had to sleep on the couch for a couple of nights, but, yes, we made it.'*

'Congratulations! Welcome to the church!' said the pastor. The pastor went to the newlywed couple and asked, *'Well, were you able to abstain from sex for two weeks?'*

'No, pastor, we were not able to go without sex for the two weeks,' the young man replied sadly.

'What happened?' inquired the pastor.

'My wife was reaching for a can of paint on the top shelf and dropped it. When she bent over to pick it up, I was overcome with lust and took advantage of her right there.'

'You understand of course, this means you will not be welcome in our church,' stated the pastor.

'We know,' said the young man sadly, *'We're not welcome at Home Depot any more either.'*

At the Bar:

Father Murphy walked into a pub in Donegal and said to the first man he met, *'Do you want to go to heaven?'*

The man replied, *'I do Father.'*

The priest said, *'Then stand over there against the wall.'*

Then the priest asked the second man, *'Do you want to go to heaven?'*

'Certainly, Father,' the man replied.
'Then stand over there against the wall,' said the priest.
Then Father Murphy walked up to O'Toole and said, 'Do you want to go to heaven?'
O'Toole said, 'No, I don't Father.'
The priest said, 'I don't believe this. You mean to tell me that when you die you don't want to go to heaven?'
O'Toole said, 'Oh, when I die, yes. I thought you were getting a group together to go right now.'

Holy Water:

A train hits a busload of Catholic schoolgirls and they all perish. They are all in heaven trying to enter the pearly gates past St. Peter. St. Peter asks the first girl, 'Jessica, have you ever had any contact with a penis?'

She giggles and shyly replies, 'Well I once touched the head of one with the tip of my finger.'

St. Peter says, 'Okay, dip the tip of your finger in The Holy Water and pass through the gate.'

St. Peter asks the next girl the same question, 'Jennifer have you ever had any contact with a penis?'

The girl is a little reluctant but replies, 'Well once I fondled and stroked one.'

St. Peter says, 'Okay, dip your whole hand in The Holy Water and pass through the gate.'

All of a sudden there is a lot of commotion in the line of girls and one girl pushes her way to the front of the line. When she reaches the front of the line St. Peter says, 'Lisa! What seems to be the rush?'

The girl replies, 'If I'm going to have to gargle that Holy Water, I want to do it before Tiffany sticks her ass in it.'

Christmas Carols for the Mentally Challenged:

Schizophrenia: Do you hear what I hear?
Multiple Personality: We three queens disoriented are.
Dementia: I think I'll be home for Christmas
Narcissistic: Hark the herald angels sing (about me)
Mania: Deck the halls and walls and house and lawn and streets and stores and offices and town or deck the halls and spare no expense!
Paranoia: Santa Clause is coming to get me.

Personality Disorder: You better watch out, I'm gonna cry, then maybe I'll tell you why.

Obsessive Compulsive: Jingle Bell, Jingle Bell, Jingle Bell Rock; Jingle Bell, Jingle Bell, Jingle Bell Rock; Jingle Bell, Jingle Bell, Jingle Bell Rock; Jingle Bell, Jingle Bell, Jingle Bell Rock; Jingle Bell, Jingle Bell, Jingle Bell Rock; Jingle Bell, Jingle Bell, Jingle Bell Rock.

Borderline Personality: Thoughts of roasting in an open fire.

Passive Aggressive: On the first day of Christmas my true love gave to me (and then took it all away).

The Twelve Days of Christmas - Revised Edition:

As a further restructuring, today's global challenges require the North Pole to continue to look for better, more competitive steps. Effective immediately, the following economic measures are to take place in the *'Twelve Days of Christmas'* subsidiary:

The partridge will be retained, but the pear tree never turned out to be the cash crop forecasted. It will be replaced by a plastic hanging plant, providing considerable savings in maintenance;

The two turtledoves represent a redundancy that is simply not cost effective. In addition, their romance during working hours can't be condoned. The positions are therefore eliminated;

The four calling birds will be replaced by the automated voice mail system, with a call-waiting option. An analysis is underway to determine who the birds have been calling, how often and how long they talked;

The Board of Directors has put the five golden rings on hold. Maintaining a portfolio based on one commodity could have negative implications for institutional investors. Diversification into other precious metals as well as a mix of T-Bills and high technology stocks appear to be in order;

The six geese a-laying constitute a luxury, which can no longer be afforded. It has long been felt that the production rate of one egg per goose per day is an example of the decline in productivity. Three geese will be let go and an upgrading in the selection procedure by personnel will assure management that from now on every goose it gets will be a good one;

The seven swans a-swimming is obviously a number chosen in better times. Their function is primarily decorative. Mechanical swans are in order. The current swans will be retrained to learn some new strokes and therefore enhance their outplacement;

As you know, the eight maids-a-milking concept has been under heavy scrutiny by the EEOC. A male/female balance in the workforce is being sought. The more militant maids consider this a dead-end job with no upward mobility. Automation of the process may permit the maids to try a-mending, a-mentoring or a-mulching;

Nine ladies dancing has always been an odd number. This function will be phased out as these individuals grow older and can no longer do the steps;

Ten Lords-a-leaping is overkill. The high cost of Lords plus the expense of international air travel prompted the Compensation Committee to suggest replacing this group with ten out-of-work congressmen. While leaping ability may be somewhat sacrificed, the savings are significant because we expect an oversupply of un-employed congressmen this year;

Eleven pipers piping and twelve drummers drumming is a simple case of the band getting too big. A substitution with a string quartet, a cutback on new music and no uniforms will produce savings that will drop right down to the bottom line.'

We can expect a substantial reduction in assorted people, fowl, animals and other expenses. Though incomplete, studies indicate that stretching deliveries over twelve days is inefficient. If we can drop ship in one day, service levels will be improved.

Regarding the lawsuit filed by the attorney association seeking expansion to include the legal profession ('thirteen lawyers-a-suing') action is pending.

Lastly, it is not beyond consideration that deeper cuts may be necessary in the future to stay competitive. Should that happen, the Board will request management to scrutinise the Snow White Division to see if seven dwarfs is the right number.

The Twelve Days of Christmas – Canuk (Canadian) Edition:

On the first day of Christmas, a Canuk sent to me one moose in a maple tree.

On the second day of Christmas, a Canuk sent to me two polar bears;

On the third day of Christmas, a Canuk sent to me three snowmen;

On the fourth day of Christmas, a Canuk sent to me four totem poles;

On the fifth day of Christmas, a Canuk sent to me five hockey sticks;

On the sixth day of Christmas, a Canuk sent to me six whales a-breaching;

On the seventh day of Christmas, a Canuk sent to me seven beavers building;

On the eighth day of Christmas, a Canuk sent to me eight lobsters nipping;

On the ninth day of Christmas, a Canuk sent to me nine Mounties riding;

On the tenth day of Christmas, a Canuk sent to me ten salmon leaping;

On the eleventh day of Christmas, a Canuk sent to me eleven sled dogs mushing;

On the twelfth day of Christmas, a Canuk sent to me one moose, two polar bears, three snowmen, four totem poles, five hockey sticks, six whales a-breaching, seven beavers building, eight lobsters nipping, nine Mounties riding, ten salmon leaping, eleven sled dogs mushing and twelve skiers skiing in a maple tree.

The Swimmer:

An atheist was swimming in the ocean. All of a sudden, he saw this shark in the water and started swimming for his boat. As he looked back, he saw the shark turn and head towards him. His boat was still a ways off and he started swimming like crazy. He was scared to death and turned to see the jaws of the great white beast open revealing its teeth in horrific splendour. The atheist screamed, *'Oh my God, save me!'*

In an instant, time froze and a bright light shone down from above. The man was motionless in the water when he heard the voice of God say, *'You are an atheist. Why do you call upon me when you do not believe in me?'*

Aghast with confusion and knowing it was true and he couldn't lie, the man replied, *'Well, that's true, I don't believe in you, but what about the shark? Can you make the shark believe in you?'*

The Lord replied, *'As you wish,'* and the light retracted back into the heavens and the man could feel the water begin to move once again.

As the atheist looked back he could see the jaws of the shark start to close down on him, when all of a sudden, the shark stops and pulls back. Shocked, the man looked at the shark as the huge beast closed his eyes and bowed his head and said, *'Thank you Lord for this food for which I am about to receive.'*

Admission Policy:

It was getting a little crowded in Heaven, so God decided to change the admission policy. The new law was that in order to get into Heaven, you had to have had a really bad day on the day you died. The policy would go into effect at noon the next day. So the next day at 12:01 a man came to the gates of Heaven, the angel at the gates remembering the new policy, promptly asked the man, *'Before I let you in, I need you to tell me how your day was going on the day you died.'*

'No problem,' the man said. *'I came home to my 25th floor apartment on my lunch hour to discover my wife having an affair. But her lover was nowhere in sight. Immediately, I began searching for him. My wife, half-naked was yelling at me as I searched the apartment. Just as I was about to give up, I happened to glance out onto the balcony and noticed that there was a man hanging off the edge by his fingertips! The nerve of that guy! Well, I ran out onto the balcony and stomped on his fingers until he fell to the ground. But wouldn't you know it, he landed in some trees and bushes that broke his fall and he didn't die.*

This ticked me off even more. In rage, I went back inside to get the first thing I could get my hands on to throw at him. Oddly enough the first thing I thought of was the refrigerator. I unplugged it, pushed it out onto the balcony and tipped it over the side. It plummeted 25 stories and crushed him. The excitement of the moment was so great that I had a heart attack and died almost instantly.'

The angel sat back and thought a moment. Technically, the guy did have a bad day. It was a crime of passion. So the angel announces, *'Okay sir, welcome to the Kingdom of heaven.'* And let him in.

A few seconds later, the next guy comes up. To the Angel's surprise it is Vernon Jordan. *'Mr. Jordan, before I can let you in, I need to hear about what your day was like before you died.'*

Jordan said, *'No problem. But you're not going to believe this. I was on the balcony of my 26th story apartment doing my daily exercises. I had been under a lot of pressure so I was pushing hard to relieve my stress. I guess I got a little carried away, slipped and accidentally fell over the side! Luckily I was* able to catch myself by the fingertips on the balcony below mine. But all of a sudden, this crazy man comes out of his apartment, starts cursing and stomps on my fingers. Well, of course I fell. I hit some trees and bushes at the bottom, which broke my fall, so I didn't die right away. As I'm lying there, face up on the ground, unable to move and in excruciating pain, I see this guy push his refrigerator - of all things - off the balcony. It falls 25 floors and lands on top of me, killing me instantly.'

The Angel quietly laughs to himself as Jordan finishes his story. *'I could get used to this new policy,'* he thinks to himself. *'Very well sir,'* the angel announces. *'Welcome to the Kingdom of Heaven,'* and he lets Jordan enter.

A few seconds later another man comes to the gate. He says, *'Please tell me what it was like the day you died.'*

The man says, *'Okay, picture this. I'm naked inside a refrigerator ...'*

Dear God

There was a man who worked for the Post Office whose job it was to process all the mail that had illegible addresses. One day, a letter came addressed in a shaky handwriting to God. He thought he should open t to see what it was about. The letter read:

Dear God,

I am an 83-year-old widow, living on a very small pension. Yesterday someone stole my purse. It had $100 in it, which was all the money I had until my next pension check. Next Sunday is Christmas and I had invited two of my friends over for dinner. Without that money, I have nothing to buy food with. I have no family to turn to and you are my only hope. Can you please help me?

Sincerely,

Edna

The postal worker was touched. He showed the letter to all the other workers. Each one dug into his or her wallet and came up with a few dollars. By the time he made the rounds, he had collected $96, which they put into an envelope and sent to the woman. The rest of the day, all the workers felt a warm glow thinking of Edna and the dinner she would be able to share with her friends.

Christmas came and went. A few days later, another letter came from the old lady to God. All the workers gathered around while the letter was opened. It read:

Dear God,

How can I ever thank you enough for what you did for me? Because of your gift of love, I was able to fix a glorious dinner for my friends. We had a very nice day and I told my friends of your wonderful gift. By the way, there was $4 missing. I think it must have been those thieving bastards at the Post Office.

Sincerely

Edna

The Nun and the Priest

A nun and a priest were crossing the Sahara desert on a camel. On the third day out the camel suddenly dropped dead without warning. After dusting themselves off, the nun and the priest surveyed their situation. After a long period of silence, the priest spoke. *'Well, sister, this looks pretty grim.'*

'I know, father. In fact, I don't think it likely that we can survive more than a day or two.'

'I agree,' said the Father. *'Sister, since we are unlikely to make it out of here alive, would you do something for me?'*

'Anything, Father.'

'I have never seen a woman's breasts and I was wondering if I might see yours.'

'Well, under the circumstances I don't see that it would do any harm.'

The nun opened her habit and the priest enjoyed the sight of her shapely breasts, commenting frequently on their beauty.

'Sister, would you mind if I touched them?'

She consented and he fondled them for several minutes.

'Father, could I ask something of you?'

'Yes, Sister?'

'I have never seen a man's penis. Could I see yours?'

'I suppose that would be okay,' the priest replied, lifting his robe.

'Oh Father, may I touch it?'

The priest consented and after a few minutes of fondling he was sporting a huge erection.

'Sister, you know that if I insert my penis in the right place, it can produce life.'

'Is that true father?'

'Yes, it is, Sister.'

'Oh Father that's wonderful, stick it in the camel and let's get the hell out of here.'

The Professional:

A woman was at work when she received a phone call that her daughter was very sick with a fever. She left her work and stopped by the pharmacy to get some medication for her daughter. When returning to her car, she found that she had locked her keys in the car. She was in a hurry to get home to her sick daughter and didn't know what to do, so she called her home and told the baby-sitter what had happened and that she didn't know what to do. The baby-sitter told her that her daughter was getting worse. She said, *'You might find a coat hanger and use that to open the door.'*

The woman looked around and found an old rusty coat hanger that had been thrown down on the ground possibly by someone else that had locked their keys in their car. She looked at the hanger and said, *'I don't know how to use this,'* and bowed her head and asked God to send her some help. Within five minutes an old rusty car pulled up, with a dirty, greasy, bearded man who was wearing an old biker skull rag on his head. The woman thought, *'Great God. This is what you sent to help me?'* But she was desperate so she was also very thankful.

The man got out of his car and asked her if he could help. She said, *'Yes my daughter is very sick. I stopped to get her some mediation and I locked my keys in my car. I must get home to her. Please, can you use this hanger to unlock my car?'*

He said, *'Sure!'* and in less than one minute the car was opened. She hugged the man and through her tears she said, *'Thank you so much. You are a very nice man.'*

The man replied, *'Lady, I'm not a nice man, see, I just got out of prison today. I was in prison for car theft and have only been out for about an hour.'*

The woman hugged the man again, looked up and with sobbing tears cried out loud, *'Thank you God, for sending me a professional.'*

The power of prayer

In church, I heard a lady in the pew next to me saying a prayer. It was so sweet and sincere that I just had to share it with you.

'Dear Lord,
This has been a tough two or three years. You have taken my favourite actor Patrick Swayze; my favourite musician Michael Jackson; my favourite blues singer Amy Winehouse; my favourite actress Elizabeth Taylor and my favourite singer Whitney Houston. I just wanted you to know who my favourite politicians are ...'

The Graveyard

Two men were walking home after a Halloween party and decided to take a shortcut through the cemetery just for laughs. Right in the middle of the cemetery they were startled by a tap-tap-tapping noise coming from the misty shadows. Trembling with fear, they found an old man with a hammer and chisel, chipping away at one of the headstones.

'Holy cow, mister,' one of them said after catching his breath, *'You scared us half to death – we thought you were a ghost! What are you doing working here so late at night?'*

'Those fools!' the old man grumbled. *'They misspelled my name.'*

Easter Jokes for the Kids:

Q. Why did the Easter egg hide?
A. He was a little chicken.
Q. Why shouldn't you tell an Easter egg a good joke?
A. It might crack up!
Q. What did one Easter egg say to the other?
A. Heard any good yolks lately?
Q. How did the soggy Easter Bunny dry himself?
A. With a hare dryer!
Q. How does the Easter bunny stay in shape?
A. Lots of eggs-ercise!
Q. What do you call a dumb bunny?
A. A hare brain.
Q. How can you tell which rabbits are the oldest in a group?
A. Just look for the gray hares.
Q. How do rabbits say good-bye to carrots?
A. It's been nice gnawing you!
Q. How does a rabbit make gold soup?
A. He begins with 24 carrots.

Oy Vey!!

Mrs. Yetta Rosenberg just off the plane from her vacation and, being tired from the flight, went to the first hotel she saw to rent a room. She walked up to the desk and said to the clerk, *'I'm Mrs. Yetta Rosenberg and I desire a room for the night.'*

The clerk looked disdainfully at her and coldly said, *'I'm sorry, madam, but our hotel is completely booked.'*

Just then, a man with his suitcase in hand, drops his key and a check at the desk and heads for the door.

'Oy, what luck,' said Mrs. Rosenberg. *'I can take his room.'*
'I'm sorry, madam,' said the clerk, *'but I thought you understood my meaning. To be blunt, we do not cater to Jews.'*

'Jews?' exclaimed Mrs. Rosenberg. *'So, who's a Jew? I'm a Cat'lic.'*

In obvious disbelief, the clerk asked her, *'If you're a Catholic, then answer this question: Who is the Son of God?'*

'That's easy,' said Mrs. Rosenberg, *'Jesus Christ.'*

The clerk, still not convinced, then asked, *'Who were Jesus' mother and father?'*

'Mary and Joseph,' replied Mrs. Rosenberg, testily.

Then the clerk asked, *'And where was Jesus born?'*

*'In a manger in a bar*n,' answered Mrs. Rosenberg, becoming agitated.

'And why was Jesus born in a manger in a barn?' asked the clerk.

'Because a shmuck like you wouldn't rent a room to Jews!!!'

Longevity

On the first day, God created the dog and said:

'Sit all day by the door of your house and bark at anyone who comes in or walks past. For this, I will give you a life span of twenty years.'

The dog said: *'That's a long time to be barking. How about only ten years and I'll give you back the other ten?'*

So God agreed. On the second day, God created the monkey and said:

'Entertain people, do tricks and make them laugh. For this, I'll give you a twenty-year life span.'

The monkey said: *'Monkey tricks for twenty years? That's a pretty long time to perform. How about I give you back ten like the Dog did?'*

And God agreed. On the third day, God created the cow and said: *'You must go into the field with the farmer all day long and suffer under the sun, have calves and give milk to support the farmer's family. For this, I will give you a life span of sixty years.'*

The cow said: *'That's kind of a tough life you want me to live for sixty years. How about twenty and I'll give back the other forty?'*

And God agreed again. On the fourth day, God created humans and said:

'Eat, sleep, play, marry and enjoy your life. For this, I'll give you twenty years.'

But the human said: *'Only twenty years? Could you possibly give me my twenty, the forty the cow gave back, the ten the monkey gave back and the ten the dog gave back; that makes eighty, okay?'*

'Okay,' said God, *'You asked for it.'*

So that is why for our first twenty years we eat, sleep, play and enjoy ourselves. For the next forty years we slave in the sun to support our family. For the next ten years we do monkey tricks to entertain the grandchildren. And for the last ten years we sit on the front porch and bark at everyone.

Life has now been explained to you. There is no need to thank me for this valuable information. I'm doing it as a public service.

A Nun Grading Papers

Can you imagine the Nun sitting at her desk grading these papers, all the while trying to keep a straight face and maintain her composure! (I know I couldn't!).

Pay special attention to the wording and spelling. If you know the bible even a little, you'll find this hilarious! It comes from a catholic elementary school test.

Kids were asked questions about the old and new testaments. The following statements about the bible were written by children. They have not been retouched or corrected. Incorrect spelling has been left in.

1. In the first book of the bible, guinessis, god got tired of creating the world so he took the sabbath off.
2. Adam and Eve were created from an apple tree. Noah's wife was Joan of Ark. Noah built an ark and the animals came on in pears.

3. Lots wife was a pillar of salt during the day, but a ball of fire during the night.
4. The Jews were a proud people and throughout history they had trouble with unsympathetic genitals.
5. Sampson was a strongman who let himself be led astray by a Jezebel like Delilah.
6. Samson slayed the Philistines with the axe of the apostles.
7. Moses led the Jews to the Red Sea where they made unleavened bread which is bread without any ingredients.
8. The Egyptians were all drowned in the dessert. Afterwards, Moses went up to Mount Cyanide to get the ten commandments.
9. The first commandment was when Eve told Adam to eat the apple.
10. The seventh commandment is thou shalt not admit adultery.
11. Moses died before he ever reached Canada. Then Joshua led the Hebrews in the battle of geritol.
12. The greatest miricle in the bible is when Joshua told his son to stand still and he obeyed him.
13. David was a Hebrew king who was skilled at playing the liar. He fought the Finkelsteins, a race of people who lived in biblical times.
14. Solomon, one of David's sons, had 300 wives and 700 porcupines.
15. When Mary heard she was the mother of Jesus, she sang the Magna Carta.
16. When the three wise guys from the east side arrived they found Jesus in the manager.
17. Jesus was born because Mary had an immaculate contraption.
18. St. John, the blacksmith dumped water on his head.
19. Jesus enunciated the golden rule, which says to do unto others before they do one to you. He also explained a man doth not live by sweat alone.
20. It was a miricle when Jesus rose from the dead and managed to get the tombstone off the entrance.
21. The people who followed the Lord were called the 12 decibels.
22. The epistels were the wives of the apostles.
23. One of the oppossums was St. Matthew, who was also a taximan.

24. St. Paul cavorted to Christianity. He preached holy acrimony which is another name for marraige.
25. Christians have only one spouse. This is called monotony.

Biblical contrasts

In her radio show, Dr Laura Schlesinger said that, as an observant Orthodox Jew, homosexuality is an abomination according to Leviticus 18:22, and cannot be condoned under any circumstance. The following response is an open letter to Dr. Laura, penned by a US resident, which was posted on the Internet. It's funny, as well as informative:

Dear Dr. Laura:
Thank you for doing so much to educate people regarding God's Law. I have learned a great deal from your show, and try to share that knowledge with as many people as I can. When someone tries to defend the homosexual lifestyle, for example, I simply remind them that Leviticus 18:22 clearly states it to be an abomination ... End of debate.

I do need some advice from you, however, regarding some other elements of God's Laws and how to follow them.

Leviticus 25:44 states that I may possess slaves, both male and female, provided they are purchased from neighbouring nations. A friend of mine claims that this applies to Mexicans, but not Canadians. Can you clarify? Why can't I own Canadians?

I would like to sell my daughter into slavery, as sanctioned in Exodus 21:7. In this day and age, what do you think would be a fair price for her?

I know that I am allowed no contact with a woman while she is in her period of Menstrual uncleanliness - Lev.15: 19-24. The problem is how do I tell? I have tried asking, but most women take offense.

When I burn a bull on the altar as a sacrifice, I know it creates a pleasing odour for the Lord - Lev.1:9. The problem is my neighbours. They claim the odour is not pleasing to them. Should I smite them?

I have a neighbour who insists on working on the Sabbath. Exodus 35:2 clearly states he should be put to death. Am I morally obligated to kill him myself or should I ask the police to do it?

A friend of mine feels that even though eating shellfish is an abomination, Lev. 11:10, it is a lesser abomination than homosexuality. I don't agree. Can you settle this? Are there 'degrees' of abomination?

Lev. 21:20 states that I may not approach the altar of God if I have a defect in my sight. I have to admit that I wear reading glasses. Does my vision have to be 20/20 or is there some wiggle-room here?

Most of my male friends get their hair trimmed, including the hair around their temples, even though this is expressly forbidden by Lev. 19:27. How should they die?

I know from Lev. 11:6-8 that touching the skin of a dead pig makes me unclean, but may I still play football if I wear gloves?

My uncle has a farm. He violates Lev.19:19 by planting two different crops in the same field, as does his wife by wearing garments made of two different kinds of thread (cotton/polyester blend). He also tends to curse and blaspheme a lot. Is it really necessary that we go to all the trouble of getting the whole town together to stone them? Lev.24:10-16. Couldn't we just burn them to death at a private family affair, like we do with people who sleep with their in-laws? (Lev. 20:14)

I know you have studied these things extensively and thus enjoy considerable expertise in such matters, so I'm confident you can help.

Thank you again for reminding us that God's word is eternal and unchanging.

Your adoring fan,

James M. Kauffman, Ed.D. Professor Emeritus, Dept. Of Curriculum, Instruction, and Special Education University of Virginia

(It would be a damn shame if we couldn't own a Canadian.)

The 'Thingy'

Why men can pee standing up:

God was just about done creating humans, but he had two parts left over. He couldn't decide how to split them between Adam and Eve, so He thought He might just as well ask them.

He told them one of the things He had left was a thingy that would allow the owner to pee while standing up. *'It's a very handy thing,' God told them, and I was wondering if either one of you had a preference for it.'*

Well, Adam jumped up and down and begged, *'Oh please give that to me! I'd love to be able to do that! It seems like just the sort of thing a man should have. Please! Pleeease! Give it to me!'* On and on he went like an excited little boy.

Eve just smiled and told God that if Adam really wanted it so badly, he could have it. So God gave Adam the thingy that allowed him to pee standing up.

Adam was so excited, he just started whizzing all over the place - first on the side of a rock, then he wrote his name in the sand and then he tried to see if he could hit a stump ten feet away – laughing with delight all the while.

God and Eve watched him with amusement and then God said to Eve. *'Well I guess you're kind of stuck with the last thing I have left.'*

'What's it called?' asked Eve.

'Brains,' said God.

Church services in the future

Preacher: Praise the Lord.
Congregation: Hallelujah!
Preacher: Can we please turn our tablet PC, iPad, cell phone, kindle Bibles to 1 Cor. 13:13. And please switch on your Bluetooth to download the sermon.
Preacher: Let us pray, committing this week into God's hands.
Open your Apps, BBM, Twitter and Facebook and chat with God.
Preacher: Please have your credit and debit cards ready as we shall now take the offering.

You can log on to the church Wi-Fi using the password Lord909887.

Ushers circulate mobile card swipe machines among the worshipers. Those who prefer to make electronic funds transfers are directed to computers and laptops at the rear of the church and those who prefer to use iPads are allowed to flip them open. Those who prefer telephone banking are allowed to take out their cell phones to transfer their contributions to the church bank account at this time.

(The holy atmosphere is truly electric as the cell phones, iPads, PCs and laptops beep and flicker!)

Announcements

This week's cell meetings shall be held on the various Facebook group pages where the usual group chatting takes place. Please don't miss out.

Wednesday's bible teachings will be held live on Skype at 1900 hrs CST. Please don't miss out.

You can follow your Preacher on Twitter this weekend for counseling and Prayers. God bless you and have a wonderful week!

Three Irishmen

Three Irishmen are sitting in the pub window seat, idly chatting and watching the front door of the brothel across the road. They see the local Methodist pastor appear, knock on the door and quickly go inside.

'Would you look at that!' exclaims the first Irishman. *'Didn't I always say what a bunch of hypocrites those Methodists are?'*

No sooner are the words out of his mouth than a Rabbi appears at the brothel door, knocks, and also disappears inside.

'Dere's another one trying to fool everyone with pious preaching and silly hats!'

They continue drinking while roundly condemning the vicar and the rabbi when they see their local Catholic priest knock on the brothel door.

'Ah, now dat's sad,' says the third Irishman, *'One of the girls must have died.'*

Getting a hairdryer through customs

In parochial school, students are taught that lying is a sin. However, instructions also advised that using a bit of imagination was okay to express the truth differently without lying. Below is a perfect example of those teachings:

An attractive young woman on a flight from Ireland asked the Priest beside her, *'Father, may I ask a favour?'*

'Of course child. What may I do for you?'

'Well, I bought my mother an expensive hair dryer for her birthday. It is unopened but well over the Customs limits and I'm afraid they'll confiscate it. Is there any way you could carry it through customs for me? Hide it under your robes perhaps?'

'I would love to help you, dear, but I must warn you, I will not lie.'

'With your honest face, Father, no one will question you.'

When they got to Customs, she let the priest go first. The official asked, *'Father, do you have anything to declare?'*

'From the top of my head down to my waist I have nothing to declare.'

The official thought this answer strange, so asked, *'And what do you have to declare from your waist to the floor?'*

'I have a marvellous instrument designed to be used on a woman, but which is, to date, unused.'

Roaring with laughter, the official said, *'Go ahead, Father. Next please!'*

What is celibacy?

Celibacy can be a choice in life, or a condition imposed by circumstances.

While attending a Marriage Weekend, my wife and I, listened to the instructor declare, *'It is essential that husbands and wives know the things that are important to each other.'*

He then addressed the men, *'Can you name and describe your wife's favourite flower?'*

I leaned over, touched my wife's hand gently, and whispered, *'Blue Ribbon Flour, isn't it?'*

And thus began my life of celibacy ...

Catholic Heart Attack

A man suffered a serious heart attack and had open heart bypass surgery. He awakened from the surgery to find himself in the care of nuns at a Catholic hospital. As he was recovering, a nun asked him questions regarding how he was going to pay for his treatment.

She asked if he had health insurance. He replied, in a raspy voice, *'No health insurance.'*

The nun asked if he had money in the bank. He replied. *'No money in the bank.'*

The nun asked, *'Do you have a relative who could help you?'*

e said, *'I only have a spinster sister, who is a nun.'*

The nun became agitated and announced loudly, *'Nuns are not spinsters! Nuns are married to God.'*

The patient replied, *'Send the bill to my brother-in-law.'*

CHAPTER 4
AT WORK

The Trouble Tree:

The carpenter I hired to help me restore an old farmhouse had just finished a rough first day on the job. A flat tire made him lose an hour of work, his electric saw quit and now his ancient pickup truck refused to start. While I drove him home, he sat in stony silence. On arriving, he invited me in to meet his family. As we walked toward the front door, he paused briefly at a small tree, touching the tips of the branches with both hands. When opening the door, he underwent an amazing transformation. His tanned face was wreathed in smiles and he hugged his two small children and gave his wife a kiss.

Afterward, he walked me to my car. We passed the tree and my curiosity got the better of me. I asked him about what I had seen him do earlier.

'Oh, that's my trouble tree,' he replied. *'I know I can't help having troubles on the job, but one thing's for sure, troubles don't belong in the house with my wife and children. So I just hang them on the tree every night when I come home. Then in the morning I pick them up again.'*

He paused. *'Funny thing is,'* he smiled, *'when I come out in the morning to pick them up, there ain't nearly as many as I remember hanging up the night before.'*

Federal Employee Performance Evaluations:

These quotes were reportedly taken from federal employee performance evaluations:

1. Since my last report, this employee has reached rock bottom and has started to dig.
2. His men would follow him anywhere, but only out of morbid curiosity.
3. I would not allow this employee to breed.
4. This employee is really not so much of a has-been, but more of a definite won't be.
5. Works well under constant supervision and cornered like a rat in a trap.
6. When she opens her mouth, it seems that it's only to change feet.

7. He would be out of his depth in a parking lot puddle.
8. This young lady has delusions of adequacy.
9. He sets low personal standards and then consistently fails to achieve them.
10. This employee is depriving a village somewhere of an idiot.
11. This employee should go far and the sooner he starts, the better.
12. Got a full 6-pack, but lacks the plastic thingy to hold it all together.
13. A gross ignoramus - 144 times worse than an ordinary ignoramus.
14. He doesn't have ulcers; he's a carrier.
15. He's been working with glue too much.
16. He would argue with a signpost.
17. He has a knack for making strangers immediately.
18. He brings a lot of joy whenever he leaves the room.
19. When his I.Q. reaches 50 we should sell.
20. A photographic memory but with the lens cover glued on.
21. A prime candidate for natural de-selection.
22. Donated his brain to science before he was done using it.
23. Gates are down, the lights are flashing, but the train isn't coming.
24. He has two brains: one is lost and the other is out looking for it.
25. If he were any more stupid, he'd have to be watered once a week.
26. If you give him a penny for his thoughts, you'd get change.
27. If you stand close enough to him, you can hear the ocean.
28. It's hard to believe that he beat out 1,000,000 other sperm.
29. One neuron short of a synapse.
30. Some drink from the fountain of knowledge; he gargled.
31. Takes him 1-½ hours to watch 60 minutes.
32. The wheel is turning, but the hamster is dead.

Three Envelops:

A fellow had just been hired as the new CEO of a large high-tech corporation. The CEO who was stepping down met with him privately and presented him with three numbered envelopes. *'Open these if you run up against a problem you don't think you can solve.'* he said.

Well, things went along pretty smoothly, but six months later, sales took a downturn and he was really catching a lot of heat. About at his wit's end, he remembered the envelopes. He went to his drawer and took out the first envelope. The message read, *'Blame your predecessor.'*

The new CEO called a press conference and tactfully laid the blame at the feet of the previous CEO. Satisfied with his comments, the press - and Wall Street - responded positively, sales began to pick up and the problem was soon behind him.

About a year later, the company was again experiencing a slight dip in sales, combined with serious product problems. Having learned from his previous experience, the CEO quickly opened the second envelope. The message read, *'Reorganise.'* This he did and the company quickly rebounded.

After several consecutive profitable quarters, the company once again fell on difficult times. The CEO went to his office, closed the door and opened the third envelope. The message read, *'Prepare three envelopes ...'*

The Cake

A man walked into a bakery and said, *'I want a birthday cake baked for me in the shape of the letter S.'*

The baker nodded, *'I'll have that ready by three this afternoon. But it will cost extra for the S shape.'*

'Money is no object,' said the customer.

At three o'clock the customer was back. The cake was proudly presented in all its serpentine glory and the man lost his temper. *'Not an ordinary S, you idiot,'* he shouted. *'I want a beautiful flowing S in script.'*

The baker said, *'But you didn't say so. If you can come back at eight this evening, I'll have it for you, but it's going to cost extra.'*

The customer was back at eight. Another cake was presented. He looked at it critically and said, *'I don't like the way the 'Happy Birthday' looks. Can you rewrite it? I'll pay extra for your trouble.'*

'I can fix that in no time. Come back in half an hour,' said the baker.

By eight thirty, he was back and the cake was perfect. With a sigh of relief, the baker pulled a box down and prepared to package the cake.

'Hold it,' said the customer said as he paid him, *'I don't need a box. I'm eating it here!'*

5 Minute Management Course

Lesson 1:

A priest offered a Nun a lift. She got in and crossed her legs, forcing her gown to reveal a leg. The priest nearly had an accident. After controlling the car, he stealthily slid his hand up her leg ...

The nun said, *'Father, remember Psalm 129?'*

The priest removed his hand. But, changing gears, he let his hand slide up her leg again. The nun once again said, *'Father, remember Psalm 129?'*

The priest apologised *'Sorry sister but the flesh is weak.'*
Arriving at the convent, the nun sighed heavily and went on her way.

On his arrival at the church, the priest rushed to look up Psalm 129. It said, *'Go forth and seek, further up, you will find glory.'*

Moral of the story: *If you are not well informed in your job, you might miss a great opportunity.*

Lesson 2:

A sales rep, an administration clerk and the manager are walking to lunch when they find an antique oil lamp.

They rub it and a Genie comes out and says, *'I'll give each of you just one wish.'*

'Me first! Me first!' says the admin clerk. *'I want to be in the Bahamas, driving a speedboat, without a care in the world.'* Poof! She's gone.

'Me next! Me next!' says the sales rep. *'I want to be in Hawaii, relaxing on the beach with my personal masseuse, an endless supply of Pina Coladas and the love of my life.'* Poof! He's gone.

'Okay, you're up,' the Genie says to the manager. The manager says, *'I want those two back in the office after lunch.'*

Moral of the story: *Always let your boss have the first say.*

Lesson 3

An eagle was sitting on a tree resting, doing nothing. A small rabbit saw the eagle and asked him, *'Can I also sit like you and do nothing?'*

The eagle answered: *'Sure, why not.'*

So, the rabbit sat on the ground below the eagle and rested. All of a sudden, a fox appeared, jumped on the rabbit and ate it.

Moral of the story: *To be sitting and doing nothing, you must be sitting very, very high up.*

Lesson 4

A turkey was chatting with a bull. *'I would love to be able to get to the top of that tree'* sighed the turkey, *'but I haven't got the energy.'*

'Well, why don't you nibble on some of my droppings?' replied the bull. *'It's full of nutrients.'*

The turkey pecked at a lump of dung and found it actually gave him enough strength to reach the lowest branch of the tree.

The next day, after eating some more dung, he reached the second branch.

Finally after a fourth night, the turkey was proudly perched at the top of the tree.

He was promptly spotted by a farmer, who shot him out of the tree.

Moral of the story: *'Bull Shit might get you to the top, but it won't keep you there ...'*

Lesson 5

A little bird was flying south for the winter. It was so cold the bird froze and fell to the ground into a large field.

While he was lying there, a cow came by and dropped some dung on him. As the frozen bird lay there in the pile of cow dung, he began to realise how warm he was. The dung was actually thawing him out!

He lay there all warm and happy and soon began to sing for joy. A passing cat heard the bird singing and came to investigate. Following the sound, the cat discovered the bird under the pile of cow dung and promptly dug him out and ate him.

Moral of the story:
Not everyone who shits on you is your enemy.
Not everyone who gets you out of shit is your friend.
And when you're in deep shit, it's best to keep your mouth shut!

The Baker's Assistant:

Many years ago, a baker's assistant (Richard the Pourer) whose job it was to pour the dough mixture in the making of sausage rolls, noted that he was running low on one of the necessary spices. He sent his apprentice to the store to buy more.

Unfortunately, upon arriving at the shop, the young man realised that he had forgotten the name of the ingredient. All he could do was to tell the shopkeeper ... it was for Richard the Pourer, for batter for wurst.

Bank Strike:

Bank employees went on strike leaving the bank officers to do the teller's tasks. While the strike was on, this customer called the bank and asked if they were open. They told her they had two windows open. The she asked, *'Can't I just come in through the front door?'*

Employee's Lingo:

- I'm extremely adept at all manner of office organisation: I've used Microsoft Office.
- I'm honest, hard working and dependable: I pilfer office supplies.
- My pertinent work experience includes: I hope you don't ask me about all the McJobs I've had.
- I take pride in my work: I blame others for my mistakes.
- I'm personable: I give lots of unsolicited personal advice to co-workers.
- I'm extremely professional: I carry a Day-Timer.
- I'm adaptable: I've changed jobs a lot.
- I'm on the go: I'm never at my desk.
- I'm highly motivated to succeed: The minute I find a better job, I'm outta there!

Vocabulary additions:

- Blamestorming: Sitting around in a group, discussing why a deadline was missed or a project failed and who was responsible.
- Seagull Manager: A manager, who flies in, makes a lot of noise, craps on everything and then leaves.
- Chainsaw Consultant: An outside expert brought in to reduce the employee headcount, leaving the top brass with clean hands.
- Cube farm: An office filled with cubicles.
- Idea Hamsters: People who always seem to have their generators running.

- Mouse Potato: The on-line, wired generation's answer to the couch potato.
- Prairie Dogging: When someone yells or drops something loudly in a cube farm and people's heads pop up over the walls to see what's going on.
- Sitcom: (Single Income, Two Children, Oppressive Mortgage). What yuppies turn into when they have children and one of them stops working to stay home with the kids.
- Squirt the Bird: To transmit a signal to a satellite.
- Starter Marriage: A short-lived first marriage that ends in divorce with no kids, no property and no regrets.
- Stress Puppy: A person who seems to thrive on being stressed out and whiny.
- Swiped Out: An ATM or credit card that has been rendered useless because the magnetic strip is worn away from extensive use.
- Tourists: People who take training classes just to get a vacation from their jobs.
- Treeware: Hacker slang for documentation or other printed material
- Zerox Subsidy: Euphemism for swiping free photocopies from one's workplace.
- Going Postal: Euphemism for being totally stressed out, for losing it. Makes reference to the unfortunate track record of postal employees who have snapped and gone on shooting rampages.
- Alpha Geek: The most knowledgeable, technically proficient person in an office or work group.
- Arssmosis: The process by which some people seem to absorb success and advancement by kissing up to the boss rather than working hard.
- Chips and Salsa: Chips = hardware, Salsa = software.
- Flight Risk: Used to describe employees who are suspected of planning to leave a company or department soon.
- Good job: A get-out-of-debt job. A well-paying job people take in order to pay off their debts; one that they will quit as soon as they are solvent again.
- Uninstalled: Euphemism for being fired.
- CLM: Career limiting move.

- Irritainment: Entertainment and media spectacles that are annoying but you find yourself unable to stop watching them. The O.J. trials were a prime example as was Bill Clinton's trial.
- Percussive maintenance: The fine art of whacking the heck out of an electronic device to get it to work again.
- Vulcan Nerve Pinch: The taxing hand position required to reach all the appropriate keys for certain computer commands.
- Yuppie food Stamps: The ubiquitous $20 bills spewed out of ATMs everywhere. Often used when trying to split the bill after a meal.
- Salmon Day: The experience of spending an entire day swimming upstream only to get screwed and die in the end.

S.H.I.T.

In order to assure the highest level of quality work and productivity from employees, it would be our policy to keep all employees well trained through our program of Special High Intensity Training (S.H.I.T.). We are trying to give our employees more S.H.I.T. than anyone else.

If you feel that you do not receive your share of S.H.I.T. on the job, please see your manager. You will be immediately placed at the top of the S.H.I.T. list and our managers are especially skilled in seeing that you get all the S.H.I.T. you can handle.

Employees who do not take their S.H.I.T. will be placed in Departmental Employee Evaluation Programs (D.E.E.P. S.H.I.T.). Those who fail to take D.E.E.P. S.H.I.T. seriously will have to go to Employee Attitude Training (E.A.T. S.H.I.T.).

Since our managers took S.H.I.T. before they were promoted, they do not have to do S.H.I.T. any more, as they are all full of S.H.I.T. already.

If you are full of S.H.I.T., you may be interested in training others. We can add your name to our Basic Understanding Lecture List (B.U.L.L. S.H.I.T.). Those who are full of B.U.L.L. S.H.I.T. will not get the S.H.I.T. jobs and can apply for promotion to Director of Intensity Program (D.I.P. S.H.I.T.).

If you have further questions, please direct them to our Head of Training Special High Intensity Training (H.O.T. S.H.I.T.).
Thank you,
Boss In General (B.I.G. S.H.I.T)

Business Jargon:

The following have been used in advertisements for staff. What they say and what they mean are seldom the same:

- Competitive Salary: We remain competitive by paying less than our competitors.
- Join our fast-paced team: We have no time to train you.
- Casual Work Atmosphere: We don't pay enough to expect that you'll dress up; well, a couple of the real daring guys wear earrings.
- Must be deadline oriented: You'll be six months behind schedule the day you start.
- Some overtime required: Some time each night and some time each weekend.
- Duties will vary: Anyone in the office can boss you around.
- Must have an eye for detail: We have no quality control staff.
- Career-Minded: Female applicants must be childless (and remain that way).
- Apply in person: If you're old, fat or ugly you'll be told the position has been filled.
- No Phone calls please: We've filled the job; our call for resumes is just a legal formality.
- Seeking candidates with a wide variety of experience: You'll need it to replace the three people who just left.
- Problem-solving skills a must: You're walking into a company in perpetual chaos.
- Requires team leadership skills: You'll have the responsibilities of a manager, without the pay or respect.
- Good communication skills: Management communicates, you listen, figure out what they want and do it!

The Salesman:

The toothbrush salesman (who has a lisp) comes into his manager's office to give a report on his first week at work. *'Well, how'd you do?'* asks the manger.

'Well, thir, I thold two toothbrutheth.' replied the salesman.

'Two!' shouts the manager. *'You're never going to make a living that way.'*

'Well thir, I don't know what to do, people juth won't buy my toothbrutheth.'

The manager thinks and says, *'Sounds to me like you need a gimmick.'*

The salesman asks, *'Wath's a gimmick?'*

The manager explains, *'A gimmick is something you use to entice, excite and motivate your customer about your product or service. A jingle, a slogan, something to make your customer feel the need for your product or service.'*

The salesman goes, *'Hmm, I gueth I'll have to get me a gimmick,'*

The salesman returns at the end of the next week and gives his report. *'Well thir, I thold 185,353 toothbrutheth.'*

The manager leaps up, *'My gosh, what did you do?'*

The salesman grins and says, *'I took your advith and got me a gimmick.'*

The manager, excited now, says, *'Well, out with it son. What's the gimmick? We need to pass this on to the rest of the staff. We'll make millions!'*

The salesman says, *'Well thir, I found me a real bithy thtreet corner and I thet up a table and a chair. On the table I put out thum chipth and dip. People would come up to the corner waiting to croth the thtreet and I would thay, 'Hey, while you're waiting, how about thum chipth and dip?' They would thay, 'Thure!' Then they would take a chip, get 'em thum dip and thtart to eat it. Then they would say, 'Hey thith thayths like thit!' I would say, 'It ith thit. Want to buy a toothbruth?'*

The Horth Whithperer

A guy calls his buddy the horse rancher and says he's sending a friend over to look at a horse. His buddy asks, *'How will I recognise him?'*

'That's easy; he's a midget with a speech impediment.'

So, the midget shows up and the guy asks him if he's looking for a male or female horse. *'A female horth.'* He shows him a prized filly.

'Nith lookin horth. Can I thee her eyeth?'

The guy picks up the midget and he gives the horse's eyes the once over. *'Nith eyeth, can I thee her earzth?'*

He picks the little fella up again and shows him the horse's ears. *'Nith earzth, can I see her mouf?'*

The rancher is getting pretty brassed off at this point, but he picks him up again and shows him the horse's mouth. *'Nice mouf, can I see her twat?'*

Totally furious at this point, the rancher grabs him under his arms and rams the midget's head as far as he can up the horse's twat, pulls him out and slams him on the ground.

The midget gets up, sputtering and coughing. *'Perhapth I should rephrase that. Can I thee her wun awound a widdlebit?'*

Disgusted construction workers

An Irishman, a Mexican and an Alabama redneck were doing construction work on scaffolding on the 20th floor of a building. They were eating lunch and the Irishman said, *'Corned beef and cabbage! If I get corned beef and cabbage one more time for lunch, I'm going to jump off this building.'*

The Mexican opened his lunch box and exclaimed, *'Burritos again! If I get burritos one more time, I'm going to jump off, too.'*

The Alabama redneck opened his lunch and said, *'Bologna again! If I get a bologna sandwich one more time I'm jumping too.'*

The next day, the Irishman opens his lunch box, sees corned beef and cabbage - and jumps to his death. The Mexican opens his lunch, sees a burrito and jumps too. The Alabama redneck opens his lunch, sees the bologna and jumps at his death also.

At the funeral, the Irishman's wife is weeping. She says, *'If I'd known how really tired he was of corned beef and cabbage I never would have given it to him again!'*

The Mexican's wife also weeps and says, *'I could have given him tacos or enchiladas! I didn't realise he hated burritos so much.'*

Everyone turned and stared at the Alabama redneck's wife. *'Hey, don't look at me, he makes his own lunch!'*

When Fishermen Meet (Best said out loud.)

'Hiyamac'
'Lobuddy'
'Binearlong?'
'Coplours'
'Cetchenny?'
'Goddafew'
'Kindarthay?'
'Bassencarp'
'Ennysizetoom?'
'Couplapowns'

'Hittinhard?'
'Sordalike'
'Wachoosen?'
'Gobbawurms'
'Fishanonaboddum?'
'Rydononaboddum'
'Whatchadrinkin?'
'Jugajimbeam'
'Igoddago'
'Tubad'
'Seeyaroun'
'Yeahtakideezy'
'Guluck'

Harassment:

A man walks up to a tall woman in his office and tells her that her hair smells nice. The woman immediately goes into her boss's office and tells him that she wants to file sexual harassment charges and explains why.

The supervisor is puzzled by this time and says, *'What's wrong with a co-worker telling you your hair smells nice?'*
The woman replied, *'He's a midget.'*

Looking for her Dad:

The boss of a big company needed to call one of his employees about an urgent problem with one of the main computers. He dialled the employee's home and was greeted with a child's whispered, *'Hello.'*

Feeling put out at the inconvenience of having to talk to a youngster, the boss asked, *'Is your Daddy home?'*

'Yes,' whispered the small voice.

'May I talk to him?' the man asked. To the surprise of the boss, the small voice whispered, *'No.'*

Wanting to talk with an adult, the man asked, *'Is your Mommy there?'*

'Yes,' Came the answer.

'May I talk with her?'

Again the whispered reply, *'No.'*

Knowing that it was not likely that a young child would be left at home alone, the boss decided he would just leave a message with the person who should be there watching over the child. *'Is there any one there besides you?'* the boss asked the child.

'Yes,' whispered the child, *'A policeman.'*

Wondering what a cop would be doing at his employee's home, the boss asked, *'May I speak with the policeman?'*

'No, he's busy,' whispered the child.

'Busy doing what?' asked the boss.

'Talking to Daddy and Mommy and the Fireman,' Came the whispered answer.

Growing concerned and even worried as he heard what sounded like a helicopter through the phone the boss asked, *'What is that noise?'*

'A hello-copper,' answered the whispering voice.

'What's going on there?' asked the boss, now alarmed.

In an awed whispering voice, the child answered, *'The search team just landed the hello-copper.'*

Alarmed, concerned and more than just a little frustrated, the boss asked, *'Why are they there?'*

Still whispering, the young voice replied along with a muffled giggle, *'They're looking for me!'*

The Plan:

In the beginning, there was the plan. And then came the assumptions. And the assumptions were without form and the plan was without substance. And darkness was upon the face of the workers. And they spoke amongst themselves and said, *'This is a crock of shit and it stinks.'* And the workers went unto their Supervisors and said, *'It is a pail of dung and we can't live with the smell.'*

And the Supervisors went unto their Managers and said, *'It is a container of strong excrement and none may abide by it.'*

And the Managers went to their Directors and said, *'It is a vessel of fertiliser and none may abide its strength.'*

And the Directors spoke amongst themselves and said to one another, *'It contains that which aids plant growth and is very strong.'*

And the Directors went to the Vice Presidents and said unto them, *'It promotes growth and it is very powerful.'*

And the Vice Presidents went to the President and said unto him, *'This new plan will actively promote growth and vigour of the company with very powerful effects.'*

And the President looked upon the plan and said that it was good. And the plan became policy.

And this, my friends, is how shit happens!

Hot Air Balloonist:

A man is flying in a hot air balloon and realises he is lost. He reduces height and spots a man down below. He lowers the balloon further and shouts, *'Excuse me. Can you tell me where I am?'*

The man below says, *'Yes, you're in a hot air balloon hovering thirty feet above this field.'*

'You must be an engineer,' says the balloonist.

'I am,' replies the man. *'How did you know?'*

'Well,' says the balloonist, *'everything you've told me is technically correct, but it's no use to anyone.'*

The man below says, *'You must be in upper management.'*

'I am,' replies the balloonist, *'But how did you know?'*

'Well,' says the man, *'you don't know where you are or where you're going, but you expect me to be able to help. You're in the same position you were before we met, but now it's all my fault.'*

The Marine:

It was 5:00 in the morning at the U.S. Marine boot camp, well below freezing and the soldiers were asleep in their barracks. The drill sergeant walks in and bellowed, *'This is a birthday suit inspection! I wanna see you's all formed up outside buck naked - now!'*

So, the soldiers quickly jumped out of their warm beds, naked and shivering and ran outside to form up in their three ranks. The sergeant walked out and yelled, *'Close up the ranks, conserve your body heat!'*

So they close in slightly ... The captain comes along with his swagger stick. He goes to the first soldier and whacks him right across the chest with it.

'Did that hurt?' he yelled.

'No sir!' Came the reply.

'Why not?'

'Because I'm a U.S. Marine, Sir!'

The captain is impressed and walks on to the next man. He takes a stick and whacks the soldier right across the rear. *'Did that hurt?'* he shouted.

'No Sir!'
'Why not?'
'Because I'm a U.S. Marine, Sir!'

Still extremely impressed, the captain walks to the third guy and sees he has an enormous erection. Naturally, he gave his target a huge whack with the swagger stick. *'Did that hurt?'*
'No Sir!'
'Why not?'
'Because it belongs to the guy behind me, Sir!'

Life Raft:

Seems that a year ago, some Boeing employees on the field decided to steal a life raft from one of the parked 747s. They were successful in getting it out of the plane and home. When they took it for a float on the river, they were quite surprised by a Coast Guard helicopter coming towards them. It turned out that the chopper was homing in on the emergency locator that is activated when the raft is inflated. The would-be rafters are no longer employed at Boeing.

Why I fired my secretary:

Two weeks ago was my 44th birthday and I wasn't feeling too hot that morning. I went down to breakfast knowing my wife would be pleasant and say, 'Happy Birthday' and probably have a present for me. She didn't even say, *'Good morning,'* let alone any, *'Happy Birthday!'*

I thought, *'Well, that's wives for you. The children will remember.'*

The children came down to breakfast and didn't say a word. When I started to the office, I was feeling pretty low and despondent. As I walked into my office, my secretary, Janet said, *'Good morning, boss, Happy Birthday!'* I felt a little better. Someone had remembered. I worked until noon, then Janet knocked on my door and said, *'You know, it is such a beautiful day outside and it's your birthday, let's go to lunch, just you and me.'*

I said, *'By George, that's the greatest thing I've heard all day. Let's go.'* We went to lunch. We didn't go where we normally go. We went out into the country to a little private place. We had two martinis and enjoyed lunch tremendously. On the way back to the office, she said, *'You know, it's such a beautiful day, we don't need to go back to the office, do we?'*

I said, *'No, I guess not.'*

She said, *'Let's go to my apartment.'*

After arriving at her apartment, she said, *'Boss, if you don't mind, I think I'll go into the bedroom and slip into something more comfortable.'*

'Sure,' I excitedly replied.

She went into the bedroom and in about six minutes she came out carrying a big birthday cake, followed by my wife, children and dozens of our friends. They were all singing *'Happy Birthday'* and there I sat on the couch - naked.

We've always done it that way!

(By Howard Winsett NASA Flight Research Centre)

The US standard railway gauge (distance between the rails) is 4 feet, 8.5 inches. That is an exceedingly odd number. Why was the gauge used? Because that is the way they built them in England and English expatriates built the US railroads.

Why did the English build them like that? Because the first rail lines were built by the same people who built the pre-railroad tramways and that is the gauge they used. Why did 'they' use that gauge then? Because the people who built the tramways used the same jigs and tools that they used for building wagons, which used the same wheel spacing.

Okay! Why did the wagons have that particular odd wheel spacing? Well, if they tried to use any other spacing, the wagon wheels would break on some of the old, long-distance roads in England, because that's the spacing of the wheel ruts. So who built those old rutted roads? Imperial Rome built the first long-distance roads in Europe (and England) for their legions. The roads have been used ever since.

And the ruts in the roads? Roman war chariots formed the initial ruts, which everyone else had to match for fear of destroying their wagon wheels. Since the chariots were made for (or by) Imperial Rome, they all had the same wheel spacing. The United States standard railroad gauge of 4 feet, 8.5 inches is derived from the original specification for an Imperial Roman war chariot.

Specifications and bureaucracies live forever. So the next time you are handed a specification and wonder what horses ass came up with it, you may be exactly right. This is because the Imperial Roman war chariots were made just wide enough to accommodate the back ends of two war-horses.

Now, the twist to the story. There's an interesting extension to the story about railroad gauges and horses' behinds. When we see a Space Shuttle sitting on its launch pad, there are two big booster rockets attached to the sides of the main tank. These are solid rocket boosters or SRBs. 'Thiokol' makes the SRBs at their factory at Utah. The engineers who designed the SRBs might have preferred to make them a bit fatter, but the SRBs had to be shipped by train from the factory to the launch site.

The railroad line from the factory happens to run through a tunnel in the mountains. The SRBs had to fit through the tunnel. The tunnel is slightly wider than the railroad track and the railroad track is about as wide as two horses' behinds. So, a major design feature of what is arguably the world's most advanced transportation system was determined over two thousand years ago by the width of two horses' asses!

The Old Petrol Station

The service station trade was slow.
The owner sat around,
With sharpened knife and cedar stick.
Piled shavings on the ground.
No modern facilities had they,
The log across the rill
Led to a shack, marked His and Hers
That sat against the hill.
'Where is the ladies restroom, sir?'
The owner leaning back,
Said not a word but whittled on,
And nodded toward the shack.
With quickened step she entered there
But only stayed a minute,
Until she screamed, just like a snake
Or spider might be in it.
With startled look and beet red face
She bounded through the door,
And headed quickly for the car.
Just like three gals before.
She tripped and fell - got up,
and then in obvious disgust,
Ran to the car, stepped on the gas,
And faded in the dust.
Of course we all desired to know

What made the gals all do
The things they did and then we found
The whittling owner knew.
A speaking system he'd devised
To make the thing complete,
He tied a speaker on the wall
Beneath the toilet seat.
He'd wait until the gals got set
and then the devilish guy,
would stop his whittling long enough,
to speak into the mike.
And as she sat, a voice below struck terror,
fright and fear
'Will you please use the other hole?
We're painting under here'

Banker's Plunge

The chairman of a large bank treated his family to a weekend away on a yacht. All was going well, until the sea started to get a bit choppy and he fell overboard. While his wife and children searched frantically for a lifebuoy, the skipper called out: *'Hey, can you float alone?'*

'Of course I can,' Gasped the floundering banker, *'but this is a hell of a time to talk business.'*

12 good (unintentional) double-entendres ever aired on British TV and radio

1. Ted Walsh - Horse Racing Commentator - *'This is really a lovely horse. I once rode her mother.'*
2. New Zealand Rugby Commentator - *'Andrew Mertens loves it when Daryl Gibson comes inside of him.'*
3. Pat Glenn, weightlifting commentator - *'And this is Gregoriava from Bulgaria. I saw her snatch this morning and it was amazing!'*
4. Harry Carpenter at the Oxford-Cambridge boat race 1977 - *'Ah, isn't that nice. The wife of the Cambridge President is kissing the Cox of the Oxford crew.'*
5. US PGA Commentator - *'One of the reasons Arnie (Arnold Palmer) is playing so well is that, before each tee shot, his wife takes out his balls and kisses them. Oh my God!! What have I just said?'*

6. Carenza Lewis about finding food in the Middle Ages on *'Time Team Live'* said: *'You'd eat beaver if you could get it.'*
7. A female news anchor who, the day after it was supposed to have snowed and didn't, turned to the weatherman and asked, *'So Bob, where's that eight inches you promised me last night?'* Not only did HE have to leave the set, but half the crew did too, because they were laughing so hard!
8. Steve Ryder covering the US Masters: *'Ballesteros felt much better today after a 69 yesterday.'*
9. Clair Frisby talking about a jumbo hot dog on 'Look North' said: *'There's nothing like a big hot sausage inside you on a cold night like this. '*
10. Mike Hallett discussing missed snooker shots on 'Sky Sports': *'Stephen Hendry jumps on Steve Davis's misses every chance he gets.'*
11. Michael Buerk on watching Philippa Forrester cuddle up to a male astronomer for warmth during BBC1's UK eclipse coverage remarked: *'They seem cold out there. They're rubbing each other and he's only come in his shorts.'*
12. Ken Brown commentating on golfer Nick Faldo and his caddie Fanny Sunneson lining-up shots at the Scottish Open: *'Some weeks Nick likes to use Fanny; other weeks he prefers to do it by himself.'*

CHAPTER 5

GENIES

The Right Man:

A woman was walking along the beach when she stumbled upon a Genie's lamp. She picked it up and rubbed it and lo-and-behold a Genie appeared. The amazed woman asked if she got three wishes. The Genie said, *'Nope ... due to inflation, constant downsizing, low wages in third-world countries and fierce global competition, I can only grant you one wish. So, what'll it be?'*

The woman didn't hesitate. She said, *'I want peace in the Middle East. See this map? I want these countries to stop fighting with each other.'*

The Genie looked at the map and exclaimed, *'Gadzooks, lady! These countries have been at war for thousands of years. I'm good, but not that good! I don't think it can be done. Make another wish.'*

The woman thought for a minute and said, *'Well, I've never been able to find the right man. You know, one that's considerate and fun, likes to cook and helps with the housecleaning, is good in bed and gets along with my family, doesn't watch sports all the time and is faithful. That's what I wish for a good mate.'*

The Genie let out a long sigh and said, *'Let me see that map again.'*

More Genies

A man walks into a bar and finds a Genie in a lamp. The Genie will only grant him one wish. The man wishes to be a million times smarter than any man on earth. *poof* the Genie turns him into a woman.

A fellow finds a bottle and when he opens it, a Genie pops out and grants him three wishes. But whatever he wished for - his wife would get double. *'I would like a million dollars,'* he says. *poof* he has a million dollars but his ex gets two! *'I would like a big house'* he says. *poof* he gets a big house and his ex-wife gets two. 'And your third wish?' asks the Genie. *'Beat me half to death.'*

A king travels through the desert, when he suddenly discovers a man captured under a big rock. He throws a rope around the rock, ties it to his horse and pulls the rock off the man. The man, grateful as he is, tells the king that he's really a great sorcerer and gives the king three wishes.

The king looks at the sorcerer and says, *'I wish to be immortal.'*

The sorcerer goes *poof* and it is done. The king takes a knife and stabs himself and nothing happens. Then he says, *'Next I want my horse to be immortal.'*

The sorcerer goes *poof* and it's done. The king, happy as can be, stabs his horse and nothing happens. Then he says, *'Now I want my horse's genitals.'* The sorcerer goes *poof* and it's done.

The king, still happy, jumps on his horse and rides back to his castle. In the doorway, he meets his friend Paul, jumps off the horse and tells Paul that he's now immortal. Paul laughs, but the king gives Paul his knife and says, *'Here stab me with the knife.'*

Paul stabs the king as ordered and nothing happens then the same thing happens with his horse. *'That's not even the best part - look at this!'* and the king drops his pants. Peter looks at the naked king and screams out loud, *'Damn that's the biggest female crotch I've ever seen!'*

A man has spent many days crossing the desert without finding a source of water. It gets so bad that his camel dies of thirst. He's crawling through the sand, certain that he has breathed his last, when he spots a shiny object sticking out of the sand ahead of him.

He crawls to the object, pulls it out of the sand and discovers that he has a Manischevitz wine bottle. It appears that there may be a drop or two left in the bottle, so he unscrews the top and out pops a Genie. But this is no ordinary Genie. This Genie appears to be a Hassidic Rabbi, complete with black alpaca coat, black hat, side curls, etc.

'Well kid,' says the Genie. *'You know how it works. You have three wishes.'*

'I'm not going to trust you,' says the man. *'I'm not going to trust a Jewish Genie!'*

'What do you have to lose? It looks like you're a goner anyway!'

The man thinks about this for a minute and decides that the Genie is right. *'Okay, I wish I were in a lush oasis with plentiful food and drink.'* *poof.* The man finds himself in the most beautiful oasis he has ever seen. And he is surrounded with jugs of wine and platters of delicacies.

'Okay kid, what's your second wish?'

'My second wish is that I was rich beyond my wildest dreams.' *poof.* The man finds himself surrounded by treasure chests filled with rare gold coins and precious gems.

'Okay kid, you have just one more wish. Better make it a good one!'

After thinking for a few minutes, the man says, 'I wish I were white and surrounded by beautiful women.' *poof.* The man is turned into a tampon.

The moral of the story is: Be careful of what you wish for. There may be a string attached!

A man is walking down the beach and comes across an old bottle. He picks it up, pulls out the cork and out pops a Genie. The genie says, 'Thank you for freeing me from the bottle. In return I will grant you three wishes.'

The man says, 'Great. I always dreamed of this and I know exactly what I want. First, I want one billion dollars in a Swiss bank account.' *poof* there is a flash of light and a piece of paper with account numbers appears in his hand.

He continues, 'Next, I want a brand new red Ferrari right here.' *poof* there's a flash of light and a bright red brand-new Ferrari appears right next to him.

He continues, 'Finally, I want to be irresistible to women' *poof* there's a flash of light and he turns into a box of chocolates.

Two Aussies, Ferret and Knackers, were adrift in a life boat. While rummaging through the boat's provisions, Ferret stumbled across an old lamp. He rubbed it vigorously and sure enough out popped a genie

This genie, however was a little different. He stated he could only deliver one wish, not the standard three. Without giving much thought, Ferret blurted out, 'Turn the entire ocean into beer. Make that Victoria Bitter!'

The genie clapped his hands with a deafening crash and immediately the sea turned into that hard-earned thirst quencher. The genie vanished.

Only the gentle lapping of beer on the hull broke the stillness as the two men considered their circumstances.

Knackers looked disgustedly at Ferret whose wish it was had been granted. After a long, tension-filled moment Knackers said, *'Nice going Dickhead! Now we're going to have to piss in the boat.'*

The Golf Course:

A couple was golfing one day on a very, very exclusive golf course, lined with million-dollar houses. On the third tee, the husband said, *'Honey, be careful when you drive the ball. Don't knock out any windows. It'll cost us a fortune to fix.'*

The wife teed up and shanked it right through the window of the biggest house on the course. The husband cringed and said, *'I told you to watch out for the houses. All right, let's go up there, apologise and see how much this is going to cost.'*

They walked up, knocked on the door and heard a voice say, *'Come on in.'*

They opened the door and saw glass all over the floor and a broken bottle lying on its side in the foyer. A man on the couch said, *'Are you the people that broke my window?'*

'Uh, yeah. Sorry about that.' The husband replied.

'No, actually I want to thank you. I'm a genie that was trapped for a thousand years in that bottle. You've released me. I'm allowed to grant three wishes. I'll give you each one wish and I'll keep the last one for myself.'

'Oh, great!' exclaimed the husband. *'I want a million dollars a year for the rest of my life.'*

'No problem - it's the least I can do. And you, what do you want?' the Genie said, looking at the wife.

'I want a house in every country of the world,' she said.

'Consider it done.' The Genie replied.

'And what is your wish, Genie?' the husband asked.

'Well, since I've been trapped in that bottled, I haven't had sex with a woman in a thousand years. My wish is to sleep with your wife.'

The husband looks at the wife and said, *'Well, we did get a lot of money and all those houses, honey. I guess I don't care.'*

The Genie took the wife upstairs and ravished her for two hours and said, *'How old is your husband, anyway?'*

'35,' she replied.

'And he still believes in Genies? That's amazing!'

CHAPTER 6

IS THAT RIGHT?

Figure this out:
- A door that's open is ajar; what is it called when a jar is open?
- Would you buy a solar-powered flashlight?
- They call it a hot-water-heater, but why would you need to heat hot water?
- They call it a building, but after it's completed shouldn't they call it a built?
- Why do women wear evening gowns to nightclubs ... shouldn't they wear nightgowns?
- If pro is the opposite of con, then what is the opposite of progress?
- If vegetarians eat only vegetables, then what do humanitarians eat?
- If a person kills his/her clone, is it murder or suicide?
- What does the Q in Q-tip stand for?
- Why do they call warm water, luke-warm ... did someone named Luke discover it?
- What do you call two Mexicans playing basketball? Juan on Juan.
- What do you see when the Pillsbury Dough Boy bends over? Doughnuts.
- Why did OJ Simpson want to move to West Virginia? Everyone has the same DNA.
- What does it mean when the flag at the Post Office is flying at half-mast? They're hiring.
- How do they get a deer to cross at that yellow road sign?
- What do they use to ship Styrofoam?
- Why is there no Disneyland in China? No one's tall enough to go on the good rides.
- Why do bagpipers walk when they play? To get away from the noise.
- If you throw a cat out a car window does it become kitty litter?
- If there is no God, who pops up the next Kleenex in the box?
- Why is abbreviation such a long word?

- Why is there only one Monopolies Commission?
- Why do they put Braille on the number pads of drive-through bank machines?
- If nothing sticks to Teflon, how do they stick Teflon to the pan?
- Why is there an expiration date on my sour cream container?
- Why do kamikaze pilots wear helmets?
- Why do they call it taking a dump instead of leaving a dump?
- Why do they say new and improved ... because how can it be new if it was improved?
- If you worked at a fire hydrant plant, where would you park?
- What happens to that other sock you lost in the laundry?
- Why is it that when you're at the beach swimming and it starts to rain, everyone gets up and leaves?
- Why when a kid is running, will his mother say, *'Don't come running to me if you break your leg?'*
- Why does a serving of frosted flakes have the same number of calories as regular flakes?
- Why do people look up when they think?
- Why do women wear shoes that hurt their feet?
- Why do men wear something that resembles a hangman's noose?
- Why does 1 kilogram of groceries generate 50 kilograms of garbage and 4 kilos on your weight?
- Do you park in a driveway and drive on a parkway?
- What do you plant to grow a seedless watermelon?
- Why are they called apartments when they're so close together?
- Why do you need a driver's license to buy liquor when you can't drink and drive?
- Why isn't phonetic spelled the way it sounds?
- Why are there interstate highways in Hawaii and Singapore?
- How do you know when it's time to tune your bagpipes?
- Is it true that cannibals don't eat clowns because they taste funny?
- Where do forest rangers go to get away?
- If this is the land of the free, why is someone always trying to sell me something?
- Why do they sterilise needles for lethal injections?

- If it's tourist season, why can't I shoot them?
- Why do they call it a TV set, when there's only one of them?
- Why do people who know the least, know it the loudest?
- How do you know when you've run out of invisible ink?
- If a vampire can't see himself in a mirror, why is his hair always so neat?
- Why do women have a pair of underwear, but just one bra?
- If a 7-11 is open 24 hours a day, 365 days of the year, why are there locks on the doors?
- How does the guy who drives the snow plow get to work in the morning?
- The 50-50-90 rule: Anytime you have a 50-50 chance of getting something right, there's a 90% probability you'll get it wrong.
- It is said that if you line up all the cars in the world end to end, someone would be stupid enough to try and pass them.
- It is hard to understand how a cemetery raised its burial cost and blamed it on the cost of living.
- You know that little indestructible black box used on planes? Why can't they make the whole plane out of the same substance?
- Why is it that when you're driving and looking for an address, you turn down the radio volume?
- I know what you're thinking and you should be ashamed of yourself.
- Despite the cost of living, have you noticed how it remains so popular?
- You have the right to remain silent. Anything you say will be misquoted then used against you.
- I wonder how much deeper the ocean would be without sponges.
- I want to die in my sleep like my grandfather - not screaming and yelling like the passengers in his car.
- What's the difference between snowmen and snowwomen? Snowballs.
- What was the best thing before sliced bread?
- If you choke a smurf, what colour does it turn?
- I have six locks on my door all in a row. When I go out, I lock every other one. I figure no matter how long somebody stands there picking the locks, they are always locking three.
- What do you call cheese that isn't yours? Nacho Cheese.

- What do you call Santa's helpers? Subordinate Clauses.
- Ever wonder if illiterate people get the full effect of alphabet soup?
- What do Eskimos get from sitting on the ice too long? Polaroids.
- What do you call four bullfighters in quicksand? Quatro sinko.
- What do you get from a pampered cow? Spoiled milk.
- What do you get when you cross a snowman with a vampire? Frostbite.
- What do you get when you cross an elephant and a skin doctor? A pachydermatologist.
- What has four legs is big, green, fuzzy and if it fell out of a tree would kill you? A pool table.
- Did you hear about the Buddhist who refused his dentist's Novocain during root canal work? He wanted to transcend dental medication!
- What kind of coffee was served on the Titanic? Sanka. And what kind of lettuce? Iceberg.
- What lies at the bottom of the ocean and twitches? A nervous wreck.
- What's the difference between an oral thermometer and a rectal one? The taste.
- What's the difference between roast beef and pea soup? Anyone can roast beef.
- Where do you find a no-legged dog? Right where you left him.
- Where do you get virgin wool from? Ugly sheep.
- Why are there so many Smiths in the phone book? They all have phones.
- Why do gorillas have big nostrils? Because they have big fingers ...
- What is a zebra? 26 sizes larger than an 'A' bra.
- If you yelled for 8 years, 7 months and 6 days you would have produced enough sound energy to heat one cup of coffee. (Hardly seems worth it.)
- If you farted consistently for 6 years and 9 months, enough gas is produced to create the energy of an atomic bomb. (Now that's more like it!)
- If Barbie is so popular, why do you have to buy her friends?
- Corduroy pillows: They're making headlines!
- I intend to live forever - so far, so good.

- Support bacteria - they're the only culture some people have.
- Early bird gets the worm, but the second mouse gets the cheese.
- Beauty is in the eye of the beer holder.
- Many people quit looking for work when they find a job.
- Everyone has a photographic memory. Some just don't have film.
- Energizer Bunny arrested - charged with battery.
- I poured Spot remover on my dog. Now he's gone.
- I used to have an open mind, but my brains kept falling out.
- Shin: a device for finding furniture in the dark.
- Join the Army, meet interesting people and kill them.
- Wear short sleeves! Support your right to bare arms!
- The Human heart creates enough pressure when it pumps out to the body to squirt blood 30 feet. (O.M.G.!)
- All those who believe in psychokinesis raise my hand.
- A cockroach will live nine days without its head before it starves to death! (Creepy!)
- Banging your head against a wall uses 150 calories an hour. (Don't try this at home - maybe at work.)
- The male praying mantis cannot copulate while its head is attached to its body. The female initiates sex by ripping the male's head off. *('Honey, I'm home. What the ....?!')*
- The flea can jump 350 times its body length. It's like a human jumping the length of a football field.
- The catfish has over 27,000 taste buds. (What could be so tasty on the bottom of a pond?)
- Some lions mate over 50 times a day. (Wow)
- Butterflies taste with their feet. (Something I always wanted to know.)
- The strongest muscle in the body is the tongue. (Hmmmmmm ...)
- Right-handed people live, on average, nine years longer than left-handed people. So if you're ambidextrous - do you split the difference?
- Polar bears are left-handed. (If they switch, they'll live a lot longer.)
- Elephants are the only animals that cannot jump. Okay - so that would be a good thing.
- A cat's urine glows under a black light. (I wonder who was paid to figure that out?)

- An ostrich's eye is bigger than its brain. (I know some people like that.)
- Starfish have no brains. (I know some people like that too).
- Humans and dolphins are the only species that have sex for pleasure.
- A snail can sleep for three years!
- 'Stewardesses' is the longest word typed with only the left hand and 'lollipop' with your right.
- 'Typewriter' is the longest word that can be made using the letters only on one row of the keyboard.
- The sentence: 'The quick brown fox jumps over the lazy dog' uses every letter of the alphabet.
- It's impossible to sneeze with your eyes open.
- Maine is the only state with a name that's just one syllable.
- No word in the English language rhymes with month orange, silver or purple.
- 'Dreamt' is the only English word that ends in the letters 'mt.'
- Our eyes are always the same size from birth, but our nose and ears never stop growing. (Ugh!)
- The words 'race car,' 'kayak' and 'level' are the same whether they are read left to right or right to left (palindromes).
- There are only four words in the English language that end in 'dous:' tremendous, horrendous, stupendous and hazardous.
- There are two words in the English language that have all five vowels in order: 'abstemious' and 'facetious.'
- All 50 states are listed across the top of the Lincoln Memorial on the back of the US $5 bill.
- A dime has 118 ridges around the edge.
- A cat has 32 muscles in each ear.
- A crocodile cannot stick out its tongue. (But who really cares?)
- A dragonfly has a life span of 24 hours.
- A 'jiffy' is an actual unit of time for 1/100th of a second.
- A shark is the only fish that can blink with both eyes.
- Almonds are members of the peach family.
- Al Capone's business card said he was a used furniture dealer.
- Babies are born without kneecaps. They don't appear until the child reaches 2 to 6 years of age. (I didn't know that!)

- Cats have over one hundred vocal sounds. Dogs only have about ten.
- February 1865 is the only month in recorded history not to have a full moon.
- In the last 4,000 years, no new animals have been domesticated.
- If the population of China walked past you, eight abreast - the line would never end because of the rate of reproduction. (How do they do that standing up and walking?)
- If you are an average person living in a developed country, in your whole life, you will spend an average of six months waiting at red lights.
- Leonardo Da Vinci invented the scissors. (I didn't know that either!)
- On the old Canadian two-dollar bill, the flag flying over the Parliament building was an American flag. (Canada now has $2 coins - nicknamed toonies - could that be why?)
- Peanuts are one of the ingredients of dynamite!
- Rubber bands last longer when refrigerated.
- The average person's left hand does 56% of the typing.
- The cruise liner, QE2, moves only six inches for each gallon of diesel that it burns.
- The microwave was invented after a researcher walked by a radar tube and a chocolate bar melted in his pocket. (Good thing he did that.)
- The winter of 1932 was so cold that Niagara Falls froze solid.
- There are more chickens than people in the world (so far).
- Tigers have striped skin, not just striped fur.
- Winston Churchill was born in a ladies' room during a dance.
- Women blink nearly twice as much as men.
- Your stomach has to produce a new layer of mucus every two weeks; otherwise it will digest itself. (Yuck!)
- If you take an Oriental person and spin him around several times, does he become disoriented?
- If people from Poland are called Poles, why aren't people from Holland called Holes?
- If FedEx and UPS were to merge, would they call it Fedup?
- Do Lipton Tea employees take coffee breaks?
- What hair colour do they put on the driver's licenses for bald men?

- Why do we say something is out of whack? What's a whack?
- Do infants enjoy infancy as much as adults enjoy adultery?
- If a pig loses its voice, is it disgruntled?
- When someone asks you, *'A penny for your thoughts,'* and you put your two cents in, what happens to the other penny?
- Why is the man who invests all your money called a broker?
- Why do croutons come in airtight packages? It's just stale bread to begin with.
- When cheese gets its picture taken, what does it say?
- Why is a person who plays piano called a pianist, but a person who drives a race car not called a racist?
- Why are a wise man and a wise guy opposites?
- Why do overlook and oversee mean opposite things?
- Why isn't 11 pronounced onety-one?
- *'I am'* is reportedly the shortest sentence in the English language. Could it be that *'I do'* is the longest sentence?
- If lawyers are disbarred and clergymen are defrocked, doesn't it follow that electricians can be delighted, musicians denoted, cowboys deranged, models deposed, tree surgeons debarked and dry cleaners depressed?
- Do older people read the Bible a whole lot more as they get older because they're cramming for their final exam?
- If mothers feed their babies with tiny forks and spoons, what do Chinese mothers use? Toothpicks?
- Why do they put pictures of criminals up in the Post Office? What are we supposed to do - write to them? Why don't they just put their pictures on the postage stamps so the mailmen can look for them while they deliver mail?
- If it's true that we are here to help others, then what exactly are the others here for?
- You never really learn to swear until you learn to drive.
- Nobody ever says, *'It's only a game,'* when their team is winning.
- Ever wonder what the speed of lightning would be if it didn't zigzag?
- Latest survey shows that 3 out of 4 people make up 75% of the world's population.
- The things that come to those that wait may be the things left by those who got there first.
- A fine is a tax for doing wrong. A tax is a fine for doing well.

- It was recently discovered that research causes cancer in rats.
- Everybody lies, but it doesn't matter, since nobody listens.
- I wish the buck stopped here, as I could use a few.
- I started out with nothing and I still have most of it.
- Light travels faster than sound. This is why some people appear bright until you hear them speak.
- The statistics on sanity are that one out of every four is suffering from some form of mental illness. Think of your three best friends. If they're okay - then it's you.
- I always wanted to be somebody, but I should have been more specific.
- Did you hear about the guy who lost his left arm and leg in a car crash? He's all right now.
- How do crazy people go through the forest? They take the psycho path.
- How do you get holy water? Boil the Hell out of it.
- What did the fish say when he hit a concrete wall? 'Dam.'
- What do prisoners use to call each other? Cell phones.
- Two wrongs don't make a right, but three rights make a left.
- Why don't blind people sky dive? Because it scares the hell out of the dog.
- Person #1: *'Do you know what the capital of Alaska is?'*
  Person #2: *'Juneau?'*
  Person #1: *'If I knew, I wouldn't be asking you!'*
- How do you confuse a retard? Put him in a round room and tell him to pee in a corner. How do you confuse him even more? Ask him what corner he peed in.
- What do you call a boomerang that doesn't come back? A stick.
- When is Mother's Day? Nine months after Father's Night!
- What's the difference between an evening gown and a nightgown? About fifteen minutes if you're lucky.
- What do all constipated people have in common? None of them give a crap!
- How did Dairy Queen get pregnant? Burger King forgot to wrap his Whopper.
- Notice: To person or persons who took the large pumpkin on Highway 87 near Southridge Storage, please return the pumpkin and be checked. Pumpkin may be radioactive. All other plants in vicinity are dead.
- If a cow laughed, would milk come out of her nose?

- Whatever happened to Preparations A through G?
- Last night I played a blank tape at full blast. The mime next door went nuts.
- If a person with multiple personalities threatens suicide, is that considered a hostage situation?
- I went for a walk last night and my kids asked me how long I'd be gone. I replied, *'The whole time.'*
- So what's the speed of dark?
- How come you don't ever hear about gruntled employees? And who has been dissing them anyhow?
- After eating, do amphibians need to wait an hour before getting out of the water?
- Why don't they just make mouse-flavoured cat food?
- I just got skylights put into my place. The people who live above me are furious.
- Do they have reserved parking for non-handicapped people at the Special Olympics?
- Isn't Disney World a people-trap operated by a mouse?
- Whose cruel idea was it for the word 'lisp' to have an 's' in it?
- If it's zero degrees outside today and it's supposed to be twice as cold tomorrow, how cold is it going to be?
- Why do you press harder on the remote control when you know the battery is dead?
- Why do banks charge you a non-sufficient funds fee on money they already know you don't have?
- Do fish get cramps after eating?
- If the universe is everything and scientists say that the universe is expanding, what is it expanding into?
- If you got into a taxi and the driver started driving backward, would the taxi driver end up owing you money?
- What would a chair look like if your knees bent the other way?
- If a tree falls in the forest and no one is around to see it, do the other trees make fun of it?
- Why is a carrot more orange than an orange?
- When two airplanes almost collide why do they call it a near miss? It sounds like a near hit to me!
- Why are there five syllables in the word 'monosyllabic?'
- Why do they call it the Department of Interior when they are in charge of everything outdoors?
- When I erase a word with a pencil, where does it go?

- Why do scientists call it research when looking for something new?
- Tell a man there are 400 billion stars and he'll believe you. Tell him a bench has wet paint and he has to touch it.
- What would you call it when an Italian has one arm shorter than the other? A speech impediment.
- Did you hear about the Chinese couple that had a retarded baby? They name him 'Sun Ting Wong.'
- How come Superman could stop bullets with his chest, but always ducked when someone threw a gun at him?
- Why is it lemon juice contains mostly artificial ingredients, but dishwashing liquid contains real lemons?
- Why buy a product that it takes 2,000 flushes to get rid of?
- Why do we wash bath towels? Aren't we clean when we use them?
- Why do we wait until a pig is dead to 'cure' it?
- Why do we put suits in a garment bag and put garments in a suitcase?
- Why doesn't glue stick to the inside of the bottle?
- Do Roman paramedics refer to IV's as '4's?'
- What do little birdies say when they get knocked unconscious?
- Why doesn't Tarzan have a beard?
- If man evolved from monkeys and apes, why do we still have monkeys and apes?
- Is boneless chicken considered to be an invertebrate?
- Do married people live longer than single people or does it just seem longer?
- I went to the bookstore and asked the saleswoman, *'Where's the self-help section?'* She replied, *'If I told you, it would defeat the purpose.'*
- Two Eskimos sitting in a kayak were chilly, but when they lit a fire in the craft - it sank proving once and for all that you can't have your kayak and heat it too.
- If all those psychics know the winning lottery numbers, why are they all still working?
- Isn't the best way to save face to keep the lower part shut?

Interesting facts:

- Rabbits can live up to ten years.
- It takes the Hubble telescope about 97 minutes to complete an orbit of the Earth. On average, the Hubble uses the

- equivalent amount of energy as 30 household light bulbs to complete an orbit.
- The expression in cooking 'al dente' means 'to the tooth.' What this means is that the pasta should be somewhat firm and offer some resistance to the tooth, but should also be tender.
- A chicken with red earlobes will produce brown eggs and a chicken with white earlobes will produce white eggs.
- To clean artificial flowers – put them into a large paper bag containing salt and give them a good shake.
- Unpeeled ripe bananas can be sealed in airtight containers or freezer bags then thawed before mashing for use in banana cakes or muffins. Or they can be frozen and peeled for use in smoothies.
- The spray WD-40 got its name because there were forty attempts needed before the creation of the 'water displacing' substance.
- The average life span of a single red blood cell is 120 days.
- Over 250 million Slinky toys have been sold since its debut in 1946.
- There are 500,000 detectable earthquakes each year.
- The last thing Elvis Presley ate before he died was four scoops of ice cream and 6 chocolate chip cookies.
- Some Chinese chopsticks contain gold as one of their materials.
- The chance of making two holes-in-one in a round of golf are one in 67 million.
- Black pepper is the most popular spice in the world.
- There are over one hundred billion galaxies with each galaxy having billions of stars.
- The highest bridge in the world is located in the Himalyan Mountains. It was built by the Indian Army in 1982 and is about 5,600 metres above sea level.
- Actress Meryl Streep holds the record for the most Oscar nominations as an actress, with a record of 13 nominations.
- Enamel is the hardest substance in the human body.
- Leonardo Da Vinci invented the scissors.
- Thomas Edison designed a helicopter that would work with gunpowder. It ended up blowing up along with his factory.
- In China, people eat one bar or chocolate for every thousand chocolate bars eaten by the British.
- The wheelbarrow was invented by the Chinese.

- The Australian Snowy Mountains receive more snowfall in a year than the Swiss Alps.
- The manufacturers of the Pac Man video game estimate that the original game has been played over a billion times by individuals.
- In Ivrea, Italy, thousands of citizens celebrate the beginning of Lent by throwing oranges at one another.
- The sloth moves so slowly that green algae grows in the groves of their hair.
- In the world, the United States and France have the most pet dogs. Approximately one out of every three families has a pet dog. Switzerland and Germany are the lowest, with only one dog per every ten families.
- During the making of the movie *'Flight Club,'* actor Brad Pitt chipped his tooth. However, he did not get his tooth capped until after the movie was completed as he thought it would look better chipped for his character.
- In ancient Rome, it was considered a sign of leadership to be born with a crooked nose.
- Carbon monoxide can kill a person in less than 15 minutes.
- A common drink for Tibetans is Butter Tea which is made out of butter, salt and brick tea.
- Crabs have very small hairs on their claws and other parts of their body to help detect water currents and vibrations.
- The colour blue has a calming effect by causing the brain to release calming hormones.
- Bourbon was first made by a Baptist minister from Bourbon County in Kentucky in 1789. That is how it got its name.
- Vampire Bat saliva has been responsible for many advances in research to stroke recovery.
- McDonald restaurants serve food and drink to an amazing 43 million customers on a daily basis.
- The aorta, which is the largest artery in the body, is about the diameter of a garden hose.
- The game Monopoly was once very popular in Cuba; however, Fidel Castro ordered that all games be destroyed.
- The longest section of straight railway track in the world is the 478 kilometres across the Nullarbor Plain in South Australia to Western Australia.
- During the era of Louis XIV, women used lemons to redden their lips.
- 70% of the poor people in the world are female.

- An oyster can change its gender
- Australia is the only continent without an active volcano.
- Queen Elizabeth always wears a necklace with a little perfume bottle everywhere she goes.
- Polar bear livers contain so much Vitamin A that it can be fatal if eaten by a human.
- In the year 1900, for a woman to be a telephone operator, she had to be between the ages of 17 and 26 and not married.
- Bubble gum contains rubber.
- It takes glass one million years to decompose, which means it never wears out and can be recycled an infinite amount of times!
- Gold is the only metal that doesn't rust, even if it's buried in the ground for thousands of years.
- Your tongue is the only muscle in your body that is attached at only one end.
- If you stop getting thirsty, you need to drink more water. When a human body is dehydrated, its thirst mechanism shuts off.
- Each year 2,000,000 smokers either quit smoking or die of tobacco-related diseases.
- Zero is the only number that cannot be represented by Roman numerals.
- Kites were used in the American Civil War to deliver letters and newspapers.
- The song, Auld Lang Syne is sung at the stroke of midnight in almost every English-speaking country in the world to bring in the New Year.
- Drinking water after eating reduces the acid in your mouth by 61 percent.
- Peanut oil is used for cooking in submarines because it doesn't smoke unless it's heated above 450F.
- The roar that we hear when we place a seashell next to our ear is not the ocean, but rather the sound of blood surging through the veins in the ear.
- Nine out of every 10 living things live in the ocean.
- The banana cannot reproduce itself. It can be propagated only by the hand of man.
- Airports at higher altitudes require a longer airstrip due to lower air density.
- The University of Alaska spans four time zones.

- The tooth is the only part of the human body that cannot heal itself.
- In ancient Greece, tossing an apple to a girl was a traditional proposal of marriage. Catching it meant she accepted.
- Warner Communications paid $28 million for the copyright to the song Happy Birthday.
- Intelligent people have more zinc and copper in their hair.
- A comet's tail always points away from the sun.
- The Swine Flu vaccine in 1976 caused more death and illness than the disease it was intended to prevent.
- Caffeine increases the power of aspirin and other painkillers; that is why it is found in some medicines.
- The military salute is a motion that evolved from medieval times, when knights in armour raised their visors to reveal their identity.
- If you get into the bottom of a well or a tall chimney and look up, you can see stars, even in the middle of the day.
- When a person dies, hearing is the last sense to go. The first sense lost is sight.
- In ancient times strangers shook hands to show that they were unarmed/
- Strawberries are the only fruit where seeds grow on the outside.
- Avocados have the highest calories of any fruit at 167 calories per hundred grams.
- The moon moves about two inches away from the Earth each year.
- The Earth gets 100 tons heavier every day due to falling space dust.
- Due to earth's gravity it is impossible for mountains to be higher than 15,000 meters.
- Mickey Mouse is known as 'Topolino' in Italy.
- Soldiers do not march in step when going across bridges because they could set up a vibration which could be sufficient to knock the bridge down.
- Everything weighs one percent less at the equator.
- For every extra kilogram carried on a space flight, 530 kg of excess fuel are needed at lift-off.

Amazing simple home remedies:

These really work!! Or maybe not!!

1. To avoid cutting yourself when slicing vegetables, get someone else to hold the vegetables while you chop.
2. To avoid arguments with the females about lifting the toilet seat- use the sink.
3. For high blood pressure sufferers ~ simply cut yourself and bleed for a few minutes, thus reducing the pressure on your veins. (Remember to use a timer.)
4. A mouse trap placed on top of your alarm clock will prevent you from rolling over and going back to sleep after you hit the snooze button.
5. If you have a bad cough, take a large dose of laxatives – you'll be afraid to cough.
6. You only need two tools in life – WD-40 and duct tape. If it doesn't move and should, use the WD-40. If it shouldn't move and does, use the duct tape.
7. If you can't fix it with a hammer, you've got an electrical problem.
8. How to get rid of ants. Sprinkle artificial sweetener (such as equal and NutraSweet or any artificial sweeteners near them or put small piles of cornmeal where you see ants. They eat it, take it home, can't digest it so it kills them. It may take a week or so, especially if it rains, but it works and you don't have the worry about pets or small children being harmed! (Makes you wonder what those sweeteners do to us who use them every day doesn't it?)

Paraprosdokians are figures of speech in which the latter part of a sentence or phrase is surprising or unexpected, frequently humourous. (Winston Churchill loved them.)

1. Where there's a will, I want to be in it.
2. The last thing I want to do is hurt you, but it's still on my list.
3. I didn't say it was your fault; I said I was blaming you.
4. Women will never be equal to men until they can walk down the street with a bald head and a beer gut and still think they were sexy.
5. If I agreed with you, we'd both be wrong.
6. We never really grow up. We only learn how to act in public.
7. Behind every successful man is his woman. Behind the fall of a successful man is usually another woman.

8. War does not determine who is right – only who is left.
9. Knowledge is knowing a tomato is a fruit. Wisdom is not putting it in a fruit salad.
10. A clear conscience is the sign of a fuzzy memory.
11. They begin the evening with *'Good Evening,'* then proceed to tell you why it isn't.
12. To be sure of hitting a target, shoot first, then call whatever you hit the target.
13. To steal ideas from one person is plagiarism. To steal from many is research.
14. Money can't buy happiness, but it sure makes misery easier to live with.
15. Buses stop in bus stations. Trains stop in train stations. On my desk is a work station.
16. There's a fine line between cuddling and holding someone down so they can't get away.
17. I thought I wanted a career, It turns out I just wanted paycheques.
18. I used to be indecisive. Now I'm not sure.
19. In filling out an application, where it says, 'In case of emergency, notify:' I put 'Doctor.'
20. You're never too old to learn something stupid.
21. Nostalgia isn't what it used to be.
22. Change is inevitable except from a vending machine.
23. Going to church doesn't make you a Christian any more than standing in a garage makes you a car.

Bumper Stickers:

- Constipated people don't give a shit!!
- If it has boobs or wheels, it's gonna give you problems.
- Seen on a biker's vest - If you can read this - my wife fell off.
- If sex is a pain in the ass, then you're doing it wrong.
- Fight crime - shoot back!
- Sarcasm: Is just one more service we offer.
- Please tell your pants it's not polite to point!
- He who laughs last; thinks slowest.
- Everyone has a photographic memory. Some don't have film.
- A day without sunshine is like, well, night.
- All stressed out and no one to choke!
- And your point is?

- Don't upset me. I'm running out of places to hide the bodies!
- The sex was so good that even the neighbours had a cigarette.
- I don't suffer from insanity; I enjoy every minute of it.
- I work hard because millions on welfare depend on me.
- Some people are alive only because it's illegal to kill them.
- I used to have a handle on life, but it broke.
- Don't take life too seriously; you won't get out alive.
- Wanted: Meaningful overnight relationship.
- You're just jealous because the voices talk only to me.
- I wouldn't need to manage my anger if people could learn how to manage their stupidity.
- Some day when you have your own kids, you will understand why mommy drinks.
- Women are not moody! We simply have days when we are less inclined to put up with your shit.
- A husband is someone who, after taking out the garbage, gives the impression that he's just cleaned the entire house.
- Men think a woman's dream is to find a perfect man. Every woman's dream is to eat anything she wants without gaining weight.
- Beer: It's not just for breakfast anymore.
- I got a gun for my wife - best trade I ever made.
- So you're a feminist - isn't that cute!
- Beauty is in the eye of the beer holder.
- Earth is the insane asylum for the universe.
- To all you virgins, thanks for nothing.
- I'm not a complete idiot; some parts are missing.
- I'm just driving this way to piss you off.
- Out of my mind. Back in five minutes.
- As long as there are tests, there will be prayer in public schools.
- I don't have to be dead to donate my organ.
- God must love stupid people, he made so many of them.
- The gene pool could use a little chlorine.
- Change is inevitable, except from a vending machine.
- It is bad what you think and they are out to get you.
- I took an IQ test and the results were negative.
- It's lonely at the top, but you eat better.
- Give me ambiguity or give me something else.
- Elvis is dead and I'm not feeling too good myself.

- Always remember, you're unique, just like everyone else.
- Very funny, Scotty. Now beam up my clothes.
- Consciousness: that annoying time between naps.
- Ever stop to think and forget to start again?
- Beer - the reason I get up each afternoon.
- I must be a proctologist because I work with assholes.
- I'm out of bed and dressed. What more do you want?
- Remember my name. You'll be screaming it later.
- Welcome to Shit Creek. Sorry, we're out of paddles.
- If you think I'm a bitch, you should have met my mother!
- On the other hand, you have different fingers.
- I just got lost in thought. It was unfamiliar territory.
- When the chips are down, the buffalo is empty.
- Seen it all, done it all, can't remember most of it.
- Those who live by the sword get shot by those who don't.
- I feel like I'm diagonally parked in a parallel universe.
- He's not dead, he's electroencephalographically challenged.
- Honk if you love peace and quiet.
- I'm one of those bad things that happen to good people.
- If they don't have chocolate in Heaven - I ain't going!
- How can I miss you if you won't go away?
- Sorry if I looked interested. I'm not.
- $o many men ... $o few who can afford me!
- If we are what we eat ... I'm fast, cheap and easy.
- Guys have feelings too, but like ... who cares?
- Next mood swing: six minutes.
- Coffee, chocolate, men. Some things are just better rich.
- Nothing is foolproof to a sufficiently talented fool.
- Just remember - if the world didn't suck, we'd all fall off.
- You can't have everything. Where would you put it?

Newspaper ads 'For Sale:'

- 1 Man, 7 women hot tub - $850/best offer.
- Amana washer $100. Owned by clean bachelor who seldom washed.
- Free puppies: ½ Cocker Spaniel - ½ sneaky neighbour dog.
- Snow blower for sale - only used on snowy days.
- Eye of round roast - $1.99 lb. - boneless.
- 2 wire mesh butchering gloves, 1 5-finger, 1-3 finger, pair $15
- Our sofa seats the whole mob - and it's made of 100% Italian leather.

- Joining nudist colony, must sell washer and dryer - $300.
- Tickle Me Elmo, still in box, comes with its own 1988 mustang, excellent condition $6,800.
- Tickle Me Elmo - new in box, hardly tickled, $700.
- 2 Tinkle Me Elmo Dolls - best offer.
- Black face cows, calves. Also 1 gay bull for sale.
- '83 Toyota Hunchback - $2,000.
- Do something special for your valentine - have your septic tank pumped.
- Free Yorkshire Terrier. 8 years old - unpleasant little dog.
- Soft and genital bath or facial tissues - 89 cents.
- German Shepherd. 85 lbs. Neutered. Speaks German. Free.
- Full-sized mattress. 20 year warranty - like new - slight urine smell.
- Free 1 can of pork and beans with purchase of 3-bedroom 2-bath home.
- For sale: Lee Majors (6 million dollar man) - $50.
- Nordic Track $300 - hardly used - call Chubbie at xxx-1275.
- Bill's septic cleaning - *'We haul American-made products.'*
- Shakespeare's pizza - free chopsticks.
- Found: dirty white dog - looks like a rat - been out a while - better be a reward.
- Hummels - largest selection ever - *'If it's in stock, we have it!'*
- Get a little John - the travelling urinal - holds 2 ½ bottles of beer.
- Harrisburg postal employees gun club.
- Georgia peaches - California grown - 89 cents lb.
- Cute kitten for sale, 2 cents or best offer.
- Nice parachute - never opened - used once - slightly stained
- Whirlpool built in oven - frost free!
- Barbie Country Ride - (Note most dolls cannot pedal the bike).
- '93 Pontiac Lemon - low miles.
- Free, farm kittens. Ready to eat.
- Kittens 8 weeks old - seeking good Christian home.
- Ground beast: 99 cents lb.
- Free puppies - Part German Shepherd, part dog.
- Open house - body shapers toning salon - free coffee and donuts.
- Kellogg's pot tarts - $1.99 box.
- Alzheimer's Centre prepares for *'An Affair to Remember.'*

- Gas cloud clears out Taco Bell.
- Battery charger for sale - batteries not included.
- Lost: small apricot poodle. Reward. Neutered. Like one of the family.
- A superb and inexpensive restaurant. Fine food expertly served by waitresses in appetising forms.
- Dinner Special - Turkey $2.35; Chicken $2.25: Children $2.00.
- For sale: Antique desk suitable for lady with thick legs and large drawers.
- Wanted: 50 girls for stripping machine operators in factory.
- We do not tear our clothing with machinery. We do it carefully by hand.
- For sale: Three canaries of undetermined sex.
- Get rid of your aunts: Zap does the job in 24 hours.
- Great Dames for sale.
- Stock up and save. Limit: one.
- Dog for sale: Eats anything and is fond of children.
- Mt. Kilimanjaro, the breathtaking backdrop for the Serena Lodge. Swim in the lovely pool while you drink it all in.
- The hotel has bowling alleys, tennis courts, comfortable beds and other athletic facilities.
- Sheer stockings. Designed for fancy dress, but so serviceable that lots of women wear nothing else.
- Men wanted to work in dynamite factory. Must be willing to travel.
- Three-year-old teacher needed for pre-school. Experience preferred.
- And now, the Superstore - unequalled in size, unmatched in variety, unrivalled inconvenience.
- Our bikinis are exciting. They are simply the tops.
- Wanted. Man to take care of cow that does not smoke or drink.
- Our experienced Mom will take care of your child. Fenced yard, meals and smacks included.
- Illiterate? Write today for free help.
- Auto repair service. Free pick-up and delivery. Try us once; you'll never go anywhere again.
- Mixing bowl set designed to please a cook with a round bottom for efficient beating.

- Semi-annual after-Christmas sale.

Answering Machine Messages:

'Hi, this is John. If you are the phone company, I already sent the money. If you are my parents, please send money. If you are my financial aid institution, you didn't lend me enough money. If you are my friends, you owe money. If you are a female, don't worry, I have plenty of money.'

'Hi. Now you say something.'

'Hi. I'm not home right now, but my answering machine is, so you can talk to it instead. Wait for the beep.'

'Hello, I'm David's answering machine. What are you?'

(From Japanese/English person) 'He-lo! This is Sa-to. If you leave message, I call you soon. If you leave *sexy* message, I call sooner!'

'Hi! John's answering machine is broken. This is his refrigerator. Please speak very slowly and I'll stick your message to myself with one of those magnets.'

'Hello, this is Sally's microwave. Her answering machine just eloped with her tape deck, so I'm stuck with taking her calls. Say, if you want anything cooked while you leave your message, just hold it up to the phone.'

'This is not an answering machine - this is a telepathic thought-recording device. After the tone, think about your name, your reason for calling and a number where I can reach you and I'll think about returning your call.'

'Hello. I'm home right now, but cannot find the phone. Please leave a message and I will call you as soon as I find it.'

I can't come to the phone right now because I have amnesia and feel stupid talking to people I don't remember. I'd appreciate it if you would help me out by leaving my name and telling me something about myself. Thanks.'

'I can't come to the phone right now because I'm down in the basement printing up a fresh batch of twenty dollar bills. If you need any money or if you just want to check out my handiwork, please leave your name, number and how much cash you need after the tone. If you're from the Department of Treasury, please ignore this message.

'Hi. I'm probably home, but am just avoiding someone I don't like. Leave me a message and if I don't call back, it's you.'

'Hello, this is Ron. I'm not home right now, but I can take a message. Hold on a second while I get a pencil.' (Open a drawer *and shuffle stuff around)* '*Okay, what would you like me to tell me?*'

(Noisy pick-up of phone.) *Hi, I'm a burglar and I was just about to steal Troy's answering machine. If you give me your name and number I'll....I'll post it on the fridge where he'll see it. Uh ... By the way, where did you say you live?*'

'*Now I lay me down to sleep; leave a message at the beep. If I die before I wake, remember to erase this tape.*

'*How do you leave a message on this thing? I can't understand the instructions. Hello. Testing 1 2 3. I wonder what happens if I touch this ... YOW!*'

'*Hi, this is George. I'm sorry I can't answer the phone right now. Leave a message and then wait by your phone until I call you back.*'

'*If you're a burglar, then we're probably at home cleaning our weapons right now and can't come to the phone. Otherwise, we probably aren't home and it's safe to leave us a message.*'

'*You're growing tired. Your eyelids are getting heavy. You feel very sleepy now. You are gradually losing your willpower and your ability to resist suggestions. When you hear the tone, you will feel helplessly compelled to leave your name, number and a message.*'

(For telemarketers*)* '*You have reached the CPX-2000 Voice Blackmail System. Your voice patterns are now being digitally encoded and stored for later use. Once this is done our computers will be able to use the sound of your voice for literally thousands of illegal and immoral purposes. There is no charge for this initial consultation. However our staff of professional extortionists will contact you in the near future to further explain the benefits of our service and to arrange for your schedule of payment. Remember to speak clearly at the sound of the tone. Thank you.*'

'*Hello, you are talking to a machine. I am capable of receiving messages. My owners do not need siding, windows or a hot tub and their carpets are clean. They give to charity through the office and don't need their picture taken. If you are still with me, leave your name and number and they will get back to you.*'

(Very fast) *Thank you for calling 555-5555. If you wish to speak to Tim, push 1 on your touch-tone phone now. If you wish to speak to Lynn, push 2 on your touch-tone phone now. If you have a wrong number, then press 6 and dial your number. If you want to leave your name and just a message, press star, press 6 for extension 4443, then leave your name and message. If you want to leave your number and the time you called, please press star twice, spin in a circle, press 1 twice, talk loud and beep.*

School Answering Machine

This is the message that the Pacific Palisades High School (California) staff voted unanimously to record on their school telephone answering machine. This is the actual answering machine message for the school. This came about because they implemented a policy requiring students and parents to be responsible for their children's absences and missing homework. The school and teachers are being sued by parents who want their children's failing grades changed to passing grades - even though those children were absent 15-30 times during the semester and did not complete enough schoolwork to pass their classes.

The outgoing message: 'Hello! You have reached the automated answering service of your school. In order to assist you in connecting to the right staff member, please listen to all the options before making a selection:

1. To lie about why your child is absent - Press 1
2. To make excuses for why your child did not do his work- Press 2
3. To complain about what we do - Press 3
4. To swear at staff members - Press 4
5. To ask why you didn't get information that was already enclosed in your newsletter and several flyers mailed to you - Press 5
6. If you want us to raise your child - Press 6.
7. If you want to reach out and touch, slap or hit someone - Press 7
8. To request another teacher, for the third time this year - Press 8
9. To complain about bus transportation - Press 9
10. To complain about school lunches - Press 0
11. If you realise this is the real world and your child must be accountable and responsible for his/her own behaviour, class work, homework and that it's not the teachers' fault for your child's lack of effort: Hang up and have a nice day!
12. If you want this in Spanish, you must be in the wrong country'

What do you call a group of:
- Ape: A shrewdness of apes.
- Baboon: A troup of baboons.
- Bacteria: A culture of bacteria.
- Badger: A cete of badgers.
- Bear: A sleuth or sloth of bears.
- Beaver: A colony of beavers.
- Boar: A sounder of boars.
- Caterpillar: An army of caterpillars
- Cat: A slowder or clutter of cats.
- Clam: A bed of clams.
- Cobra: A quiver of cobras.
- Cow: A kine of cows [twelve cows are a flink.
- Crocodile: A float of crocodiles.
- Crow: A murder of crows.
- Dove: A dule of doves.
- Ferrett; A business or fesnyng of ferrets.
- Finch: A charm of finches.
- Fox: A skulk or leash of foxes.
- Frog: An army or colony of frogs.
- Geese: A flock, gaggle or skein [in flight] of geese
- Hare: A down or husk of hares.
- Hawk: A cast or kettle of hawks.
- Hog: A drift or parcel of hogs.
- Hound: A pack, mute or cry of hounds.
- Jellyfish: A smack of jellyfish.
- Leopard: A leap of leopards.
- Magpie: A tiding of magpies.
- Owl: A parliament of owls.
- Partridge: A covey of partridges.
- Peacock: A muster or ostentation of peacocks.
- Plover: A wing or congregation of plovers.
- Rattlesnake: A rhumba of rattlesnakes.
- Swan: A bevy, herd, lamentation or wedge of swans.
- Toad: A knot of toads.
- Trout: A hover of trout.
- Turkey: A rafter of turkeys.
- Turtledove: A pitying or dule of turtledoves.
- Turtle: A bale of turtles.
- Woodpecker: A descent of woodpeckers.

Words of wisdom:
- Feel safe tonight ... sleep with a cop.
- Remember folks: Stop lights timed for 60 kph are also timed for 120 kph.
- Sign seen in restaurant: guys: No shirt, no shoes - no service. Gals: No shirt - no charge.
- If walking is so good for you, then why does my mailman look so bad?
- Impotence: Nature's way of saying, *'No hard feelings.'*
- Necrophilia: That uncontrollable urge to crack open a cold one.
- We have enough youth, how about a fountain of smart?
- Very funny, Scotty. Now beam down my clothes.
- Cat: the other white meat.
- Caution - Driver legally blonde!
- Don't be a sexist - broads hate that.
- Eat well, stay fit and die anyway.
- Heart attacks - God's revenge for eating his animal friends.
- Honk if you've never seen an Uzi fired from a car window.
- If you lived in your car, you'd be home by now.
- I'm an imbecile and I vote.
- Money isn't everything, but it sure keeps the kids in touch.
- Saw it - wanted it - had a fit - got it!
- Do not walk behind me, for I may not lead. Do not walk ahead of me, for I may not follow. Do not walk beside me either, just leave me alone.
- The journey of a thousand miles begins with a broken fan belt and a flat tyre.
- The darkest hours come just before the dawn. So if you're going to steal your neighbour's milk and newspaper, that's the time to do it.
- Sex is like air. It only becomes really important when you aren't getting any.
- Don't aspire to become irreplaceable. If you can't be replaced, you can't be promoted.
- Remember, no one is listening until you fart.
- Never test the depth of the water with both feet.
- If you think nobody cares whether you're dead or alive, try missing a couple of mortgage payments.
- If at first you don't succeed, avoid skydiving.
- Don't worry; it only seems kinky the first time.

- A closed mouth gathers no feet.
- Before you judge someone, you should walk a mile in his or her shoes. That way, when you judge them, you're a mile away and you have their shoes.
- Give a man a fish and he will eat for a day. Teach him how to fish and he will sit in a boat and drink beer all day.
- Have you ever lent someone $20 and never seen that person again? It was probably worth it.
- If you tell the truth, you don't have to remember anything.
- Some days we are the flies; some days we are the windscreens.
- Good judgment comes from experience; experience comes from bad judgment.
- The quickest way to double your money is to fold it in half and put it back in your pocket.
- There are two theories about how to win an argument with a woman. Neither one works.
- Generally speaking, you aren't learning much if your lips are moving. Never miss a good chance to shut up.
- Experience is something you don't get until just after you need it.
- When we are born we are naked, wet, hungry and we get smacked on our arse. From there on in, life gets worse.
- The most wasted day of all is one in which we have not laughed.
- Remember not to forget that which you do not need to know.

Why fishing is better than making love:

When you go fishing and you catch something - that's good. If you're making love and you catch something - that's bad.

Fish don't compare you to other fishermen and want to know how many other fish you caught.

In fishing, you lie about the one that got away. In loving you lie about the one you caught.

You can catch and release a fish; you don't have to lie and promise to still be friends after you let it go.

You don't have to necessarily change your line to keep catching fish. You can catch a fish on a 20-cent night crawler. If you want to catch a woman you're talking dinner and a movie minimum.

Fish don't mind if you fall asleep in the middle of fishing.

A real friend test!!

A simple friend, when visiting, acts like a guest. A real friend opens your refrigerator and helps himself.

A simple friend has never seen you cry. A real friend has shoulders soggy from your tears.

A simple friend doesn't know your parents' first names. A real friend has their phone numbers in his address book.

A simple friend brings a bottle of wine to your party. A real friend comes early to help you cook and stays late to help you clean.

A simple friend hates it when you call after he has gone to bed.   A real friend asks you why you took so long to call.

A simple friend seeks to talk with you about their problems. A real friend seeks to help you with your problems.

A simple friend wonders about your romantic history. A real friend could blackmail you with it.

A simple friend thinks the friendship is over when you have an argument. A real friend calls you after you had a fight.

A simple friend expects you to always be there for them. A real friend expects to always be there for you!

Politically Correct

30 Politically Correct ways to say someone is stupid:
1. Not the sharpest knife in the drawer.
2. A few clowns short of a circus.
3. A few fries short of a Happy Meal.
4. An experiment in artificial stupidity.
5. A few beers short of a six-pack.
6. A few peas short of a casserole.
7. Doesn't have all his cornflakes in one box.
8. One Fruit Loop shy of a full bowl.
9. One taco short of a combination plate.
10. A few feathers short of a whole duck.
11. All foam, no beer.
12. The cheese slid off his cracker.
13. Body by Fisher, brains by Mattel.
14. Warning: Objects in mirror are dumber than they appear.
15. Couldn't pour water out of a boot with instructions on the heel.
16. He fell out of the Stupid tree and hit every branch on the way down. n
17. An intellect rivalled only by garden tools.

18. Chimney's clogged.
19. Doesn't know much but leads the league in nostril hair.
20. Elevator doesn't go all the way to the top floor.
21. Her sewing machine's out of thread.
22. His antenna doesn't pick up all the channels.
23. His belt doesn't go through all the loops.
24. Missing a few buttons on his remote control.
25. No grain in the silo.
26. Proof that evolution can go in reverse.
27. Receiver is off the hook.
28. Several cards short of a full deck.
29. Skylight leaks a little.
30. Too much yardage between the goal posts.

Southern Slang:

(Most effective if said out loud)
Heidi - howdy or hi
Hire yew - how are you
Bard - borrowed
Jawjah - Georgia
Birminhayum Bammer - Birmingham, Alabama
Munts - months
Thank - think
Bare - beer
Ignernt - ignorant
Ranch - wrench
All - oil
Far - fire
Tar - tire
Retard - retired
Fat - fight
Rats - rights
Farn - foreign
Ear - air
Bob war - barbed wire
Jew here - did you hear
Haze - he's
Seed - to see
View - have you
Gubmint - government

What's the difference between a northern fairytale and a southern fairytale? A northern fairytale begins, *'Once upon a time ...'* a southern fairytale begins, *'Y'all ain't gonna believe this s--t!'*

Mixed Words:

The following are exceptionally clever. Someone out there either has far too much time on his or her hands or they're not so good at Scrabble. When you re-arrange the letters:

WORD	BECOMES
Dormitory:	Dirty Room
Evangelist:	Evil's Agent
Desperation:	A rope ends it
The Morse Code:	Here come dots
Slot Machines:	Cash lost in 'em
Animosity:	Is no amity
Mother-in-Law:	Woman Hitler
Snooze Alarms:	Atlas! No more Z's
Alec Guinness:	Genuine Class
Semolina:	Is no meal
The Public Art Galleries:	Large picture halls, I bet
A Decimal Point:	I'm a Dot in place
The Earthquakes:	That Queer Shake
Eleven plus Two:	Twelve plus one
Contradiction:	Accord not in it

And for the grand finale:
President Clinton of the USA: To copulate he finds interns

Oxymorons:

Military intelligence
Jumbo shrimp
Postal worker
Student teacher
Civil war

English is a crazy language

There is no egg in eggplant, nor ham in hamburger; neither apple nor pine in pineapple. English muffins weren't invented in England or French Fries in France. Sweetmeats are candies while sweetbreads, which aren't sweet, are meat; quicksand can work slowly, boxing rings are square and a guinea pig is neither from Guinea, nor is it a pig.

And why is it that writers write but fingers don't fing; grocers don't groce and hammers don't ham. If the plural of tooth is teeth, why isn't the plural of booth, beeth. One goose, two geese. So one moose, two meese? One index, two indices? Doesn't it seem crazy that you can make amends but not one amend? If you have a bunch of odds and ends and get rid of all but one of them, what do you call it?

If teachers taught, why don't preachers praught? If a vegetarian eats vegetables, what does a humanitarian eat? In what language do people recite at a play and play at a recital? Ship by truck and send cargo by ship. Have noses that run and feet that smell?

How can a slim chance and a fat chance be the same, while a wise man and a wise guy are opposites? Your house can burn up as it burns down; where you fill in a form by filling it out and in which an alarm goes off by going on. Why doesn't Buick rhyme with quick?

Here are some more oddities in the language:

1. The bandage was wound around the wound.
2. The farm was used to produce produce.
3. The dump was so full that it had to refuse more refuse.
4. We must polish the Polish furniture.
5. He could lead if he would get the lead out.
6. The soldier decided to desert his dessert in the desert.
7. Since there is not time like the present, he thought it was time to present the present.
8. A bass was painted on the head of the bass drum.
9. When shot at, the dove dove into the bushes.
10. I did not object to the object.
11. The insurance was invalid for the invalid.
12. There was a row among the oarsmen about how to row.
13. They were too close to the door to close it.
14. The buck does funny things when the does are present.
15. A seamstress and a sewer fell down into the sewer line.
16. To help with planting, the farmer taught his sow to sow.
17. The wind was too strong to wind the sail.
18. Upon seeing the tear in the painting, I shed a tear.
19. I had to subject the subject to a series of tests.
20. How can I intimate this to my most intimate friend?

Council Complaints:

- I want some repairs done to my cooker as it has backfired and burned my knob off.
- I wish to complain that my father hurt his ankle very badly when he put his foot in the hole in his back passage.
- Their 18-year-old son is continuously banging his balls against my fence. Not only is this making a hell of a noise, but the fence is now sagging in the middle.
- This is to let you know there is a smell coming from the man next door.
- I am writing on behalf of my sink, which is running away from the wall.
- I wish to report that tiles are missing from the roof of the outside toilet and I think it was bad wind the other night that blew them off.
- I request your permission to remove my drawers in the kitchen.
- The toilet is blocked and we cannot bath the children until it is cleared.
- Will you please send a man to look at my water - it is a funny colour and not fit to drink.
- Would you please send a man to repair my spout? I am an old-aged pensioner and need it straight away.
- I want to complain about the farmer across the road. Every morning at 5:30 his cock wakes me up and it's getting too much. It's all right when my husband is on day shift, but when he's on back-shifts or nights, I get it several times a week from Mr. Docherty next door and at my age it's too much.
- The man next door has a large erection in his back garden, which is unsightly and dangerous.
- Our kitchen floor is very damp. We have two children and would like a third, so will you please send someone to do something about it.
- The toilet seat is cracked. Where do I stand?
- I'm a single woman living in a downstairs flat and would be pleased if you could do something about the noise made by the man I have on top of me every night.
- Please send a man with clean tools to finish the job and satisfy the wife.

- I have had the Clerk of the Works down on the floor six times and still have no satisfaction.
- Can you send a carpenter to the house? When the woman next door closed the door the other night, she pulled at my knob too hard and now it's ready to fall off.

How to keep a healthy level of insanity and drive other people insane:

1. At lunchtime, sit in your parked car and point a hair dryer at passing cars to see if they slow down.
2. Page yourself over the intercom. (Don't disguise your voice).
3. Insist that your e-mail address be: Zena-goddess-of-fire@companyname.com or Elvis-the-king@companyname.com
4. Every time someone asks you to do something, ask if they want fries with that.
5. Encourage your colleagues to join you in a little synchronised chair dancing.
6. Put your garbage can on your desk and label it 'in.'
7. Develop an unnatural fear of staplers.
8. Put decaf in the coffee maker for three weeks. Once everyone has gotten over his or her caffeine addiction, switch to espresso.
9. In the memo field of all your cheques, write, *'For sexual favours.'*
10. Reply to everything someone says with, *'That's what you think.'*
11. Finish all your sentences with, *'In accordance with the prophecy.'*
12. Adjust the tint on your monitor so that the brightness level lights up the entire working area. Insist to others that you like it that way.
13. Don't use any punctuation or capital letters.
14. As often as possible, skip rather than walk.
15. Ask people what sex they are.
16. Specify that your drive-through order is a 'to go.'
17. Sing along at the opera.
18. Go to a poetry recital and ask why the poems don't rhyme.
19. Find out where your boss shops and buy exactly the same outfits. Wear them one day after your boss does. (This is especially effective if your boss is the opposite gender.)

20 Send e-mail to the rest of the company and tell them what you're doing. For example: *'If anyone needs me, I'll be in the bathroom.'*
21 Put mosquito netting around your cubicle.
22 Five days in advance, tell your friends you can't attend their party because you're not in the mood.

Laws of the Universe

Law of Mechanical Repair: After your hands become coated with grease, your nose will begin to itch or you'll have to pee.

Laws of the Workshop: Any tool, when dropped, will roll to the least accessible corner. Any small, extremely expensive part that is accidentally dropped, will disappear from view ... forever!

Law of Probability: The probability of being watched is directly proportional to the stupidity of your act.

Law of the Telephone: When you dial a wrong number, you never get a busy signal.

Laws of Bathing: When the body is fully immersed in water, the telephone inevitably rings.

Law of Proving Something: When you try to prove to someone that a machine won't work – it will.

Law of Seating: At any event, the people whose seats are furthest from the aisle arrive last.

Law of Coffee: As soon as you sit down to enjoy a cup of hot coffee, your boss will ask you to do something that will last until the coffee is cold.

7 Secrets to Success

Roof said: Aim high
Fan said: Be cool
Clock said: Every minute is precious
Mirror said: Reflect before you act
Window said: See the world
Calendar said: Be up-to-date
Door said: Push hard to achieve your goals
The moment you're ready to quit is usually the moment right before a miracle happens. Don't give up!

The Circle of Life

What is Success? (A Simple Explanation)
At the age of 3, success means: not shitting in your pants.
At the age of 12, success means: having friends.
At age of 18, successmeans having a driver's licence.
At the age of 20, success means: having sex.
At the age of 35, success means having money.
At the age of 50, success means having money.
At the age of 60, success means having sex.
At the age of 70, success means having a driver's licence.
At the age of 75, success means having friends.
At the age of 80, success menas not shitting your pants.
There you have it ... Enjoy Success!

Truths for Mature Humans

1. I think part of a best friend's job should be to immediately clear your computer history within minutes after you die.
2. Nothing sucks more than that moment during an argument when you realise you're wrong.
3. I totally take back all those times I didn't want to nap when I was younger.
4. There is great need for a sarcasm font.
5. How the hell are you supposed to fold a fitted sheet?
6. Map Quest really needs to start their directions on # 5. I'm pretty sure I know how to get out of my neighbourhood.
7. Obituaries would be a lot more interesting if they told you how the person died.
8. Bad decisions make good stories.
9. You never know when it will strike, but there comes a moment at work when you know that you just aren't going to do anything productive for the rest of the day.
10. Can we all just agree to ignore whatever comes after Blue Ray? I don't want to have to restart my collection ... again.
11. I'm always slightly terrified when I exit out of Word and it asks me if I want to save any changes to my ten-page technical report that I swear I did not make any changes to.
12. *'Do not machine wash or tumble dry'* means I will never wash this - ever.
13. I hate leaving my house, confident and looking good and then not seeing anyone of importance the entire day. What a waste.
14. I think the freezer deserves a light as well.

15. I wish Google Maps had an *'Avoid - you're not safe here'* routing option.
16. I keep some people's phone numbers in my phone just so I know not to answer when they call.
17. I hate when I just miss a call by the last ring (Hello? Hello? Damn it!) but when I immediately call back, it rings nine times and goes to voice mail. What did you do after I didn't answer? Drop the phone and run away?
18. Sometimes, I'll watch a movie that I watched when I was younger and suddenly realise I had no idea what the heck was going on when I first saw it.
19. I would rather try to carry 10 over-loaded plastic bags in each hand than take 2 trips to bring my groceries in.
20. The only time I look forward to a red light is when I'm trying to finish a text. (Before the law passed banning it that is.)
21. How many times is it appropriate to say *'What?'* before you just nod and smile because you still didn't hear or understand a word they said?
22. I love the sense of camaraderie when an entire line of cars team up to prevent a jerk from cutting in at the front. Stay strong, brothers and sisters!
23. Shirts get dirty. Underwear gets dirty. Pants? Pants never get dirty and you can wear them forever. (Must have been written by a man.)
24. Is it just me or do high school kids get dumber and dumber every year?
25. There's no worse feeling than that millisecond you're sure you are going to die after leaning your chair back a little too far.
26. As a driver I hate pedestrians and as a pedestrian I hate drivers, but no matter what the mode of transportation, I always hate bicyclists.
27. Sometimes I'll look down at my watch three consecutive times and still not know what time it is.
28. Even under ideal conditions people have trouble locating their car keys in a pocket, finding their cell phone and Pinning the Tail on the Donkey - but I'd bet my ass everyone can find and push the snooze button from 3 feet away, in about 1.7 seconds, eyes closed, first time, every time!

CHAPTER 7

MISCELLANEOUS

Under the kilt

A kilted Scotsman was walking down a country path after finishing off a large amount of whisky at a local pub. As he wandered down the road, he felt quite sleepy and decided to take a nap with his back against a tree. As he slept, two young female French tourists walked down the road and heard him snoring loudly.

When they came to the source of the noise, one said, *'I've always wondered what a Scotsman wears under his kilt.'* So she boldly walked over to the sleeper, raised his kilt and saw what nature had provided him with.

Her friend said, *'Well, he has solved a great mystery for us! Let's thank him for the education!'* Whereupon, she took a pretty blue ribbon from her hair and gently tied it around what nature had provided to the Scotsman.

Some time later, the Scotsman was awakened by the call of nature. He walked around to the other side of the tree, raised his kilt and bewilderment filled his mind at the sight of the bright blue ribbon tied neatly in a bow. After several moments passed, he said, *'I dinno know where y'been lad ... but it's nice ta' se y'won first prize.'*

A Scotsman and an Englishman were leaning against the counter in a store when a bandit walked in and brandished his gun. The Scot, a quick thinker, hauld out his money and handed it to his English friend. He said, *'Here's the fifty dollars you lent me.'*

Little Kid

The speaker told her audience that to have a balanced life, everyone needed to let the little kid in themselves out to play at least once a week. One participant replied, *'But they're too young!'*

Chess Players:

A group of chess enthusiasts had checked into a hotel and were standing in the lobby discussing their recent tournament victories. After about an hour, the manager came out of his office and asked them to leave. *'But why?'* they asked. *'Because,'* he said, *'I can't stand chess nuts boasting in an open foyer.'*

Memorial:

It is with the saddest heart that I have to pass on the following. Please join me in remembering a great icon. Veteran Pillsbury spokesperson.

The Pillsbury Doughboy, died yesterday of a severe yeast infection and complications from repeated pokes to the belly. He was 71. Doughboy was buried in a slightly greased coffin. Dozens of celebrities turned out including Mrs. Butterworth, the California Raisins, Hungry Jack, Betty Crocker, the Hostess Twinkies, Captain Crunch, Vegemite and many others.

The graveside was piled high with flours as long-time friend; Aunt Jemima delivered the eulogy, describing Doughboy as a man who *'never knew how much he was kneaded.'* Doughboy Rose quickly in show business and his later life was filled with many turnovers. He was not considered a very smart cookie, wasting much of his dough on half-baked ideas. Despite being a little flaky at times, as a crusty old man, he was considered a roll model for millions.

Towards the end, it was thought he'd rise once again, but he was no tart. Doughboy is survived by his wife, Play Dough. They have two children and one in the oven. The funeral was held at 2:00 for about 20 minutes.

Cannibal's Canoe

Cannibals captured a Frenchman, an Englishman and a New Yorker. The chief comes to them and says, *'The bad news is that now we've caught you - we're going to kill you. We will put you in a pot, cook you, eat you and then we're going to use your skins to build a canoe. The good news is that you can choose how to die.'*

The Frenchman says, *'I take ze sword.'* The chief gives him a sword and the Frenchman says, *'Vive la France!'* and runs himself through.

The Englishman says, *'A pistol for me please.'* The chief gives him a pistol. The Englishman points it at his head and says, *'God save the queen!'* and blows his brains out.

The New Yorker says, *'Gimme a fork!'* The chief is puzzled, but he shrugs and gives him a fork. The New Yorker takes the fork and starts jabbing himself all over - in the stomach, the sides, the chest, everywhere. There is blood gushing out all over - it's horrible. The chief is appalled and asks, *'My God, what are you doing?'* and the New Yorker responds, *'So much for your canoe you stupid cannibal!'*

Two cannibals, a father and son, were elected by the tribe to go out and get something to eat. They walked deep unto the jungle and waited by a path. Before long along came this little old man. The son said, *'Oh dad, there's one!'*

'No,' his father said, *'there's not enough meat on that one to even feed the dogs. We'll just wait.'*

A little while later, along came this really fat man. The son said, *'Hey dad, he's plenty big enough.'*

'No,' the father said, *'We'd all die of a heart attack from the fat in that one. We'll just wait.'*

About an hour later, along came an absolutely gorgeous woman. The son said, *'Now there's nothing wrong with that one dad. Let's eat her.'*

'No,' said the father. *'We won't eat her either.'*

'Why not?' asked the son.

'Because, we're going to take her back alive and eat your mother.'

Set it Free:

If you love something, set it free.
If it comes back, it will always be yours.
If it doesn't come back, it was never yours to begin with.
But, if it just sits in your living room, messes up your stuff, eats your food, uses your telephone, takes your money and doesn't appear to realise that you had set it free - you either married it or gave birth to it!

Carpet Layer

A carpet layer had just finished installing carpet for a lady. He stepped out for a smoke, only to realise he'd lost his cigarettes. In the middle of the room, under the carpet, was a bump. *'No sense pulling up the entire floor for one pack of smokes.'* He said to himself. He got out his hammer and flattened the bump.

As he was cleaning up, the lady came in. *'Here,'* she said, handing him his pack of cigarettes. *'I found them in the hallway.'*

'Now,' she said, *'if only I could find my parakeet.'*

The Aliens

Two aliens landed in the desert near an abandoned gas station. They approached one of the petrol pumps and one of them said to it, *'Greetings, earthling. We come in peace. Take us to your leader.'*

The petrol pump, of course, didn't respond. The alien repeated the greeting. There was no response. The alien, annoyed by what he perceived to be the petrol pump's haughty attitude, drew his ray gun and said impatiently, *'Earthling, how dare you ignore us in this way! Take us to your leader or I will fire!'*

The other alien shouted to his comrade, *'No, you mustn't anger him!'* But before he finished his warning, the first alien fired. There was a huge explosion that blew both of them 200 meters into the desert, where they landed in a heap. When they finally regained consciousness, the one who fired turned to the other and said, *'What a ferocious creature. It nearly killed us! But how did you know he was so dangerous?'*

The other alien answered, *'If there's one thing I've learned during all my travels through the galaxy, it's that if a guy has a penis he can wrap around himself twice and then stick into his own ear, you don't mess with him!'*

The Salesman:

A keen country lad applied for a salesman's job at a city department store. In fact, it was the biggest store in the world - you could get almost anything there. The boss asked him, *'Have you ever been a salesman before?'*

'Yes, I was a salesman in the country,' replied the lad.

The boss took an immediate liking to him and said, *'You can start tomorrow and I'll come by and see you when we close up.'*

The day was long and arduous for the young man, but finally 5 o'clock came round. The boss duly closed up and asked the lad, *'How many sales did you make today?'*

'One,' said the young salesman.

'Only one?' blurted the boss, *'Most of my staff make 20 or 30 sales a day. How much was the sales worth?'*

'Three hundred thousand, three hundred and thirty four dollars,' said the young man.

'How did you manage that?' asked the flabbergasted boss.

'Well,' said the salesman, *'this guy came in and I sold him a small fish hook, then a medium hook and finally a really large*

hook. Then I sold him a small fishing line, a medium one and a huge big one. I asked him where he was going fishing and he said down the coast. I said he would probably need a boat, so I took him down to the boat department and sold him that twenty-foot schooner with the twin engines. Then he said his Honda Civic probably wouldn't be able to pull it, so I took him to the vehicle department and sold him a new Ford Expedition.'

The boss took two steps back and asked in astonishment, 'You sold all that to a guy who came in for a fish hook?'

'No...' answered the salesman. 'He didn't come in to buy a fish hook. He came in to buy a box of tampons for his wife and I said to him, 'your weekend's shot, you might as well go fishin.''

Euro-English: The five-year plan for universal Language:

The European Commission has just announced an agreement whereby English will be the official language of the EU, rather than German, which was the other possibility. As part of the negotiations, Her Majesty's government conceded that English spelling had some room for improvement and has accepted a 5-year phase-in plan that would be known as 'Euro-English.'

In the first year, 'S' will replace the soft 'C.' Sertainly, this will make the sivil servants jump with joy. The hard 'C' will be dropped in favour of the 'K.' This would klear up konfusion and keyboards kan have one less letter.

There will be growing publik enthusiasm in the sekond year, when the troublesome 'PH' will be replased with the 'F.' This will make words like fotograf 20% shorter.

In the third ear publik akseptanse of the new speling kan be expekted to reach the stage where more komplikated changes are possible. Government will enkourage the removal of double letters, which have always been a deterent to akurate speling. Also, al wil agre that the horible mes of the silent 'E' in the languag is disgrasful and they should go away.

By the forth yar, people wil be reseptiv to steps such as replasing 'TH' with 'Z,' and 'W' with 'V.'

During ze fifz yar, ze unesesary 'O' can be dropd from vords kontaining 'OU' and similar changes vud of kors be aplid to ozer kombinations of leters.

After zis fifz yar, ve vil hav a rel sensible riten styl. Zer vil no mor trubls or difikiltis and evrivun vil find it ezi to understand ech ozer.

Ze drem vil finl kum tru!

[Author's note: my spell checker went crazy when I edited this portion!]

How much do you know?

Answer the following 11 questions, then scroll down and check your answers. Don't cheat! When you're done, count the number correct and see how you compare with others. Okay here we go:

1. Is there a 4th of July in England? Yes or No?
2. How many birthdays does the average man have?
3. Some months have 31 days. How many have 28?
4. Is it legal for a man in California to marry his widow's sister?
5. Take the number 30, divide it by * and then add 10. What do you get?
6. There are 3 apples and you take two away. How many apples are you left with?
7. A doctor gives you three pills and tells you to take one every half hour. How long will the pills last?
8. A farmer has 17 sheep. All but 9 of them die. How many sheep are left?
9. How many animals of each sex did Moses bring with him on the ark?
10. A butcher in the market is 5' 10' tall. What does he weigh?
11. How many 2-cent stamps are there in a dozen?

So how did you do?

1. Yes. It comes right after the 3rd.
2. One (1). You can only be born once.
3. Twelve (12). All of them have at least 28 days.
4. No. He must be dead, if it is his widow!
5. Seventy (70). 30 divided by * is 60.
6. Two (2). You take two apples, therefore - you have two apples.
7. One hour. If you take the first pill at 1:00, the second at 1:30 and the third at 2:00, the pills have run out and only an hour has passed.
8. Nine (9). Like I said, all but nine die.
9. None. I didn't know that Moses had an ark?
10. Meat ... that is self-explanatory.
11. Twelve (12). How many eggs are in a dozen? Twelve ... it's a dozen!

So how did you do?

11 correct - genius - you are good!
9-10 correct - above average ....but don't let it go to your head
5-9 correct – average ... but who wants to be average?
3-4 correct - slow ... pay attention to the question
2-3 correct – idiot ... what else can I say?
1 correct - congratulations, you're a certified moron!!!

Bus Conversation:

A bus stops and two Italian men get on. They seat themselves and engage in animated conversation. The lady sitting behind them ignores their conversation at first, but her attention is galvanised when she hears one of them say the following: *'Emma, she comsa firsta. Den I come. Two asses, dey comsa together. I comsa again. Two asses, dey comsa together again. I some again anda pee twice. Then I comsa once-a more.'*

'You foul-mouthed swine', retorted the lady indignantly. 'In this country we don't talk about our sex lives in public.'

'Hey, calma down lady,' said the man. *'I'ma justa telling my friend howa to spell Mississippi.'*

Tight skirt:

In a crowded city, at a crowded bus stop, a beautiful young woman was waiting for the bus. She was decked out in a tight leather mini-skirt. As the bus rolled up and it became her turn to get on, she became aware that her skirt was too tight to allow her leg to come up to the height of the first step on the bus. Slightly embarrassed and with a quick smile to the bus driver, she reached behind her and unzipped her skirt a little thinking that this would give her enough slack to raise her leg.

Again she tried to make the step onto the bus, only to discover that she still couldn't! So, a little more embarrassed, she once again reached behind her and unzipped her skirt a little more and for a third time attempted the step and once again, much to her chagrin, she couldn't raise her leg. After she unzipped her skirt a third time, the big Texan behind her in the line picked her up easily from the waist and placed her lightly at the top step of the bus.

Well, she went ballistic and turned on the would-be hero, screeching at him, *'How dare you touch my body!!! I don't even know who you are!'*

At this the Texan drawled, *'Well ma'am ... normally I would agree with you, but after you unzipped my fly three times, I kinda figured that we was friends.'*

Santa Claus:

A beautiful innocent girl wants to meet Santa Claus, so she puts on a robe and stays up late on Christmas Eve. Santa arrives, climbs down the chimney and begins filling the stockings. He is about to leave, when the girl (who happens to be a gorgeous redhead) says in a sexy voice, *'Oh Santa, please stay. Keep the chill away.'*

Santa replies, *'Ho Ho Ho - gotta go, gotta go, gotta get the presents to the children, you know.'*

The girl drops the robe to reveal a sexy bra and panties and says in an even sexier voice, *'Oh Santa, don't run a mile; just stay for a while ...'*

Santa begins to sweat, but replies, *'Ho Ho Ho, gotta go, gotta go, gotta get the presents to the children, you know.'*

She takes off her bras and says, *'Oh Santa ... Please stay.'*

Santa, with sweat pouring off his brow, says, *'Hey Hey Hey, gotta go, gotta go, gotta get the presents to the children, you know.'*

She loses the panties and says, *'Oh Santa ... Please stay.'*
Santa, with the sweat pouring off his brow, says, *'Hey, Hey, gotta stay, gotta stay. Can't get up the chimney with my pecker this way!'*

'Twas the dive before Christmas and all through the deep,
The morays were dozing; the sharks were asleep.
I in my wetsuit, my wife in her gear,
Dropped over the side for the last time that year.
The oysters were nestled all snug in their beds,
Waiting for Santa on his undersea sled.
When what to our wondering eyes should appear?
But the jolly old elf in his red scuba gear!

Visiting each hole in his bright Christmas hues,
And deftly delivering the Bottom Time News,
The fish were excited as they read it with glee,
'Look,' cried a 'cuda,' *'That's a picture of me!'*

And as we ascended on that wondrous night,
We heard the fish singing Christmas songs with delight.
Santa then surfaced as we climbed on the boat.

Removing his mouthpiece and clearing his throat.

'Merry Christmas to you and all others that dive,
Who visit the reefs and leave them alive.'
Then we heard him exclaim as he dropped from our sight,
'Merry Christmas, keep diving and I beg you good night!'

Trivia:

Why do things appear darker when they're wet?

Grab a white shirt, dip it in water and voila, it turns grey right before your eyes. If we hadn't all seen it much too often, it would make for an impressive magic trick. Since we have, it's an excellent trivia questions.

What causes this optical transformation is simple science. When fabric gets wet, light coming towards it refracts within the water, dispersing the light. In addition, the surface of the water causes incoherent light scattering. The combination of these two effects causes less light to reflect to your eyes and makes the wet fabric appear darker.

Why doesn't drinking water cool your mouth after eating spicy food?

The spices in most of the hot foods that we eat are oily and like our elementary school science teacher taught you, oil and water don't mix. In this case, the water just rolls over the oily spices.

So what can you do to calm your aching tongue? Try one of these three methods. Eat bread. The bread will absorb the oily spices. A second solution is to drink milk. Milk contains a substance called 'casein' which will bind to the spices and carry them away. Finally, you could drink something alcoholic. Alcohol will dissolve the oily spices.

[I like the last solution!]

They weren't invented in France, so why does everybody call them 'French fries?'

It's true; the French fry wasn't invented in France. (Its origin is probably Belgium.) But the 'French' in French fries doesn't refer to its country of origin. It refers to the way in which this side dish is prepared. Food that is cut into strips is said to be 'Frenched.' Since French fries are strips of potato that have been fried, they became known as 'French fries.'

Why is it called a 'hamburger' if it doesn't contain ham?

At first glance, it seems that the word 'hamburger' is a combination of the words 'ham' and 'burger.' Therefore, one naturally assumes that a hamburger is a burger that contains ham. But the word 'hamburger' actually traces its roots back to Hamburg Germany, where people used to eat a similar food called the 'Hamburg steak.' Eventually, the Hamburg steak made its way to the United States, where people shortened its name to 'hamburger.'

[**Note**: Do you remember the character in Perry Mason whose name was Hamilton Berger? Imagine what his nickname was?]

Were hot dogs ever made of dogs?

Nah. But when they were first introduced, people wouldn't touch hot dogs for fear that they were made of dogs.

How'd the hot dog get its strange name?

The hot dog was originally called 'frankfurter' after Frankfurt, Germany, its birthplace. But from the beginning people called it 'dachshund sausage,' because it looked like the long, thin dog.

In the US, the German sausage was especially popular with New York baseball fans, who bought the newfangled sandwich from vendors who sold them by selling, *'Get your dachshund sausages while they're red hot.'*

Ted Dorgan, a leading cartoonist, thought these vendors were so comical, that he decided to lampoon them. In his cartoon, they were shown selling REAL dachshund dogs in a roll, yelling, *'Get your hot dogs!'* at each other. The name stuck and the rest is history.

How do astronauts go to the bathroom?

Thanks to gravity, we here on earth take going to the bathroom for granted, but using the toilet in space isn't nearly as easy.

For a long time, says NASA, astronauts actually taped a plastic bag to their backsides to collect faeces and used a hose-and-bag device to urinate. Then, in the early 70's, NASA improved bathroom technology with its vacuum toilet. To defecate, astronauts now sit on this toilet and turn the vacuum on. Urination is done through what looks like your vacuum cleaner's hose attachment. Using this toilet is a bit tricky, so part of the preparation for space travel includes potty training, but it sure beats the old bag system.

Diary of a Snow Shoveller

December 8: 6:00 pm it started to snow. The first snow of the season and the wife and I took our cocktails and sat for hours by the window watching the huge soft flakes drift down from Heaven. It looked like a Grandma Moses print. So romantic we felt like newlyweds again. I love snow!

December 9: We woke to a beautiful blanket of crystal white snow covering every inch of the landscape. What a fantastic sight! Can there be a lovelier place in the whole world? Moving here was the best idea I've ever had. Shovelled for the first time in years and felt like a boy again. I did both our driveway and the sidewalks. This afternoon, the snow plow came along and covered up the sidewalks and closed in the driveway, so I got to shovel again. What a perfect life!

December 12: The sun melted all our lovely snow. Such a disappointment. My neighbour tells me not to worry we'll definitely have a white Christmas. No snow on Christmas would be awful! Bob says we'll have so much snow by the end of winter that I'll never want to see snow again. I don't think that's possible. Bob is such a nice man. I'm glad he's our neighbour.

December 14: Snow, lovely snow! 8' last night. The temperature dropped to -20. The cold makes everything sparkle so. The wind took my breath away, but I warmed up by shovelling the driveway and sidewalks. This is the life! The snow plow came back this afternoon and buried everything again. I didn't realise I would have to do quite this much shovelling, but I'll certainly get back in shape this way. I wish I wouldn't huff and puff so.

December 15: 20 inches of snow forecast. I sold my van and bought a 4x4 Blazer. Bought snow tires for the wife's car and two extra shovels. Stocked the freezer. The wife wants a wood stove in case the electricity goes out. I think that's silly. We aren't in Alaska, after all.

December 16: Ice storm this morning. Fell on my ass on the ice in the driveway putting down salt. Hurt like Hell. The wife laughed for an hour, which I think is very cruel.

December 17: Still way below freezing. Roads are too icy to go anywhere. Electricity was off for five hours. I had to pile the blankets on to stay warm. Nothing to do but stare at the wife and try not to irritate her. Guess I should have bought a wood stove, but won't admit it to her. God I hate it when she's right. I can't believe I'm freezing to death in my own living room!

December 20: Electricity is back on, but had another 14' of the damn stuff last night. More shovelling. Took all day. Goddamn snow plow came by twice. Tried to find a neighbour kid to shovel, but they say they're too busy playing hockey. I think they're lying. Called the only hardware store around to see about buying a snow blower but they've sold out. Might have another shipment in March. I think they're lying. Bob says I have to shovel or the city will have it done and bill me. I think he's lying.

December 22: Bob was right about a white Christmas because 13 more inches of the white shit fell today and it's so cold it won't probably melt till August. Took me 45 minutes to get all dressed up to go out to shovel and then I had to pee. By the time I got undressed, peed and got dressed again, I was too tired to shovel. Tried to hire Bob who has a plow on his truck for the rest of the winter; but says he's too busy. I think the asshole is lying.

December 23: Only 2' of snow today and it warmed up to 0. The wife wanted me to decorate the front of the house this morning. What - is she nuts!!!? Why didn't she tell me to do that a month ago? She says she did, but I think she's lying.

December 24: 6' of snow packed so hard by the snow plow that I broke the shovel. Thought I was having a heart attack. If I ever catch that son of a bitch who drives that snow plow, I'll drag him through the snow by his balls. I know he hides around the corner and waits for me to finish shovelling and then he comes down the street at 100 miles per hour and throws snow all over where I've just been! Tonight the wife wanted me to sing Christmas carols with her and open our presents, but I was busy watching for the goddamn snow plow.

December 25: Merry Christmas. 20 more inches of the !+$#@?*# slop tonight. Snowed in. The idea of shovelling makes my blood boil. God I hate the snow! Then the snow plow driver came by asking for a donation, I hit him over the head with my shovel. The wife says I have a bad attitude. I think she's an idiot. If I have to watch *'It's a wonderful Life?'* One more time, I'm going to kill her.

December 26: Still snowed in. Why the Hell did I ever move here? It was all her idea. She's really getting on my nerves.

December 27: Temperature dropped to –50 and the pipes froze.

December 28: Warmed up to above –30. Still snowed in. the bitch is driving me crazy.

December 29: 10 more inches. Bob says I have to shovel the roof or it will cave in. That's the silliest thing I ever heard. How dumb does he think I am?

December 30: Roof caved in. The snow plow driver is suing me for a million dollars for the bump on his head. The wife went home to her mother. 9' snow predicted.

December 31: Set fire to what's left of the house. No more shovelling.

January 8: I feel so good. I just love those little white pills they keep giving me. Why am I tied to the bed?

Vanity License Plates:

Plate: icncydu - I see inside you (a radiologist's plate)
oh2b39 - Oh to be 39
cyimbrk - See Why I'm broke (found on a cherry red 95 ford three-quarter ton truck).
yurnext - On the car of an undertaker
av8rx - Aviatrix (female pilot)
toolong - On a Lincoln super-log limo
w8n4fri - Waitin' for Friday
cmegobyu - See me go by you!
cme4ad8 - See me for a date
cme4dk - See me for decay (dentist's car)

A hundred year-old man

A hundred year-old man has broken a mirror and looks very pleased about it.

'*Why are you so pleased?*' people asked him, '*You'll have seven years of bad luck!*'

He answered, '*But, it means I'll live another seven years!*'

Ole, Lena and Sven:

Ole, Lena and Sven were lost in the woods of Northern Minnesota and were becoming desperate having run out of food several days ago. It was winter, the snow was deep and their situation was looking very bleak. When Ole dug down into the snow to look for nuts, he found an oil lamp and rubbed it to get the snow off. A Genie came out and said, *'I am da great Genie of Nordern Minnesooota and I can grant each of you vun vish.'*

Ole says, *'I vish I vas back on da farm.'* Poof, Ole was gone.

Lena quickly says, *'I vish I vas back on da farm wit Ole.'* Poof, Lena was gone.

Sven was sitting there looking sad and the Genie finally says, *'Sven, vat is your vish?'* and Sven says, *'Gee I'm really lonely. I vish Ole and Lena vere here with me.'*

Sven was going for his morning walk one day when he walked past Ole's house and saw a sign that said 'Boat for Sale.' This confused Sven because he knew that Ole didn't own a boat, so he decided to ask Ole about it. *'Hey Ole,'* said Sven, *'I noticed a sign in your yard dat says 'Boat for Sale,' but ya don't even have a boat. All ya have is your old John Deere tractor and combine.'*

Ole replied, *'Yup and they're boat for sale.'*

One day Ole goes in to see his doctor. Ole says, *'Doc, I just don't know vat to do. Lena and me, vell, our sex life just ain't going dat vell.'*

The doctor says, *'Ole, all you need is some exercise. I want you to walk ten miles every day. You give me a call in a week and let me know how you're doing.'*

So, a week later the phone rings and the doctor answers it. A voice on the other end says, *'Doc, dis is Ole.'*

The doctor says, *'Hello Ole. Have you been walking ten miles every day?'*

Ole says, *'Yes.'*

The doctor asks, *'And has your sex life improved?'*

Ole replies, *'Well, how the Hell vould I know? I'm seventy miles avay from home!'*

Ole and Lena were sitting down to their usual cup of morning coffee while listening to the weather report coming over the radio: *'There will be three to five inches of snow today and a snow emergency has been declared. To avoid a snow-bird parking ticket and/or a tow to the city impound lot, you must park your cars on the odd numbered side of the street.'*

Ole gets up from his coffee and, on his way to the door, announces, *'Uff da, Lena. I gotta go move da car.'*

Two days later, as they again are drinking their morning coffee, the radio forecaster says, *'There will be two to four inches* of snow today and a snow emergency has been declared. You must park your car on the even numbered side of the street.'

Ole gets up from his coffee and announces, *'Moure snow, Lena. I gotta move da car again.'*

Three days later, same setting worse forecast: *'There will be six to eight inches of snow today and a snow emergency has been declared. You must park your cars on the ...'*

Just then the power went out, preventing Ole from getting the rest of the parking instructions. *'Lena, vat am I going to do now?'*

Lena replies, *'Oh Ole! Just leave da car in da garage.'*

Lena passed away and Ole called emergency services. The operator told Ole that she would send someone out right away. *'Where do you life?'* asked the operator.

Ole replied, *'At da end of Eucalyptus Drive.'*

The operator asked, *'Can you spell that for me?*

There was a long pause and finally Ole said, *'How 'bout if I drag her over to Oak Street and you pick her up der?'*

Ole was fishing with Sven in a rented boat. They could not catch a thing. Ole said, *'Let's go a vit furder down stream.'* So they did and they caught many monstrous fish. They had their limit so they went home.

Ole said, *'How are we going to remember where we caught the fish?'*

Sven replied, *'I marked de spot in de middle of de boat, Ole.'*

'You stupid,' said Ole, *'How do you know ve vill get da same boat next time?'*

The African King:

The beautiful secretary of the president of the bank goes on a sightseeing tour with a very rich African king who was a very important client. The client, out of the blue, asks her to marry him. Naturally, the secretary is quite taken aback. However, she remembers what her boss told her ... don't reject the guy outright. So she tries to think of a way to dissuade the king from wanting to marry her.

After a few minutes, the woman says, *'I will only marry you under three conditions. First, I want my engagement ring to be a 75-carat diamond ring with a matching 200-carat diamond tiara.'*

The African king pauses for a while. Then he nods his head and says, *'No problem! I have. I have!'*

Realising her first condition was too easy; the woman says to the man, *'I want you to build me a 100-room mansion in New York. As a vacation home, I want a chateau built in the middle of the best wine country in France.'*

The African king pauses for a while. He whips out his cellular phone and calls some brokers in New York and in France. He looks at the woman, nods his head and says, *'Okay, okay. I build. I build.'*

Realising that she only has one last condition, the secretary knows that she'd better make this a good one. She takes her time to think and finally she gets an idea, a sure-to-work condition. She squints her eyes, looks at the man and says, rather coldly, *'Since I like sex, I want the man I marry to have a 10-inch penis.'* The man seems disturbed. He cups his face with his hands and rests his elbows on the table. All the while muttering in African dialect.

Finally, after what seemed like forever, the king shakes his head, looking really sad and says to the woman, *'Okay, okay. I cut. I cut.'*

Manipulation:

A man called his mother and asked, *'Mother, how are you doing?'*

She replied, *'Not too good. I've been very weak.'*

The son becomes concerned and asked, *'Why are you so weak?'*

'Because I haven't eaten in 38 days,' she said.

'What!' he shouted, jumping to his feet, *'How come you haven't eaten in 38 days?'*

His mom replied, *'Because I didn't want my mouth to be filled with food when you called.'*

Watson:

The legendary detective, Sherlock Holmes, along with his constant companion and confidant, Dr. Watson, went on a camping trip. After a good meal, they lay down for the night and went to sleep. Some hours later, Holmes awoke and nudged his faithful friend, *'Watson, look up at the sky and tell me what you see?'*

Watson replied, *'I see millions and millions of stars.'*

'What does that tell you?'

Watson pondered for a minute. *'Astronomically, it tells me that there are millions of galaxies and potentially billions of planets. Horologically, I deduce that the time is approximately a quarter past three. Theologically, I can see that God is all-powerful and that we are small and insignificant. Meteorologically, I suspect that we will have a beautiful day tomorrow. What does it tell you?'*

Holmes was silent for a minute, then spoke, *'Watson, you idiot, someone has stolen our tent.'*

Chinese Jews

Sid and Al were sitting in a Chinese restaurant. *'Sid,'* asked Al, *'Are there any Jews in China?'*

'I don't know,' Sid replied. *'Why don't we ask the waiter?'*

'I don't know sir, let me ask,' the waiter replied and he went into the kitchen. He returned in a few minutes and said, *'No, sir. No Chinese Jews.'*

'Are you sure?' Al asked.

'I will check again, sir,' the waiter replied and went back to the kitchen.

While he was still gone, Sid said, *'I cannot believe there are no Jews in China. Our people are scattered everywhere.'*

When the waiter returned he said, *'Sir, no Chinese Jews.'*

'Are you really sure?' Al asked again. *'I cannot believe there are no Chinese Jews.'*

'Sir, I ask everyone,' the waiter replied exasperated. *'We have Orange Jews, Prune Jews, Tomato Jews and Grape Jews, but no Chinese Jews!'*

Chinese Proverbs:

- Virginity like bubble, one prick, all gone.
- Man who run in front of car, get tired.
- Man who run behind car, get exhausted.
- Man with hand in pocket, feel cocky all day.
- Foolish man give wife grand piano. Wise man give wife upright organ.
- Man who walk through airport turnstile sideways, going to Bangkok.
- Man with one chopstick go hungry.
- Man who scratch ass should not bite fingernails.
- Man who eat many prunes get good run for money.

- Baseball is wrong. Man with four balls cannot walk.
- Panties not best thing on earth, but next to best thing on earth.
- Wife who put husband in doghouse soon finds him in cat house.
- Man who fight with wife all day get no piece at night.
- It takes many nails to build crib, but one screw to fill it.
- Man who drive like Hell bound to get there.
- Man who stand on toilet is high on pot.
- Man who live in glass house, should change clothes in basement.
- Man who fish in other man's well often catch crabs.
- Crowded elevator, smell different to midget.

Chinese to English Translation:

(Must be said out loud):
- Dung On Mi Shu - I stepped in excrement.
- Ai Wan Tu Bang Yu - Let's sleep together.
- Ar U Wun Tu? - A gay liberation greeting.
- Chin Tu Fat - You need a face-lift.
- Chow Mai Dong - Romantic proposition.
- Dum Gai - A stupid guy.
- Wel Hung Gai - Is that a banana in your pocket?
- Gun Pao Der - An ancient Chinese invention.
- Hi Flung Dung - Which one of you fertilised the field?
- Lin Ching - An illegal execution.
- Shai Gai - A bashful man.
- Wan Bum Lung - A person with T.B.
- Yu Mai Te Tan - Your vacation in Hawaii agrees with you.
- Wai So Dim - Are you trying to save electricity?
- Wai U Shao Ting - There's no reason to raise your voice.

Chinese Doctor:

While in China, a man is very sexually promiscuous and does not use a condom all the time. A week after arriving back home in the States, he wakes one morning to find his penis covered with bright green and purple spots.

Horrified, he immediately goes to see a doctor. The doctor, never having seen anything like this before orders some tests and tells the man to return in two days for the results.

The man returns a couple of days later and the doctor says: *'I've got bad news for you - you've contracted Mongolian VD. It's* very rare and almost unheard of here. We know very little about it.'

The man looks a little perplexed and says: *'Well, give me a shot or something and fix me up, Doc.'*

The doctor answers: *'I'm sorry, there's no known cure. We're going to have to amputate your penis.'*

The man screams in horror, *'Absolutely not! I want a second opinion.'*

The doctor replies: *'Well, it's your choice. Go ahead if you want but surgery is your only choice.'*

The next day, the man seeks out a Chinese doctor, figuring that he'll know more about the disease. The Chinese doctor examines his penis and proclaims: *'Ah, yes, Mongolian VD. Vely lare disease.'*

The guy says to the doctor: *'Yeah, yeah, I already know that, but what can we do? My American doctor wants to operate and amputate my penis!'*

The Chinese doctor shakes his head and laughs: *'Stupid Amelican docta, always want to opelate. Make more money that way. No need to opelate!'*

'Oh, Thank God!' the man replies.

'Yes,' says the Chinese doctor, *'You no worry! Wait two weeks. Faw off by itself!'*

The secret of enjoying good red wine

1. Open the bottle to allow it to breathe.
2. If it doesn't look like it's breathing, give it mouth to mouth resuscitation.

The other day someone told me that I could make ice cubes with leftover wine. I was confused ... What leftover wine?

The American Soldier:

An American soldier, serving in World War II, had just returned from several weeks of intensive action on the Italian front lines. He had finally been granted rest and relaxation and had made it to England, to board a train bound for a few days in London. The train was very crowded, so the soldier walked the length of the train, looking for an empty seat.

The only seat unoccupied was directly across from a well-dressed middle-aged lady and was being used by her little dog. The war-weary soldier asked, *'Please ma'am, may I sit in that seat?'*

The English woman looked down her nose at the soldier, sniffed and said, *'You Americans are such a rude class of people. Can't you see that my little Fifi is using that seat?'*

The soldier walked away, determined to find a place to rest. But after another trip down to the end of the train, once again he found himself again facing the woman with the dog in the opposite seat. Again he asked, *'Please lady. Can I sit there? I'm very tired.'*

The English woman wrinkled her nose and snorted, *'You Americans! Not only are you rude, you are also quite arrogant. Imagine!'*

The soldier leaned against the swaying wall of the train and again asked if he could please sit down. The lady replied, *'Not only are you Americans rude and arrogant, you're also very inconsiderate.'*

Without warning, the soldier leaned over, picked up the little dog and tossed it out the window of the moving train. He sat down in the empty seat across to the speechless woman. An English gentlemen sitting across the aisle, motioned and remarked, *'You know sir, you Americans do seem to have a penchant for doing the wrong thing. You eat holding the fork in the wrong hand. You drive your autos on the wrong side of the road. And now, sir you've thrown the wrong bitch out of the window!'*

Creative Obituary:

Your great-great uncle, Remus Starr (a fellow lacking in character) was hanged for horse stealing and train robbery in Montana in 1889. A cousin has supplied you with the only known photograph of Remus, showing him standing on the gallows. On the back of the picture are the words: *'Remus Starr: Horse thief, sent to Montana Territorial Prison, 1885. Escaped 1887, robbed the Montana Flyer six times. Caught by Pinkerton detectives, convicted and hanged, 1889.'*

A pretty grim situation - right? But, let's revise things a bit. We simply crop the picture, scan in an enlarged image and edit it with image processing software so that all that is seen is a head shot.

Next, we re-write the text: *'Remus Starr was a famous cowboy in the Montana Territory. His business empire grew to include acquisition of valuable equestrian assets and intimate dealings with the Montana railroad. Beginning in 1885, he devoted several years of his to life to service at a government facility, finally taking leave to resume his dealings with the railroad. In 1887, he was a key player in a vital investigation run by the renowned Pinkerton Detective Agency. In 1889, Remus passed away during an important civic function held in his honour when the platform upon which he was standing collapsed.'*

Cinderella

Cinderella wants to go to the ball, but her wicked stepmother won't let her. As Cinderella sits crying in the garden, her Fairy Godmother appears and promises to provide Cinderella with everything she needs to go to the ball, but only on two conditions. *'First, you must wear a diaphragm.'*

Cinderella agrees. *'What's the second condition?'*

'You must be home by 2:00 am. Any later and your diaphragm will turn into a pumpkin.'

Cinderella agrees to be home by 2:00 am. The appointed hour comes and goes and Cinderella doesn't show up. Finally, at 5:00 am, Cinderella shows up, looking love struck and **very** satisfied.

'Where have you been?' demands the Fairy Godmother. *'Your diaphragm was supposed to turn into a pumpkin three hours ago.'*

'I met a prince, Fairy Godmother. He took care of everything.'

'I know of no prince with that kind of power! Tell me his name.'

'I can't remember exactly. Peter, Peter, something or other ...'

Mickey & Minnie:

Mickey Mouse and Minnie Mouse were in divorce court and the judge said to Mickey, *'You say here that your wife is crazy.'*

Mickey replied, *'I didn't say she was crazy, I said she's screwing Goofy.'*

Little Red Riding Hood

Little Red Riding hood was walking through the woods when suddenly the Big Bad Wolf jumped out from behind a tree and, holding a sword to her throat, said, *'Red, I've going to screw your brains out!'*

To that, Little Red Riding Hood calmly reached into her picnic basket and pulled out a .44 magnum and pointed it at him and said, *'No, you're not. You're going to eat me, just like it says in the book!'*

Pinocchio

Pinocchio had a human girlfriend who would sometimes complain about splinters when they were having sex. Pinocchio, therefore, went to visit Gepetto to see if he could help. Gepetto suggested he try a little sandpaper wherever indicated and Pinocchio skipped away enlightened.

A couple of weeks later, Gepetto saw Pinocchio bouncing happily through town and asked him, *'How's the girlfriend?'* Pinocchio replied, *'Who needs a girlfriend?'*

Snow White saw Pinocchio walking through the woods so she ran up behind him, knocked him flat on his back and then sat on his face crying, *'Lie to me! Lie to me!'*

Tarzan & Jane

One day Jane met Tarzan in the jungle. She was very attracted to him and during her questions about his life; she asked him how he managed for sex.

'What's that?' he asked.

She explained to him what sex was and he said, *'Oh, I use a hole in the trunk of a tree.'*

Horrified, she said, *'Tarzan you have it all wrong, but I will show you how to do it properly.'*

She took off her clothes, lay down on the ground and spread her legs wide. *'Here,'* she said, *'You must put it in here.'*

Tarzan removed his loincloth, stepped closer and then gave her an almighty kick in the crotch. Jane rolled around in agony. Eventually she mentioned to gasp, *'What the Hell did you do that for?'*

'Just checking for bees.' said Tarzan.

My neighbour asked if she could use my vacuum cleaner. I said, *'Sure, as long as you don't take it out of my house.'*

World's worst puns:

- I changed my iPad's name to Titanic. It's syncing now.
- When chemists die, they barium.
- Jokes about German sausage are the wurst.

- I know a guy who's addicted to brake fluid. But he says he can stop any time.
- How does Moses make his tea? Hebrews it.
- I stayed up all night to see where the sun went. Then it dawned on me.
- This girl said she recognised me from the vegetarian club, but I'd never met herbivore.
- I'm reading a book about anti-gravity. I just can't put it down.
- I didn't like my beard at first. Then it grew on me.
- When you get a bladder infection, urine trouble.
- Broken pencils are pointless.
- I tried to catch some fog, but I mist.
- What do you call a dinosaur with an extensive vocabulary? A thesaurus.
- I used to be a banker, but then I lost interest.
- A man's home is his castle, in a manor of speaking.
- Dijon vu - the same mustard as before.
- Practice safe eating - always use condiments.
- Shotgun wedding - A case of wife or death.
- A man needs a mistress just to break the monogamy.
- A hangover is the wrath of grapes.
- Dancing cheek-to-cheek is really a form of floor play.
- Does the name Pavlov ring a bell?
- Condoms should be used on every conceivable occasion.
- Reading while sunbathing makes you well red.
- When two egotists meet, it's an I for an I.
- A bicycle can't stand on its own because it is two tired.
- What's the definition of a will? It's a dead give away.)
- Time flies like an arrow. Fruit flies like a banana.
- In democracy your vote counts. In feudalism your count votes.
- She was engaged to a boyfriend with a wooden leg but broke it off.
- A chicken crossing the road is poultry in motion.
- If you don't pay your exorcist, you get repossessed.
- With her marriage, she got a new name and a dress.
- The man who fell into an upholstery machine is fully recovered.
- You feel stuck with your debt if you can't budge it.
- Local Area Network in Australia - the LAN down under.
- Every calendar's days are numbered.

- A lot of money is tainted - taint yours and taint mine.
- A boiled egg in the morning is hard to beat.
- A midget fortune-teller who escapes from prison is a small medium at large.
- Once you've seen one shopping centre, you've seen a mall.
- Bakers trade bread recipes on a knead-to-know basis.
- Santa's helpers are subordinate clauses.
- Acupuncture is a jab well done.

Five festive funnies

1. There once was a Tsar in Russia whose name was Rudolph the Great. He was standing in his house one day with his wife. He looked out the window and saw something happening. He says to his wife, *'Look honey. It's raining.'* She, being the obstinate type, responded, *' I don't think so, dear. I think it's snowing.'*
But Rudolph knew better. So he says to his wife, *'Let's step outside and we'll find out.'* Lo and behold, they step outside and discover it was in fact rain. And Rudolph turns to his wife and replies, *'I knew it was raining. Rudolph the Red knows rain, dear!'*
2. How do you know Santa has to be a man? No woman is going to wear the same outfit year after year.
3. What did Adam say on Christmas night? *'It's Christmas, Eve.'*
4. An honest politician, a kind lawyer and Santa Claus were walking down the street and saw a $20 bill. Which one picked it up? Santa! The other two don't exist!
5. Do you know what would have happened if it had been Three Wise Women instead of Three Wise Men? They would have asked directions, arrived on time, helped deliver the baby, cleaned the stable, made a casserole and brought practical gifts

Doormats with a difference

- *'Come back with a warrant.'*
- *'This is not a joke. If you ever want to see these people again, bring me a 5 pound roast in a plain brown bag.'* Signed *'The dog.'*
- *'Our dog is not a biter – he's a humper.'*
- *'Nice underwear.'*

- *'I will not be a doormat. I will not be a doormat. I will not be a doormat. Oh just walk all over me!'*
- *'Go away – come back with wine.'*
- *'I'm really glad to see you, but then I'm a doormat.'*
- *'Beer gets you in the door.'*
- *'We love our vacuum cleaner: we found God; and we gave at the office.'*
- *'Please stay on the mat. Your visit is very important to us. Your knock will be answered in the order in which it was received.'*
- *'Ask not for whom the dog barks. It barks for thee.'*
- *'Beware of the cat – roar!'* (with picture of a lion).
- *'A lovely lady and a grumpy old man live here.'*
- *'Oh shit! Not you again!'*

Stinky Sailors

There's an old sea story about a ship's captain who inspected his sailors and afterwards told the first mate that his men smelled bad. The captain suggested perhaps it would help if the sailors would change underwear occasionally.

The first mate responded, *'Aye, aye sir. I'll see to it immediately!'*

He went straight to the sailors' berth deck and announced, *'The Captain thinks you guys smell bad and wants you to change your underwear.'* He continued, *'Pittman, you change with Jones, McCarthy, you change with Witkowski and Brown, you change with Schultz.'*

Texan in Australia

A Texan farmer goes to Australia for a vacation. There, he meets an Aussie farmer and gets talking. The Aussie shows off his big wheat field and the Texan says, *'Oh! We have wheat fields that are at least twice as large.'*

Then they walk around the farm a little and the Aussie shows off his herd of cattle. The Texan immediately says, *'We have longhorns that are at least twice as large as your cows.'*

The conversation has, meanwhile, almost died when the Texan sees a herd of kangaroos hopping through the field. He asked, *'And what are those?'*

The Aussie replies with an incredulous look, *'Don't you have any grasshoppers in Texas?'*

Supermarket

I was checking out at a busy supermarket and the cashier was having problems. The register ran out of paper, the scanner malfunctioned and then the cashier spilled a handful of coins.

When she totalled my order, it came to exactly $22. Trying to soothe her nerves, I said, *'That's a nice round figure.'*
Still frazzled, she glared at me and said, *'You're no bean pole yourself!'*

Copper wire

After having dug down five metres last year, French scientists found traces of copper wire dating back 200 years and concluded that their ancestors had a telephone network more than 150 years ago.

Not to be outdone, America archaeologists dug to a depth of ten metres before finding traces of 250 year-old copper wire.
Shortly afterwards, they published an article in The New York Times saying: *'American archaeologists have concluded that their ancestors already had an advanced hi-tech communications network fifty years earlier than the French.'*

A few weeks later, Aussie newspapers reported: *'After digging in the outback two years ago, Jack Daniel (Bluey) a self-taught amateur archaeologist, reported that he and found absolutely nothing. Jack has therefore concluded that 250 years ago, Australia had already gone wireless.'*

The travelling Euro

It's August. In a small town on the South Coast of France the holiday season is in full swing, but it's raining so there's not too much business happening. Everyone is heavily in debt.

One day a rich Aussie arrives in the foyer of the small local hotel. He asks for a room and puts a €100 note on the reception counter, takes a key and goes to inspect the room located up the stairs on the third floor.

The hotel owner takes the banknote and rushes to his meat supplier to whom he owes €100.

The butcher takes the money and races to his supplier to clear his debt.

The wholesaler rushes to the farmer to pay €100 for pigs he purchased some time ago.

The farmer triumphantly gives the €100 note to a local prostitute who gave him her services on credit.

The prostitute goes quickly to the hotel, as she owes €100 for her hourly room use to entertain clients.

Just as she hands the owner the cash, the rich Aussie comes back down to reception. He informs the hotel owner that the proposed room is unsatisfactory.

He takes back his €100 and departs.

Sure, there was no retained profit in these transactions, but everyone no longer has any debt and the people of the small town can look more optimistically towards their future.

Thought for the day:

Never hold farts in. They travel up your spine into your brain and that is where shitty ideas come from.

English Signs from Around the World

In a Bangkok temple:
It is forbidden to enter a woman, even a foreigner, if dressed as a man.

Doctor's office, Rome:
Specialist in women and other diseases.

Dry cleaners, Bangkok:
Drop your trousers here for the best results.

In a Nairobi restaurant:
Customers who find our waitresses rude ought to see the manager.

On the main road to Mombassa, leaving Nairobi:
Take notice: when this sign is under water, this road is impassable.

On a poster at Kencom:
Are you an adult that cannot read? If so we can help.

In a city restaurant:
Open seven days a week and weekends.

In a cemetery:
Persons are prohibited from picking flowers from any but their own graves.

Tokyo hotel's rules and regulations:
Guests are requested not to smoke or do other disgusting behaviours in bed.

On the menu of a Swiss restaurant:
Our wines leave you nothing to hope for.

In a Tokyo bar:
Special cocktails for the ladies with nuts.

Hotel , Yugoslavia:
The flattening of underwear with pleasure is the job of the chambermaid.

Hotel , Japan:
You are invited to take advantage of the chambermaid.

In the lobby of a Moscow hotel across from a Russian Orthodox monastery:
You are welcome to visit the cemetery where famous Russian and soviet composers, artists and writers are buried daily except Thursday.

A sign posted in Germany's Black Forest:
It is strictly forbidden on our black forest camping site that people of different sex, for instance, men and women, live together in one tent unless they are married with each other for this purpose.

Hotel, Zurich:
Because of the impropriety of entertaining guests of the opposite sex in the bedroom, it is suggested that the lobby be used for this purpose.

Advertisement for donkey rides, Thailand:
Would you like to ride on your own ass?

Airline ticket office, Copenhagen:
We take your bags and send them in all directions.

CHAPTER 8
HISTORY

Very interesting:
Here's a little part of US history, which makes you go hmm ...

- Abraham Lincoln was elected to congress in 1846. John F. Kennedy was elected to congress in 1946.
- Abraham Lincoln was elected president in 1860. John F. Kennedy was elected president in 1960.
- The name Lincoln and Kennedy each contain seven letters.
- Both were particularly concerned with civil rights. Both wives lost children while living in the White House.
- Both presidents were shot on a Friday. Both presidents were shot in the head.
- Lincoln's secretary was named Kennedy. Kennedy's secretary was named Lincoln.
- Both were assassinated by Southerners. Both were succeeded by Southerners.
- Both successors were named Johnson.
- Andrew Johnson, who succeeded Lincoln, was born in 1808. Lyndon Johnson, who succeeded Kennedy, was born in 1908.
- John Wilkes Booth, who assassinated Lincoln, was born in 1839.
- Lee Harvey Oswald, who assassinated Kennedy, was born in 1939.
- Both assassins were known by their three names. Both names were comprised of fifteen letters.
- Booth ran from the theatre and was caught in a warehouse. Oswald ran from a warehouse and was caught in a theatre.
- Booth and Oswald were assassinated before their trials.
- A week before Lincoln was shot; he was in Monroe, Maryland. A week before Kennedy was shot, he was in Marilyn Monroe?

Let's Imagine:
It's time to elect a world leader and your vote counts. Here's the scoop on three leading candidates:
Candidate A:
Associates with ward healers and consults with astrologists.

Has had two mistresses.
He chain smokes and drinks 8 to 10 martinis a day.

Candidate B:
Was kicked out of office twice.
Sleeps till noon,
Used opium in college,
Drinks a quart of brandy every evening.

Candidate C:
Is a decorated war hero.
He's a vegetarian,
Doesn't smoke,
Drinks an occasional beer,
Hasn't had any illicit affairs.

Which of these candidates is your choice? You don't really need any more information do you? (Oh yes, you do!)
Candidate A: is Franklin D. Roosevelt
Candidate B: is Winston Churchill
Candidate C is Adolph Hitler!

John Cleese's Address to U.S. Citizens:

In light of your failure to elect a competent President of the USA and thus to govern yourselves, we hereby give notice of the revocation of your independence, effective immediately. Her Sovereign Majesty Queen Elizabeth II will resume monarchical duties over all states, commonwealths and territories (excepting Kansas, which she does not fancy).

Your new prime minister, Tony Blair, will appoint a governor for America without the need for further elections. Congress and the senate will be disbanded. A questionnaire may be circulated next year to determine whether any of you noticed. To aid in the transition to a British Crown Dependency, the following rules will be introduced with immediate effect:

1. You should look up 'revocation' in the Oxford English Dictionary. Then look up aluminum and check the pronunciation guide.
   Author's note: Aluminum was invented in the United States – not the U.K. (They added the extra 'i' to the word.)
   You will be amazed at how wrongly you have been pronouncing and spelling it. The letter 'U' will be reinstated in words such as 'favour' and 'neighbour.'

Likewise, you will learn to spell ' doughnut' without skipping half the letters and the suffix 'ize' will be replaced by the suffix 'ise.' Generally, you will be expected to raise your vocabulary to acceptable levels. (Look up vocabulary).

2. Using the same twenty-seven words interspersed with filler noises such as 'like' and 'you know' is an unacceptable and inefficient form of communication. There is no such thing as US English. We will let Microsoft know on your behalf. The Microsoft spell-checker will be adjusted to take account of the re-instated letter 'u' and the elimination of 'ize.'

3. You will relearn your original national anthem, 'God Save the Queen.'

4. July 4th will no longer be celebrated as a holiday.

5. You will learn to resolve personal issues without using guns, lawyers or therapists. The fact that you need so many lawyers and therapists shows that you're not adult enough to be independent. Guns should only be handled by adults. If you're not adult enough to sort things out without suing someone or speaking to a therapist, then you're not grown up enough to handle a gun. Therefore, you will no longer be allowed to own or carry anything more dangerous than a vegetable peeler. A permit will be required if you wish to carry a vegetable peeler in public.

6. All American cars are hereby banned. They are crap and this is for your own good. When we show you German cars, you will understand what we mean. All intersections will be replaced with roundabouts and you will start driving on the left with immediate effect. At the same time, you will go metric with immediate effect and without the benefit of conversion tables. Both roundabouts and metrication will help you understand the British sense of humour.

7. The former USA will adopt UK prices on petrol (which you have been calling gasoline) - roughly $6/US gallon. Get used to it.

8. You will learn to make real chips. Those things you call French fries are not real chips and those things you insist on calling potato chips are properly called crisps. Real chips are thick cut, fried in animal fat and dressed - not with catsup - but with vinegar.

9. The cold tasteless stuff you insist on calling beer is not actually beer at all. Henceforth, only proper British Bitter will be referred to as beer and European brews of known

and accepted provenance will be referred to as Lager. American brands will be referred to as Near-Frozen Gnat's Urine, so that all can be sold without risk of further confusion.
10. Hollywood will be required occasionally to cast English actors as Good guys. Hollywood will also be required to cast English actors to play English characters. Watching Andie McDowell attempt English dialogue in Four Weddings and a Funeral was an experience akin to having one's ears removed with a cheese grater.
11. You will cease playing American football. There is only one kind of proper football; you call it soccer. Those of you brave enough will, in time, be allowed to play rugby (which has some similarities to American football, but does not involve stopping for a rest every twenty seconds and wearing full Kevlar body armour like a bunch of nancies).
12. Further you will stop playing baseball. It is not reasonable to host an event called the World Series for a game, which is not played outside of America. Since only 2.1% of you are aware that there is a world beyond your borders, your error is understandable.
13. You must tell us who killed JFK. It's driving us mad.
14. An internal revenue agent (i.e. tax collector) from Her Majesty's Government will be with you shortly to ensure the acquisition of all monies due (backdated to 1776).
15. Thank you for your indulgence and ultimate co-operation.

Semblance of Justice

The following has apparently been attributed to state Representative Mitchell Kaye from Georgia, USA:

'We, the sensible people of the United States, in an attempt to help everyone get along, restore some semblance of justice, avoid any more riots, keep our nation safe, promote positive behaviour and secure the blessings of debt-free liberty to ourselves and our great-great-great-grandchildren, hereby try one more time to ordain and establish some common sense guidelines for the terminally whiny, guilt-ridden, delusional and other liberal bed wetters.

'We hold these truths to be self-evident: that a whole lot of people are confused by the Bill of Rights and are so dim that they require a Bill of no Rights:'

Article I: You do not have the right to a new car, big screen TV or any other form of wealth. More power to you if you can legally acquire them, but no one is guaranteeing anything.

Article II: You do not have the right to never be offended. This country is based on freedom and that means freedom for everyone - not just you! You may leave the room, turn the channel, express a different opinion, etc., but the world is full of idiots and probably always will be.

Article III: You do not have the right to be free from harm. If you stick a screwdriver in your eye, learn to be more careful; do not expect the tool manufacturer to make you and all your relatives independently wealthy.

Article IV: You do not have the right to free food and housing. Americans are the most charitable people to be found and will gladly help anyone in need, but we are quickly growing weary of subsidising generation after generation of professional couch potatoes who achieve nothing more than the creation of another generation of professional couch potatoes.

Article V: You do not have the right to free health care. That would be nice, but from the looks of public housing, we're just not interested in public health care.

Article VI: You do not have the right to physically harm other people. If you kidnap, rape, intentionally maim or kill someone, don't be surprised if the rest of us want to see you fry in the electric chair.

Article VII: You do not have the right to the possessions of others. If you rob, cheat or coerce away the goods or services of other citizens, don't be surprised if the rest of us get together and lock you away in a place where you still won't have the right to a big screen colour TV or a life of leisure.

Article VIII: You won't have the right to demand that your children risk their lives in foreign wars to soothe your aching conscience. We hate oppressive governments and won't lift a finger to stop you from going to fight if you'd like. However, we do not enjoy parenting the entire world and do not want to spend so much of our time battling each and every little tyrant with a military uniform and a funny hat.

Article IX: You don't have the right to a job. All of us sure want you to have one and will gladly help you along in hard times, but we expect you to take advantage of the opportunities of education and vocational training laid before you to make yourself useful.

Article X: You do not have the right to happiness. Being an American means that you have the right to pursue happiness - which by the way, is a lot easier if you are unencumbered by the overabundance of idiotic laws created by those of you who were confused by the Bill of Rights.

Mozart:

When Mozart passed away, he was buried in a churchyard. A couple of days later the town drunk was walking through the cemetery and heard some strange noises coming from the area where Mozart was buried.

Terrified, the drunk ran and got the town magistrate to come and listen to it.

When the magistrate arrived, he bent his ear to the grave, listened for a moment and said, *'Ah, yes, that's Mozart's Ninth Symphony, being played backwards.'*

He listened a while longer and said, *'There's the Eighth Symphony and it's backwards, too. Most puzzling.'*

So the magistrate kept listening; *'There's the Seventh ... the Sixth ... the Fifth ...'*

Suddenly the realisation of what was happening dawned on the magistrate; he stood up and announced to the crowd that had gathered in the cemetery, *'My fellow citizens, there's nothing to worry about. It's just Mozart decomposing.'*

The IRS

As income tax time approaches, did you ever notice: When you put the two words *'The'* and *'IRS'* together it spells *'Theirs?'*

Ignorant Government Worker's:

A Washington, DC airport ticket agent offers some examples of why the U.S.A. is in trouble! It makes you wonder if any geography (even American geography) is taught at school!

1. I had a New Hampshire Congresswoman ask for an aisle seat so that her hair wouldn't get messed up by being near the window.

2. I got a call from a candidate's staffer, who wanted to go to Capetown. I started to explain the length of the flight and the passport information and then she interrupted me with, *'I'm not trying to make you look stupid, but Capetown is in Massachusetts.'* Without trying to make **her** look stupid, I calmly explained, *'Cape Cod is in Massachusetts. Capetown is in Africa.'* Her response - click.
3. A senior Vermont Congressman called, furious about a Florida package we did. I asked what was wrong with the vacation in Orlando. He said he was expecting an ocean-view room. I tried to explain that's not possible, since Orlando is in the middle of the state. He replied, *'Don't lie to me, I looked on the map and Florida is a very thin state!'*
4. I got a call from a lawmaker's wife who asked, *'Is it possible to see England from Canada?'* I said, *'No.'* She said, *'But they look so close on the map.'*
5. An aide for a cabinet member once called and asked if he could rent a car in Dallas. When I pulled up the reservation, I noticed he had only a one-hour layover in Dallas. When I asked him why he wanted to rent a car, he said, *'I heard Dallas was a big airport and we will need a car to drive between gates to save time.'*
6. An Illinois Congresswoman called last week. She needed to know how it was possible that her flight from Detroit left at 8:30 am and got to Chicago at 8:33 am. I explained that Michigan was an hour ahead of Illinois, but she couldn't understand the concept of time zones. Finally, I told her the plane went fast and she bought that.
7. A New York lawmaker called and asked, *'Do airlines put your physical description on your bag so they know whose luggage belongs to whom?'* I said, *'No, why do you ask?'* She replied, *'Well, when I checked in with the airline, they put a tag on my luggage that said (FAT) and I'm overweight. I think that's very rude!'* After putting her on hold for a minute while I looked into it (I was laughing.) I came back and explained the city code for Fresno, CA is (FAT) and the airline was just putting a destination tag on her luggage.
8. A Senator's aide called to inquire about a trip package to Hawaii. After going over all the cost info, she asked, *'Would it be cheaper to fly to California and then take the train to Hawaii?'*

9. I just got off the phone with a freshman Congressman who asked, *'How do I know which plane to get on?'* I asked him what exactly he meant, to which he replied, *'I was told my flight number is 823, but none of these planes have numbers on them.'*
10. A lady Senator called and said, *'I need to fly to Pepsi-Cola, Florida. Do I have to get on one of those little computer planes?'* I asked if she meant fly to Pensacola, Fl. on a commuter plane. She said, *'Yeah, whatever, smarty!'*
11. A senior Senator called and had a question about the documents he needed in order to fly to China. After a lengthy discussion about passports, I reminded him that he needed a visa. *'Oh, no I don't. I've been to China many times and never had to have one of those.'* I double checked and sure enough, his stay required a visa. When I told him this he said, *'Look, I've been to China four times and every time they have accepted my American Express!'*
12. A New Mexico Congresswoman called to make reservations, *'I want to go from Chicago to Rhino, New York.'* I was at a loss for words. Finally, I said, *'Are you sure that's the name of the town?'* *'Yes, what flights do you have?'* replied the lady. After some searching, I came back with, *'I'm sorry, ma'am, I've looked up every airport code in the country and can't find a Rhino anywhere.'* The lady retorted, *'Oh, don't be silly! Everyone knows where it is. Check your map!'* So I scoured a map of the state of New York and finally offered, *'You don't mean Buffalo, do you?'* The reply? *'Whatever! I knew it was a big animal'.*

Now you know why the Government is in the shape that it's in!

Life in the 1500's:

Most people got married in June because they took their yearly bath in May and still smelt pretty good by June, although they were starting to smell, so brides carried a bouquet of flowers to hide the B.O. Baths equalled a big tub filled with hot water. The man of the house had the privilege of the nice clean water, then all the other sons and men, then the women and finally the children. Last of all the babies. By then the water was so dirty you could actually lose someone in it. Hence the saying, *'Don't throw the baby out with the bath water.'*

Houses had thatched roofs. Thick straw, piled high with no wood underneath. It was the only place for animals to get warm, so all the pets - dogs, cats and other small animals, mice rats and bugs lived in the roof. When it rained it became slippery and sometimes the animals would slip and fall off the roof. Hence the saying, *'It's raining cats and dogs.'*

The floor was dirt. Only the wealthy had something other than dirt, hence the saying, *'Dirt poor.'* The wealthy had slate floors that in the winter would become slippery when wet. So they spread thresh on the floor to help keep their footing. As the winter wore on, they kept adding more thresh until when you opened the door, it would all start slipping outside. A piece of wood was placed at the entryway, hence a *'thresh hold.'*

Sometimes they would obtain pork and would feel really special when that happened. When company came over, they would bring out some bacon and hang it to show it off. It was a sign of wealth and that a man 'could really *'bring home the bacon.'* They would cut off a little to share with guests and would sit around and *'chew the fat.'*

Bread was divided according to status. Workers got the burned bottom of the loaf, the family got the middle and guests got the top or the *'upper crust.'*

Lead cups were used to drink ale or whiskey. The combination would sometimes knock them out for a couple of days. Someone walking along the road would take them for dead and prepare them for burial. They were laid on the kitchen table for a couple of days and the family would gather around and eat and drink and wait to see if they would wake up. Hence the custom of holding a *'wake.'*

England started running out of places to bury people, so they would dig up coffins and would take their bones into a house and re-use the grave. In re-opening these coffins, one out of 25 coffins were found to have scratch marks on the inside so they realised they had been burying people alive. So they thought they would tie a string on their wrist and lead it through the coffin and up through the ground and tie it to a bell. Someone would have to sit out in the graveyard all night to listen for the bell. Hence on the *'graveyard shift'* they would know that someone was *'saved by the bell'* or he was a *'dead ringer.'*

American comments made in the year 1955:

- *'I'll tell you one thing: if things keep going the way they are, it's going to be impossible to buy a week's groceries for $20.'*

- *'Have you seen the new cars coming out next year? It won't be long before $2,000 will only buy a used one.'*
- *'If cigarettes keep going up in price, I'm going to quit. A quarter a pack? It's ridiculous.' (25¢)*
- *'Did you hear the post office is thinking about charging a dime just to mail a letter?' (10¢)*
- *'If they raise the minimum wage to $1, nobody will be able to hire outside help at the store.'*
- *When I first started driving, who would have thought gas would someday cost 29 cents a gallon. Guess we'd be better off leaving the car in the garage.'*
- *'Kids today are impossible. Those duck-tail haircuts make it impossible to stay groomed. Next thing you know, boys will be wearing their hair as long as the girls.'*
- *'I'm afraid to send my kids to the movies any more. Ever since they let Clark Gable get by with saying 'damn' in 'Gone With The Wind,' it seems every new movie has either 'hell' or 'damn' in it'*
- *'I read the other day where some scientist thinks it's possible to put a man on the moon by the end of the century. They even have some fellows they call astronauts preparing for it down in Texas.'*
- *'Did you see where some baseball player just signed a contract for $75,000 a year just to play ball? It wouldn't surprise me if someday they'll be making more than the president.'*
- *'I never thought I'd see the day all our kitchen appliances would be electric. They are even making electric typewriters now.'*
- *'It's too bad things are so tough nowadays. I see where a few married women are having to work to make ends meet.'*
- *'It won't be long before young couples are going to have to hire someone to watch their kids so they can both work.'*
- *'Marriage doesn't mean a thing any more. Those Hollywood stars seem to be getting divorced at the drop of a hat.'*
- *'I'm just afraid the Volkswagen car is going to open the door to a whole lot of foreign business.'*
- *'Thank goodness I won't live to see the day when the Government takes half our income in taxes. I sometimes wonder if we are electing the best people to congress.'*

- *'The drive-in restaurant is convenient in nice weather, but I seriously doubt they will ever catch on.'*
- *'There is no sense going to Lincoln or Omaha any more for a weekend. It costs nearly $15 a night to stay in a hotel.'*
- *'No one can afford to be sick any more; $35 a day in the hospital is too rich for my blood.'*
- *'If they think I will pay 50¢ for a haircut, forget it.'*

Condom Supply:

John Key, Prime Minister of New Zealand, is rudely awoken at 4:00 am by the telephone. *'John, it's the Hilth Munister here. Sorry to bother you at this hour, but there is an emergency! I've just received word thet the Durex factory en Auckland has burned to the ground. It is istimated thet the entire New Zulland supply of condoms will be gone by the ind of the week.'*

Prime Minister: *'Shut - the economy wull niver be able to cope with all those unwanted babies. We'll be ruined!'*

Hilth Munister: *'We're going to hef to shup some in from abroad ... Brutain?'*

Prime Minister: *'No chence!! The Poms will have a field day on thus one!'*

Hilth Munister: *'What about Australia?'*

Prime Minister: *'Maybe, but we don't want them to know thet we are stuck.'*

Hilth Munister: *'You call Tony Abbott - tell hum we need one moollion condoms; ten enches long and two enches thuck! That way they'll know how bug the Kiwis really are!!'*

John calls Tony, who agrees to help the Kiwis out in their hour of need. Three days later a van arrives in Auckland - full of boxes. A delighted John rushes out to open the boxes. He finds condoms; 10 enches long and two enches thuck, all coloured green and gold. He then notices in small writing on each and ivery one ... Made in Australia - Size: Medium.

'Ozzie Ozzie Ozzie - Oy Oy Oy!'

Saddam and Clinton:

Saddam Hussein and Bill Clinton meet up in Baghdad for talks on sanctions. When Bill sits down, he notices that Saddam's chair has three buttons on the armrest.

They begin talking, but after five minutes Saddam presses a button and a boxing glove pops out of Clinton's chair and bashes him in the face. Clinton, barely believing it, carries on talking, but after another few minutes, Saddam presses a second button and out comes a large boot and kicks him up the ass. Clinton is pissed off, but still remains outwardly calm. They resume their talks, but after five minutes Saddam presses the final button and from under the table another boxing glove hits Clinton right in the nuts.

Clinton is really fed up by now and stands up to leave. *'We'll continue this talk next week in the White House,'* he says. Saddam, choking from laughing, is too proud to say no, so the appointment stands.

A week later, Clinton receives Saddam in the Oval Office and as Saddam sits down, he sees three buttons on the armrest of Clinton's chair. As the meeting goes on, Saddam sees Clinton press the first button, ducks really fast, but nothing seems to happen. This doesn't stop Clinton from laughing ... really loudly.

After this, Clinton continues where he left off until he presses another button. Saddam reacts quickly and jumps up. Absolutely nothing happens and this time Clinton falls out of his chair laughing. Saddam doesn't get it - what the Hell is happening here? But he hasn't been harmed yet, so he sits down again to talk further.

After a few minutes, Clinton presses the final button. This time, Saddam stays sitting, but Clinton isn't - he's rolling on the floor, doubled up from laughing. Saddam is really annoyed by now, so he stands up from his chair and shouts, *'I've had enough of this. I'm going back to Baghdad'*

Through tears of laughter and rolling on the floor, Clinton replies, *'Baghdad ... what Baghdad?'*

The Firing Squad:

Bill Clinton, Al Gore and George W. Bush face a firing squad in a small Central American country. Bill Clinton is first placed against the wall and just before the order to shoot him is given, he yells, *'Earthquake!'* The firing squad falls into a panic and Bill jumps over the wall and escapes in the confusion.

Al Gore is the second one placed against the wall. The squad is reassembled and Al ponders what his old boss has done. Before the order to shoot is given, Al yells, *'Tsunami!'* Again the squad falls apart and Al slips over the wall.

The last person, George W. Bush, is placed against the wall. He is thinking, *'I see the pattern here, just scream out a disaster and hop over the wall.'* As the firing squad reassembles and the rifles rise in his direction, that famous smirk comes over his face and he yells, *'Fire!'*

George W. Bush ... at school

George Bush goes to a primary school to talk about the war. After his talk he offers question time. One little boy puts up his hand and George asks him what his name is.

'Billy.'

'And what is your question, Billy?'

'I have 3 questions: First, why did the USA invade Iraq without the support of the UN? Second, why are you President when Al Gore got more votes? And third, whatever happened to Osama Bin Laden?'

Just then the bell rings for recess. George Bush informs the kiddies that they will continue after recess. When they resume George says, *'Okay, where were we? Oh that's right question time. Who has a question?'*

Another little boy puts up his hand. George points him out and asks him what his name is.

'Steve.'

'And what is your question, Steve?'

'I have 5 questions: First, why did the USA invade Iraq without the support of the UN? Second, why are you President when Al Gore got more votes? Third, whatever happened to Osama Bin Laden? Fourth, why did the recess bell go twenty minutes early? And fifth, where did Billy go?'

Breakfast:

One morning, Dick Cheney and George W. Bush were having breakfast at a restaurant. The attractive waitress asked Cheney what he would like and he replied, *'I'll have a bowl of oatmeal and some fruit.'*

'And what can I get for you, sir?' she asked George W.

He replied, *'How about a quickie?'*

'Why, Mr. President,' the waitress said, *'How rude. You're starting to act like Mr. Clinton!'* The waitress stormed away.

Cheney leaned over to Bush and whispered, *'It's pronounced 'quiche.'‛*

Air force one

The President, First Lady and Dick Cheney were flying on Air Force One. George looked at Laura, chuckled and said, *'You* know, I could throw a $1,000.00 bill out of the window right now and make somebody very happy.'

Laura shrugged her shoulders and replied, *'I could throw ten $100.00 bills out of the window and make ten people very happy.'*

Cheney added, *'That being the case, I could throw one hundred $10.00 bills out of the window and make a hundred people very happy.'*

Hearing their exchange, the pilot rolled his eyes and said to his co-pilot, *'Such big-shots back there. Hell, I could throw all of them out of the window and make 56 million people very happy!'*

Custer's Last Thought:

The curator of a Western art museum commissioned a local artist to paint a mural-sized painting of Custer's Last Thought. The artist was told to make it highly symbolic of Custer's mindset during the debacle at Little Big Horn.

Deep in thought, the artist went to her studio. After many false starts, she proceeded to paint an enormous oil painting. Finally, after many months of work, the painting was unveiled for the curator. In the foreground, a beautiful crystalline blue lake with a single fish leaping. Around the fish's head was a halo. In the background, the hills and meadows are covered with naked Native American couples copulating. The curator is both disgusted and baffled by what he sees. In a rage, he turns to the artist and asks, *'What the hell has this got to do with Custer's Last Thought?'*

The artist replied, *'Well, the way I see it, Custer's last thought had to have been: 'Holy Mackerel! Where did all those f***ing Indians come from?''*

The Ignorant Archaeologists:

A team of archaeologists was excavating in Israel when they came upon a cave. Written across the wall of the cave were the following symbols, in this order of appearance: A woman, a donkey, a shovel, a fish and a Star of David.

They decided that this was a unique find and the writings were at least three thousand years old. They chopped out the piece of stone and had it brought to the museum where archaeologists from all over the world came to study the ancient symbols. They held a huge meeting after months of conferences to discuss what they could agree was the meaning of the markings. The president of their society stood up and pointed at the first drawing and said: *'This looks like a woman. We can judge that this race was family-oriented and held women in high esteem. You can also tell they were intelligent and the next symbol resembles a donkey, so they were smart enough to have animals help them till the soil,*

'The next drawing looks like a shovel of some sort, which means they even had tools to help them. Even further proof of their high intelligence is the fish, which means that if a famine had hit the earth, whereby the food didn't grow, they would take to the sea for food. The last symbol appears to be the Star of David which means they were evidently Hebrews.'

The audience applauded enthusiastically and the president smiled and said, *'I'm glad to see that you are all in full agreement with our interpretations.'*

Suddenly a little old man stood up in the back of the room and said, *'Idiots! You are all wrong about what the writings say. First of all, everyone knows that Hebrew is not read from left to right, but from right to left. Look again. It now says: 'Holy Mackerel, dig the ass on that woman!''*

CHAPTER 9

LETTERS

Letter from Mom:

Dear Son,

I'm writing this slow, cause I know you can't read fast.

We don't live where we did when you left. Your Dad read in the paper where most accidents happen within twenty miles of home, so we moved. I won't be able to send you the address as the last Mississippi family that lived here took the numbers with them for their next house, so they wouldn't have to change their address.

This place has a washing machine; it's small. The first day I put four shirts in it, pulled the chain and haven't seen them since. It only rained twice this week, three days the first time and four days the second time.

The coat you wanted me to send you, your Aunt Sue said it would be a little too heavy to sent in the mail with them heavy buttons, so we cut them off and put them in the pockets.

We got a bill from the Funeral Home, said if we didn't make the last payment on Grandma's funeral ... .up she comes.

About your father, he has a new job, he has five hundred men under him and he's cutting grass at the cemetery.

About your sister, she had a baby this morning, haven't found out whether it's a boy or a girl, so I don't know if you are an Aunt or an Uncle.

Your Uncle Joe fell in a whiskey vat. Some men tried to pull him out, but he fought them off, so he drowned. We cremated him: he burned for three days.

Three of your friends went off the bridge in a pickup, one was driving the other two were in the back. The driver got out. He rolled the window down and swam to safety. The other two drowned, they couldn't get the tailgate down.

Not much news this time, nothing much happened.

Write more often,

Love, Mom

P/S I was going to send you some money, but the envelope was already sealed.

Bricklayer's Accident Report:

Here's a bricklayer's accident report that was printed in the newsletter of a Worker's Compensation Board:

Dear Sir:

I'm writing in response to your request for additional information. In Block #3 of the accident report form, I *put 'trying to do the job alone'* as the cause of my accident. Now you said in your letter that I should explain more fully. I trust that the following details will be sufficient.

I'm a bricklayer by trade. On the date of the accident, I was working alone on the roof of a new 6-storey building. When I completed my work, I discovered that I had about 250 kilos of brick left over. Rather than carry the bricks down by hand, I decided to lower them in a barrel by using a pulley, which was attached to the side of the building on the 6th floor.

Securing the rope at ground level, I went up to the roof, swung the barrel out and loaded the bricks onto it. Then I went back to the ground and untied the rope, holding it tightly to ensure a slow descent of the 250 kilos of brick.

Now you will note in Block #2 of the accident report form that I weigh 60 kilos. Due to the surprise at being jerked off the ground so suddenly, I lost my presence of mind and forgot to let go of the rope. Needless to say, I proceeded at a rather rapid rate up the side of the building. In the vicinity of the third floor I met the barrel coming down. This explains the fractured skull and broken collarbone.

Slowed only slightly, I continued my rapid ascent, not stopping until the fingers of my right hand were two knuckles deep in the pulley. Fortunately, by this time, I had regained my presence of mind and was able to hold tightly to the rope in spite of my pain. At approximately the same time however, the barrel of bricks hit the bottom and the bottom fell out of the barrel. Devoid of the weight of the bricks, the barrel now weighs approximately 22 kilos.

I refer you again to my weight in Block #2 of the accident report form. As you might imagine, I began a rather rapid descent of the building. Somewhere in the vicinity of the third floor, I again met the barrel coming up. This accounts for the fractured ankles and the lacerations of my legs and lower body. The encounter with the barrel slowed me enough to lessen my injuries when I fell onto the pile of bricks and fortunately only three vertebrae were cracked.

I'm sorry to report however, that as I lay there on the bricks, in pain and unable to move and watching the empty barrel six storeys above me, I again lost my presence of mind and let go of the rope. The empty barrel weighed more than the rope, so it came down and broke both my legs.

Now I hope I've furnished the information you required as to how the accident occurred, because you see, *'I was trying to do the job alone!'*

Life in the Army:

Dear Mom & Dad,
I am well. Hope youse are too. Tell me big brothers Doug and Phil that the Army is better than workin' on the farm - tell them to get in bloody quick smart before the jobs are all gone! I wuz a bit slow in settling down at first, because ya don't hafta get outta bed until 6:00 am. But I like sleeping in now, cuz all ya gotta do before brekky is make ya bed and shine ya boots and clean ya uniform. No bloody cows to milk, no calves to feed, no feed to stack - nothin'!! Blokes haz gotta shave though, but its not so bad, coz there's lotsa hot water and even a light to see what ya doing!

At brekky ya get cereal, fruit and eggs but there's no steaks or possum stew like wot Mom makes. You don't get fed again until noon and by that time all the city boys are buggered because we've been on a 'route march' - geez, its only just like walking to the windmill in the back paddock!!

This one will kill me brothers Doug and Phil with laughter. I keep getting medals for shootin' - dunno why. The bullseye is as big as a bloody possum's bum and it don't move and it's not firing back at ya like the Johnsons did when our big scrubber bull got into their prize cows last year! All ya gotta do is make yourself comfortable and hit the target - it's a piece of piss!! You don't even load your own cartridges - they comes in little boxes and ya don't have to steady yourself against the rollbar of the shooting truck when you reload! Sometimes ya gotta wrestle with the city boys and I gotta be real careful coz they break easy - it's not like fighting with Doug and Phil and Jack and Steve and Mike all at once like we do at home after the muster.

Turns out I'm not a bad boxer either and it looks like I'm the best the platoon's got and I've only been beaten by this one bloke from the Engineers - he's 6 foot 5 and 150 kilograms and three pickhandles across the shoulders and as ya know I'm only 5 foot 7 and 64 kilograms wringin' wet, but I fought him till the other blokes carried me off to the boozer.

I can't complain about the Army - tell the boys to get in quick before word gets around how bloody good it is.

Your loving daughter,
Jill

Letter from daughter:

Dear Mom and Dad,

It's been four months since I left for college. I've been remiss in writing and am very sorry for my thoughtlessness. I'll bring you up to date now, but before you read on - please sit down.

Don't read any further unless you are sitting down ... Okay? Good. I'm getting along pretty well now. The skull fracture and the concussion I got from jumping out of the window of my dormitory when it caught fire, shortly after my arrival, are pretty well healed now. I only spent two weeks in the hospital and now I can see almost normally and only get three headaches a day.

Fortunately, the fire in the dormitory and my jump were witnessed by the attendant at a nearby gas station and he was able to call the fire department and ambulance. He also visited me at the hospital and since I had nowhere to live because of the burned out dorm, he was kind enough to invite me to share his apartment with him. It's really a basement room, but it is kind of cute.

He is a very fine boy and we have fallen deeply in love and are planning to get married. We haven't set the exact date yet, but I'm sure it will be before I start to show. Yes, Mom and Dad, I'm pregnant. I know how much you are looking forward to being grandparents and I know you will give the baby the same love and devotion and tender care you gave me when I was a child.

The reason for the delay in our marriage is that my boyfriend has some minor infection, which prevents us from passing our premarital blood tests and I carelessly caught it from him. This will soon clear up, thanks to my daily penicillin injections. I know you will welcome him into our family with open arms. He is kind and although not well educated, he is ambitious. Also, he is of a different race and religion than ours, but I know that after all your years of teaching me tolerance, that you won't mind the fact that he is somewhat darker than we are.

I'm sure you will love him as I do. His family background is good too; I am told that his father is an important gun bearer in his native African village.

I guess that's it. Now that I've brought you up-to-date, I want you to know ...
- There was no dormitory fire
- I did not have a concussion or skull fracture
- I was not in the hospital
- I am not pregnant
- I am not engaged
- I do not have syphilis and
- There is no man of other race in my life.

However, I am getting a 'D' in History and an 'F' in Science and I wanted you to see these marks in their proper perspective.
Your loving daughter,
Chelsea
P.S. Stanford is great ... I love it, although I miss you both terribly ... and Socks, too!
P.S.S. (Dad, please give my best to Monica and the others.)

Bottom Dweller:

Just a word of explanation. Brian is a commercial saturation diver for Globalers out of Louisiana and performs underwater repairs on offshore drilling rigs. Below is an e-mail he sent to his sister. Any time you think you've had a bad day at the office, remember this letter:
Dear Sis,
Just another note from your bottom-dwelling brother. Last week, I had a bad day at the office. Before I can tell you what happened to me, I must first bore you with a few technicalities of my job. As you know, my office lies at the bottom of the sea. I wear a suit to the office - a wetsuit. This time of the year, the water is quite cool, so what we do to keep warm is this:

We have a diesel-powered industrial water heater. This $20,000 piece of garbage sucks the water out of the sea, heats it to a delightful temperature then pumps it down to the diver through a garden hose, which is taped to the air hose. Now this sounds like a darned good plan and I've used it several times with no complaints. What I do, when I get to the bottom and start working, is I take the hose and stuff it down the back of my neck. This floods my whole suit with warm water. It's like working in a Jacuzzi. Everything was going well until all of a sudden, my butt started to itch. So, of course I scratched it.

This only made things worse. Within a few seconds my butt started to burn. I pulled the hose out from my back, but the damage was done. In agony I realised what had happened. The hot water machine had sucked up a jellyfish and pumped it into my suit. This is even worse than the poison ivy you once had under a cast.

Now, I had that hose down my back. I don't have any hair on my back, so the jellyfish couldn't get stuck to my back. My butt crack was not as fortunate. When I scratched what I thought was an itch, I was actually grinding the jellyfish into my bottom ...

I informed the dive supervisor of my dilemma over the communication system. His instructions were unclear due to the fact that he along with five other divers were laughing hysterically. Needless to say, I aborted my dive.

I was instructed to make three agonising in-water decompression stops totalling thirty-five minutes before I could come to the surface for my chamber dry decompression. I got to the surface wearing nothing but my brass helmet. My suit and gear were tied to the bell.

When I got on board, the medic, with tears of laughter running down his face, handed me a tube of cream and told me to shove it up my butt when I got into the chamber. The cream put the fire out, but I couldn't use the bathroom for two days because my butt was swollen shut. I later found out that this could easily have been prevented if the suction hose was placed on the leeward side of the ship.

Anyway, the next time you have a bad day at the office, think of me. Think about how much your day would be if you were to have a jellyfish in your butt.
All my love,
Bill

Letter from Camp

Dear Mom and Dad,
We are having a great time here at Lake Typhoid. Scoutmaster Webb is making us all write to our parents in case you saw the flood on TV and are worried. We are okay. Only one of our tents

and two sleeping bags got washed away. Luckily, none of us got drowned because we were all up on the mountain looking for Chad when it happened.

Oh yes, please call Chad's mother and tell her he is okay. He can't write because of the cast. I got to ride in one of the search and rescue jeeps. It was neat. We never would have found him in the dark if it hadn't been for the lightening. Scoutmaster Webb got mad at Chad for going on a hike alone without telling anyone. Chad said he did tell him, but it was during the fire so he probably didn't hear him.

Did you know that if you put gas on a fire, the gas can will blow up? The wet wood still didn't burn, but one of our tents did. Also some of our clothes. Billy is going to look weird until his hair grows back.

We will be home on Saturday if Scoutmaster Webb gets the car fixed. It wasn't his fault about the wreck. The brakes worked okay when we left. Scoutmaster Webb said that a car that old you have to expect something to break down; that's probably why he can't get insurance on it. We think it's a neat car. He doesn't care if we get it dirty; and if it's hot, sometimes he lets us ride on the tailgate. It gets pretty hot with ten people in the car. He lets us take turns riding in the trailer until the highway patrolman stopped and talked to us.

Scoutmaster Webb is a neat guy. Don't worry; he is a good driver. In fact he is teaching Terry how to drive, but he only lets him drive on the mountain roads where there isn't any traffic. All we ever see up there are logging trucks.

This morning all of the guys were diving off the rocks and swimming out in the lake. Scoutmaster Webb wouldn't let me, because I can't swim and Chad was afraid he would sink because of his cast, so he let us take the canoe across the lake. It was great. You can still see some of the trees under the water from the flood. Scoutmaster Webb isn't crabby like some scoutmasters. He didn't even get mad about the life jackets.

He has to spend a lot of time working on the car, so we are trying not to cause him any trouble. Guess what? We have all passed our first aid merit badges. When Dave dove in the lake and cut his arm, we got to see how a tourniquet works.

Also Wade and I threw up. Scoutmaster Webb said it probably was just food poisoning from the leftover chicken.

I have to go now. We are going into town to mail our letters and buy bullets. Don't worry about anything. We are fine.

Love,
Johnny
P.S. How long has it been since I had a tetanus shot?

CHAPTER 10

BAR JOKES

The Bartender:

A man walked into a bar and ordered a glass of white wine. He took a sip of the wine and then tossed the remainder to the bartender's face. Before the bartender could recover from the surprise, the man began weeping. *'I'm really sorry. I keep doing that to bartenders. I can't tell you how embarrassing it is to have a compulsion like this.'*

Far from being angry, the bartender was sympathetic. Before long, he was suggesting that the man see a psychoanalyst about his problem. *'I happen to have the name of a psychoanalyst,'* the bartender said. *'My brother and my wife have both been treated by him and they say he's as good as they come.'*

The man wrote down the name of the doctor, thanked the bartender and left. The bartender smiled, knowing he'd done a good deed for a fellow human being.

Six months later, the man was back. *'Did you do what I suggested?'* the bartender asked, serving him a glass of white wine.

'I certainly did,' the man said. *'I've been seeing the psychoanalyst twice a week.'* He took a sip of the wine and threw the remainder into the bartender's face.

The flustered bartender wiped his face with a towel. *'The doctor doesn't seem to be doing you any good,'* he sputtered.

'On the contrary,' the man said, *'he's done me a world of good.'*

'But you just threw the wine in my face again!' the bartender exclaimed.

'Yes,' the man said, *'but it doesn't embarrass me any more!'*

Nuts:

A guy goes into a bar. He's sitting on the stool, enjoying his drink when he hears, *'You look great!'* He looks around - there's nobody near him. He hears the voice again, *'No really, you look terrific.'*

The guy looks around again. Nobody. He hears, *'Is that a new shirt or something. Because you're absolutely glowing!'* He then realises that the voice is coming from a dish of peanuts on the bar.

'*Hey,*' the guy calls to the bartender, '*What's with the peanuts?*'

'*Oh,*' the bartender answers, '*They're complimentary.*'

The Biker:

A drunken man walks into a biker bar, sits down at the bar and orders a drink. Looking around, he sees three men sitting at a corner table. He gets up, staggers to the table, leans over, looks the biggest, meanest, biker in the face and says: '*I went by your grandma's house today and I saw her in the hallway buck naked. Man, she is one fine looking woman!*'

The biker looks at him and doesn't say a word. His buddies are confused, because he is one bad biker and would fight at the drop of the hat.

The drunk leans on the table again and says: '*I got it on with your grandma and she is good, the best I ever had!*'

The biker's buddies are starting to get really mad, but the biker still says nothing. The drunk leans on the table one more time and says, '*I'll tell you something else boy, your grandma liked it!*'

At this point, the biker stands up, takes the drunk by the shoulders, looks him square in the eyes and says, '*Grandpa, go home - you're drunk.*'

Pppphhhhhbbbbbbttttt:

(Equals sticking your tongue between your lips and blowing air - try it now '*pppphhhhhbbbbbbttttt*')

A man walks into a bar with a Leprechaun on his shoulder. He walks up to the bar and sits down. He proceeds to order a beer for himself and for the little Leprechaun.

Well, the man and the Leprechaun drink about two beers when finally the Leprechaun jumps down off the guy's shoulder, trots down the bar and stands in front of a rather large construction worker. He looks at the construction worker and goes, '*pppphhhhhbbbbbbttttt*' right to the big guy's face.

Then, the Leprechaun trots back onto his buddy's shoulder. The construction worker is a little ticked, but decides to ignore this breach of manners.

After another beer and a half though, the Leprechaun hops down and again goes in front of the construction worker and goes, *'pppphhhhhbbbbbbttttt'* onto the construction worker's face. Then he trots back and hops onto his buddy's shoulder. The construction worker is visibly bothered, but decides not to do anything again.

Well, sure enough, the guy and the Leprechaun drink another beer. Soon enough, the Leprechaun hops down, trots in front of the construction worker and goes, *'pppphhhhhbbbbbbttttt'* to his face. Well, this time the big guy has had enough of the little guy's manners and walks over to the fellow with the Leprechaun, again on his shoulder.

The construction worker tells this fella, *'If your little friend does that again, I'm gonna cut off his little dick!'*

The fellow tells the big guy, *'Well, Leprechauns don't have dicks.'*

The big guy asks, *'Well then, how does he go pee?'*

The fellow with the Leprechaun on his shoulder looks at the big guy and does, *'pppphhhhhbbbbbbttttt.'*

Paddy

Paddy staggered home very late after another evening with his drinking Buddy, Mick. He took off his shoes to avoid waking his wife, Brigid. He tiptoed as quietly as he could towards the stairs leading to their upstairs bedroom, but misjudged the bottom step. As he caught himself by grabbing the banister, his body swung around and he landed heavily on his rump. A whiskey bottle in each back pocket broke and made the landing especially painful.

Managing not to yell, Paddy sprung up, pulled down his pants and looked in the hall mirror to see that his butt cheeks were cut and bleeding. He managed to quietly find a full box of band-Aids and began putting a Band-Aid as best he could on each place he saw blood. He then hid the now almost empty Band-Aid box and shuffled and stumbled his way to bed.

In the morning, Paddy woke up with searing pain in both his head and butt and Brigid staring at him from across the room. She said, *'You were drunk again last night weren't you Paddy?'*

Paddy said, *'Why do you say such a mean thing?'*

'Well,' Brigid said, *'it could be the open front door, it could be the broken glass at the bottom of the stairs, it could be the drops of blood trailing through the house, it could be your bloodshot eyes, but mostly - it's all those Band-Aids stuck on the hall mirror.'*

The Cowboy:

An old cowboy dressed to kill with cowboy shirt, hat, jeans, spurs and chaps went to a bar and ordered a drink. As he sat there sipping his whiskey, a young lady sat down next to him. After she ordered her drink she turned to the cowboy and asked, *'Are you a real cowboy?'*

'Well, I have spent my whole life on the ranch herding cows, breaking horses, mending fences ... I guess I am,' replied the cowboy.

After a short while, he asked her what she was. *'I've never been on a ranch so I'm not a cowboy,'* said the young woman, *'but I am a lesbian. I spend my whole day thinking about women. As soon as I get up in the morning, I think about women. When I eat, shower, watch TV, everything seems to make me think of women.'*

A short while later she left and the cowboy ordered another drink. A couple sat down next to him and asked, *'Are you a real cowboy?'*

'I always thought I was, but I just found out that I'm a lesbian.'

Best Friend:

A man is sitting at the bar in his local tavern, furiously imbibing shots of whiskey. One of his friends happens to come into the bar and sees him.

'Lou,' says the shocked friend, *'what are you doing? I've known you for over fifteen years and I've never seen you take a drink before. What's going on?'*

Without even taking his eyes off his newly filled shot glass, the man replies, *'My wife just ran off with my best friend.'* He then throws back another shot of whisky in one gulp.

'But,' says the other man, *'I'm your best friend!'*

The man turns to his friend, looks at him through bloodshot eyes, smiles and slurs, *'Not any more!'*

The Lemon

A local bar was so sure that its bartender was the strongest man around that they offered a standing $1,000 bet: The bartender would squeeze a lemon until all the juice ran into a glass and hand the lemon to a patron. Anyone who could squeeze out one more drop of juice would win the money.

Many people had tried over time (weight lifters, longshoremen, etc.) but nobody could do it. One day a scrawny little man came in wearing thick glasses and a polyester suit and said in a tiny squeaky voice, *'I'd like to try the bet.'*

After the laughter died down, the bartender said, *'Okay,'* grabbed a lemon and squeezed away, then handed the wrinkled remains of the rind to the little man.

But the crowd's laughter turned to total silence as the man clenched his fist around the lemon and six drops fell into the glass. As the crowd cheered, the bartender paid the $1,000 and asked the little man, *'What do you do for a living? Are you a lumberjack, a weight lifter or what?'*

The man replied, *'I work for the Internal Revenue Service.'*

The Head

A man is waiting for his wife to give birth. The doctor came in and informed the dad that his son was born without torso, arms or legs. The son is just a head! But the dad loves his son and raises him as well as he can, with love and compassion.

After 18 years, the son is now old enough for his first drink. Dad takes him to the bar, tearfully tells the son he is proud of him and orders up the biggest, strongest drink for his boy.

With the entire bar patrons looking on curiously and the bartender shaking his head in disbelief, the boy takes his first sip of alcohol. Swoooosh! Plop!! A torso pops out! The bar is dead silent; then bursts into whoops of joy. The father, shocked, begs his son to drink again. The patrons chant, *'Take another drink!'*

The bartender continues to shake his head in dismay. Swoooosh! Plip! Plop!! Two arms pop out.

The bar goes wild. The father, crying and wailing, begs his son to drink again. The patrons chant, *'Take another drink! Take another drink!!'*

The bartender ignores the whole affair and goes back to polishing glasses, shaking his head, clearly unimpressed by the amazing scenes.

By now the boy is getting tipsy, but with his new hands he reaches down, grabs his drink and guzzles the last of it.

Plop! Plip!! Two legs pop out. The bar is in chaos.

The father falls to his knees and tearfully thanks God. The boy stands up on his new legs and stumbles to the left then staggers to the right through the front door, into the street, where a truck runs over him and kills him instantly. The bar falls silent.

The father moans in grief. The bartender sighs and says,
(Wait for it)
(It's coming)
(Ya ready?)
'He should've quit while he was a head!'

Most Exciting Experiences:
Three old timers were relating their most exciting experiences. The first, a retired sheriff, described the terrifying excitement of a shoot-out with Bonnie and Clyde back in his younger days. The other gents nodded and agreed that that, indeed, would have been exciting.

The second, a retired fireman, related the tale of a huge fire at the university several years back. There were flames, fire trucks from several area fire departments, but the most exciting part was the naked co-eds jumping from their dorm windows into his arms. The other gents agreed that had to be a very interesting time.

The third stated, *'I was an undertaker. One night I got a call to pick up a body that was under a sheet in a hotel room. When I got there, the guy had a huge erection. I knew there was no way I could get him through the lobby like that. So I found an old broom and whacked that erection just as hard as I could to make it go down.'*

The retired fireman asked, *'So, how was that exciting?'*

The undertaker answered, *'Well, you see, I was in the wrong room.'*

Buying a Drink:
The bartender was washing his glasses and an elderly Irishman came in and with great difficulty, hoisted his bad leg over the bar stool, pulled himself up painfully and asked for a sip of Irish whiskey. The Irishman looked down the bar and said, *'Is that Jesus down there?'* The bartender nodded and the Irishman told him to give Jesus an Irish whiskey also.

The next patron was an ailing Italian with a hunched back and slowness of movement. He shuffled up to the bar stool and asked for a glass of Chianti. He also looked down the bar and asked if that was Jesus sitting there. The bartender nodded and the Italian said to give Him a glass of Chianti, also.

The third patron, an American, swaggered in dragging his knuckles on the floor and hollered, *'Barkeep, set me up a cold one. Hey, is that God's Boy down there?'* The barkeep nodded and the American told him to give Jesus a cold one too.

As Jesus got up to leave, he walked over to the Irishman and touched him and said, *'For your kindness, you are healed!'* The Irishman felt the strength come back to his leg and he got up and danced a jig to the door.

Jesus touched the Italian and said, *'For your kindness you are healed!'* The Italian felt his back straighten and he raised his hands above his head and did a cartwheel out the door.

Jesus walked toward the American who jumped back and exclaimed, *'Don't touch me, I'm drawin' disability.'*

Wearing a tie

A bloke goes into a nightclub with his shirt open at the collar and is stopped by the bouncer who tells him he has to wear a tie to get in. So the bloke goes out to his car and gets a set of jumper cables out of the boot. He ties the cables around his neck, sand manages to fashion a fairly acceptable looking knot and lets the ends dangle free.

He goes back to the nightclub. The bouncer suspiciously looks him over for a few moments and then says, *'Well, okay, I guess you can come in. Just don't start anything.'*

Professions:

Two guys and a girl were sitting at a bar talking about their professions. One guy says, *'I'm a yuppie - ya know - Young, Urban, Professional'*

The second guy says, *'I'm a dink - ya know - Double Income No Kids.'*

They ask the woman, *'What are you?'*

She replies, *'I'm a wife - ya know - Wash, Iron, Fornicate, Etc.'*

Wrong Bar

A man, who is obviously very drunk, stumbles into a bar and asks for a drink.

'Sorry,' the bartender said, *'but you look like you've already had too much.'*

Fuming, the drunk walked out the front door, but after a few moments, returns through a side *door.*

'Can I have a pint,' he asks.

'Sorry, but you can't drink here.'

The drunk leaves and a few minutes later comes back in through the back door. *'Can I please have a pint?'* he asks.

'That's enough,' the bartender screams, *'I told you, no drinks!'*

The drunk looks at the bartender closely and replies, *'Darn, how many bars do you work at?'*

Boy's Night Out

A man's wife was complaining to their friends about her husband spending all his free time at the pub. They suggested she tag along with him one night, which she did.

When they got there, he said: *'What'll you have?'*

'The same as you,' she replied.

So he ordered a couple of Jack Daniels and threw his down in one shot. His wife watched in amazement, then took a sip from her glass. She immediately spat it out. *'Yuck, that's terrible!'* she stuttered. *'How you can drink this stuff!'*

'Well, there you go,' the husband said. *'And you think I'm out here enjoying myself every night!'*

The olives

McFadden walked into a bar and ordered martini after martini – each time removing the olives and placing them in a jar.

When the jar was filled with olives and the drinks consumed, the Irishman started to leave.

'Excuse me,' said a customer, who was puzzled over what McFadden had done. *'What was that all about?'*

'Nothing.' answered the Irishman, *'My wife just sent me out for a jar of olives.'*

CHAPTER 11

HIGH TECHNOLOGY

How to handle telemarketers:

The phone rang as I was sitting down to my evening meal and as I answered it I was greeted with *'Is this Karl Brummer.'* Not sounding anything like my name, I asked who is calling.

The telemarketer said he was with The Rubber Band Powered Freezer Company or something like that. Then I asked her if she knew Karl personally and why was she calling this number.

I then said off to the side, *'Get some pictures of the body at various angles and the blood smears.'* I then turned back to the phone and advised the caller that she had entered a murder scene and must stay on the line because we had already traced this call and she would be receiving a summons to testify in this murder case.

I questioned the caller at great length as to her name, address, phone number at home, at work, whom she worked for, how she knew the dead guy and could she prove where she had been about one hour before she made this call.

The telemarketer was getting very concerned and her answers were given in a shaky voice. I then told her we had located her position and the police were entering the building to take her into custody, at that point I heard the phone fall and the scurrying of her running away.

My wife asked me as I returned to our table why I had tears streaming down my face and so help me, I couldn't tell her for about fifteen minutes. My meal was cold, but it was the best meal in a long, long time.

Here are other examples of how to deal with telemarketers:

1. If they start out with, *'How are you today?'* say, *'Why do you want to know?'* Alternatively, you can tell them, *'I'm so glad you asked, because no one these days seems to care and I have all these problems; my arthritis is acting up, my ingrown toenail hurts, my car won't start.'* When they try to sell you anything, just keep talking about your problems.
2. If they want to lend you money, tell them you just filed for bankruptcy and you could sure use some money.

3. If they say they're John Doe from XYZ Company, ask them to spell their name. Then ask them to spell the company name. Then ask them where it is located. Continue asking personal questions or questions about their company for as long as necessary.
4. This works great if you are male: Telemarketer: *'Hi, my name is Judy and I'm with XYZ Company ...'* You: (Wait for a second) and with a real husky voice ask, *'What are you wearing?'*
5. The telemarketer identifies herself as 'Judy.' Cry out in surprise, *'Judy! Is that you? Oh my God! Judy, how have you been?'* Hopefully this will give Judy a few brief moments of terror as she tries to figure out where she could know you.
6. Say, *'No,'* over and over. Be sure to vary the sound of each one and keep a rhythmic tempo, even as they are trying to speak. This is most fun if you can do it until they hang up.
7. If a healthcare service calls trying to get you to sign up for a Family and Friends plan, reply in as sinister a voice as you can, *'I don't have any family or friends. Would you be my friend?'*
8. If a rug cleaning company calls, respond, *'Can you get blood out? Goat blood? How about human blood?'*
9. After the telemarketers gives their spiel, ask them to marry you. When they get all flustered, tell them that you could not just give your credit card to complete strangers.
10. Tell the telemarketer that you work for the same company (they often can't sell to their fellow employees).
11. Answer the phone. As soon as you realise it's a telemarketer, set down the receiver and shout or scream, *'Oh my God!!!'* and then hang up.
12. Tell the telemarketer you are busy at the moment and ask them if they will give you their home phone number, you will call them back. When the telemarketer explains that they cannot give out their home number, you say, *'I guess you don't want anyone bothering you at home, right?'* The telemarketer will agree and you say, *'Now you know how I feel!'* Then hang up.
13. Ask them to repeat everything they say, several times.
14. Tell them it's dinnertime, but ask if they would please hold. Put them on your speakerphone while you continue to eat at

your leisure. Smack your food loudly and continue with your dinner conversation or watch TV.
15. Tell the telemarketer you are on 'home incarceration' and ask if they could bring you some beer.
16. Tell the telemarketer, *'Okay, I will listen to you. But I should probably warn you, I'm not wearing any clothes.'*
17. Insist that the caller is really your buddy Leon, playing a joke. *'Come on Leon, cut it out! Seriously, Leon, how's your mom?'*
18. Tell them you are hard of hearing and that they need to speak up ... louder ... louder!
19. Tell them to talk very slowly, because you want to write down every word.

Lucille:

One of my friends works in the customer service call centre of a national pager company. He deals with the usual complaints regarding poor pager operation, as well as the occasional crank caller demanding to be paged less often, more often or by more interesting people.

The best call came from a man who repeatedly complained that 'Lucille' was paging him. He was instructed that he would have to call her and tell her to stop paging him.

'She don't never leave no number, so I can't call her back,' he said.

After three such calls, someone thought to ask how he knew it was Lucille if she didn't leave a number.

'She leaves her name,' was the reply.

After establishing that the customer had a numeric-only pager, the light bulb came on. *'How does she spell her name?'* the service rep asked.

'l-o-w c-e-l-l'

Computer trouble!

I was having trouble with my computer ... So I called David, the 11 year old next door whose bedroom looks like Mission Control and asked him to come over.

David clicked a couple of buttons and solved the problem. As he was walking away, I called after him, *'So, what was wrong?'*

He replied, *'It was an ID ten T error.'*

I didn't want to appear stupid, but nonetheless inquired, *'An, ID ten T error? What's that? In case I need to fix it again.'*

David grinned. 'Haven't you ever heard of an ID ten T error before?'

'No,' I replied.

'Write it down,' he said, *'and I think you'll figure it out.'*

So I wrote down: I D 1 0 T

I used to like the little sh*t.

Aussie High Technology:
- Log on - make the barbie hotter.
- Log off - Don't add any more wood.
- Monitor - Keep an eye on the barbie.
- Floppy disc - what you get from trying to carry too much firewood.
- Window - what to shut when it's cold outside.
- Screen - what to shut in the mosquito season.
- Byte - what the mosquitoes do.
- Bit - what the mosquitoes did.
- Mega bite - what Townsville mosquitoes do.
- Chip - a bar snack.
- Micro chip - what's left in the bag after you eat the chips.
- Modem - what you did to the grass.
- Dot matrix - Old Dan's wife.
- Laptop - where the cat sleeps.
- Software - the plastic knives and forks they give you at the Red Rooster.
- Hardware - the real stainless steel cutlery.
- Mouse - what eats the grain in the shed.
- Mainframe - what holds the shed up.
- Web - what a spider makes.
- Web site - the shed or under the veranda.
- Cursor - someone who swears.
- Search engine - what you do when the ute won't go.
- Upgrade - steep hill.
- Server - the person at the hotel who brings your lunch.
- Mail server - the bloke who works for the post office.
- User - the neighbour who keeps borrowing your stuff.
- Network - when you have to repair your fishing net.
- Internet - complicated fish net repair method.

- Netscape - when a fish manoeuvres out of reach.
- Online - when you get the laundry hung out on the washing line.
- Off line - when the clothes pegs let go and the washing falls on the ground.

Hard Day

The businessman dragged himself home and barely made it to his chair before he dropped into it exhausted. His sympathetic wife was right there with a tall, cool drink and a comforting word.

'My, you look tired,' she said. *'You must have had a hard day today. What happened to make you so exhausted?'*

'It was terrible,' her husband said. *'The computer broke down and all of us had to do our own thinking.'*

American High Technology:

- Backup - What you do when you run across a skunk in the woods.
- Bar Code - Them's the fight'n rules down at the local tavern.
- Bug - The reason you give for calling in sick.
- Byte - What your pit bull dun to cousin Jethro.
- Cache - Needed when you run out of food stamps.
- Chip - Pasture muffins that you try not to step in.
- Crash - when you go to Junior's party uninvited.
- Digital - The art of counting on your fingers.
- Diskette - Female Disco dancer.
- Fax - what you lie about to the IRS.
- Hacker - Uncle Leroy after thirty-two years of smoking.
- Hardcopy - Picture looked at when selecting tattoos.
- Internet - Where cafeteria workers put their hair.
- Keyboard - Where you hang the keys to the John Deer Tractor.
- Mac - Big Bubba's favourite fast food.
- Megahertz - How your head feels after seventeen beers.
- Modem - What ya did when the grass and weeds got too tall.
- Mouse pad - Where Mickey and Minnie live.
- Network - Scoop'n up a big fish before it breaks the line.
- Online - Where to stay when taking the sobriety test.
- Rom - Where the Pope lives.
- Screen - Helps keep the skeeters off the porch.
- Serial Port - A red wine you drink with breakfast.

- Superconductor - Amtrak's Employee of the year.
- Terminal - Time to call the undertaker.

The Sailor

A man, who was previously a sailor, was very aware that ships are addressed as 'she' and 'her.' He often wondered in what gender computers should be addressed. To answer the question, he set up two groups of computer experts. The first was composed of women and the second, of men. Each group was asked to recommend whether computers should be referred to in the feminine or the masculine gender. They were asked to give four reasons for their recommendations. The group of women reported that the computers should be referred to in the masculine gender because:

1. In order to get their attention, you have to turn them on.
2. They have a lot of data, but are still clueless.
3. They are supposed to help you solve problems, but half the time they are the problem.
4. As soon as you commit to one, you realise that, if you had waited a little longer you could have had a better model.

The men, on the other hand, concluded that computers should be referred to in the feminine gender because:

1. No one but the Creator understands their internal logic.
2. The native language they use to communicate with other computers is incomprehensible to everyone else.
3. Even your smallest mistakes are stored in long-term memory for later retrieval.
4. As soon as you make a commitment to one, you find yourself spending half your paycheque on accessories for it.

Technical Help:

Jonathan asked for technical help. His problem is as follows:
Last year I upgraded Girlfriend 1.0 to Wife 1.0 and noticed that the new program began unexpected child processing that took up a lot of space and valuable resources. No mention of this phenomenon was included in the product brochure. In addition, Wife 1.0 installs itself into all other programs and launches during system initiation where it monitors all other system activity. Applications such as Poker night 10.3 and Beer bash 2.5 no longer run, crashing the system whenever selected. I cannot seem to purge wife 1.0 from my system. I am thinking about

going back to Girlfriend 1.0, but uninstall does not work on this program. Can you help me?

Dear Jonathan:
This is a very common problem men complain about, but is mostly due to a primary misconception. Many people upgrade from Girlfriend 1.0 to Wife 1.0 with the idea that Wife 1.0 is merely a 'Utilities and entertainment' program.

Wife 1.0 is an operating system and is designed by its creator to run everything. Do not try to uninstall, delete or purge the program from the system once installed. Trying to uninstall Wife 1.0 is not designed to do this. Some have tried to install Girlfriend 2.0 or Wife 2.0, but end up with more problems than the original system. Look in your manual under Warnings-Alimony/Child Support. Others have tried to run Girlfriend 1.0 in the background, while Wife 1.0 is running. Eventually Wife 1.0 detects Girlfriend 1.0 and a system conflict occurs. This can lead to a non-recoverable system crash. Some users have tried to download similar products such as 'Fling' and 'Onenitestand,' but often their systems become infected with a virus. I recommend you keep Wife 1.0 and just deal with the situation.

Having Wife 1.0 installed myself; I might also suggest you read the entire section regarding 'General Protection Faults (GPFs).' You must assume all responsibility for faults and problems that might occur. The best course of action will be to push apologise button then reset the button as soon as lockup occurs. System will run smoothly as long as you take the blame for all GPFs. Wife 1.0 is a great program but is very high maintenance.

Suggestions for improved operation of Wife 1.0:
- Monthly use utilities such as TLC and FTD.
- Frequently use Communicator 5.0.
Cheers,
Tech Assistant I

(From Tech Assistant II)

Dear Jonathan,
I agree that Wife 1.0 (or any version thereof) is most definitely an operating system with significant requirements for system resources. However, when properly installed, this OS has some highly useful functions and utilities. Because of the deceptively consistent packaging, Wife 1.0 does indeed appear to be merely a simple upgrade from Girlfriend 1.0. Do not be deceived by this

marketing tactic! It is in fact an entirely new system that will overwrite everything else, as will be evident when you actually run the installation program 'Wedding.'

The biggest flaw in that system is the lack of a command-line interface. You are stuck with a graphical interface that can be very difficult to use and interpret. There is also a notable lack of the standard communication protocol.

In contrast, the Girlfriend 1.0 program is merely an entertainment package that usually includes some attractive wallpapers and screensavers that you can dress up your system with to impress your friends. There are a few useful utilities. It has a very rudimentary command-line interface, which usually does not work well and it often produces the opposite result of what you were expecting. The command syntax and system messages change meaning at random (this bug was apparently not fixed in the Wife upgrade and the command-line interface is disabled completely). Occasionally the Girlfriend program will malfunction and begin acting like a full-blown Wife OS by consuming additional system resources and attempting to spawn child processes. This usually means that it is either time to purge the application or purchase a full upgrade. You cannot get a bootleg copy of the upgrade and the user license is very expensive.

Regardless of whichever package we wish to install (Girlfriend or Wife) we must ensure that it is compatible with our critical and necessary applications. This is very difficult, because both packages frequently advertise complete compatibility with all applications. It isn't until you try to use the application that you find terrible conflicts with subprograms running in the Wife OS. For example, the popular Sportscar 1.0 game will almost certainly conflict with wife's NewKitchen 2.5 utility. Of course you were not even aware that NewKitchen was running until you attempted to play SportsCar.

Now of course there are some applications that you will have to sacrifice. For example, StripClub 8.0 is completely incompatible with virtually any version of Girlfriend or Wife. You can try to run it during off-hours when Wife is occupied with other processing, but inevitably this hidden process will be detected by the operating system.

For me, my favourite application is Sailing 3.4. I can't tolerate any conflicts with this application. I had to uninstall Wife 1.0 because of pervasive conflicts with this and practically every other application I was running. As I mentioned earlier, uninstalling this operating system is an extremely difficult and expensive process. You need to hire outside consultants who charge very high rates to assist with this procedure. And even when removed from the system, it will continue to consume system resources, particularly if you permitted it to spawn child processes. It will also conflict with any future versions of Girlfriend or Wife that you attempt to install.

I'm presently working on a complete set of Compatibility and Benchmark tests to validate the performance of the Girlfriend, Fiancée and Wife suite. Keep tuned.
Cheers, Tech Assistant II

Computer Symbols:

We all know those cute little computer symbols called 'emoticons' where we have 'assicons.'

- (_!_) gives you: a regular ass
- (__!__) gives you: a fat ass
- (!) gives you: a tight ass
- (_*_) gives you: a sore ass
- {_!_} gives you: a swishy ass
- (_o_) gives you: an ass that's been around
- (_x_) gives you: kiss my ass
- (_X_) gives you: leave my ass alone
- (_zzz_) gives you: a tired ass
- (_^^_) gives you: a bubble ass
- (_o^^o_) gives you: a wise ass
- (_$_) gives you: money coming out of his ass
- (_?_) gives you: dumb ass

Signs of the Time:

Here are 12 signs that your life is changing:

1. You tried to enter your password on your microwave.
2. You now think of three espressos as 'getting wasted.'
3. You haven't played solitaire with a real deck of cards for years.
4. You have a list of 15 phone numbers to reach your family of 3.
5. You e-mail your son in his room to tell him that dinner is ready and he e-mails you back, *'What's for dinner?'*
6. Your daughter sells Girl Scout cookies via her web site.

7. You pull up in your own driveway and use your cell phone to see if anyone is home.
8. You didn't give your valentine a card this year, but you posted one for your e-mail buddies via a web page.
9. You chat several times a day with a stranger from South Africa, but haven't spoken to your next-door neighbour yet this year.
10. Your daughter just bought a DVD of all the records your college roommate used to play.
11. You checked the ingredients on a can of chicken noodle soup to see if it contained Echinacea.
12. Your grandmother clogs up your e-mail In Box, asking you to send her a JPEG file of your newborn so she can create a screen saver.

A neutron goes into a bar and asks the bartender, *'How much for a beer?'* The bartender replies, *'For you, no charge.'*

The Unstoppable Virus

I thought you would want to know about this e-mail virus. Even the most advanced programs from Norton or McAfee cannot take care of this one. It appears to affect those who were born prior to 1965. The symptoms are:

1. Causes you to send the same e-mail twice. (Done that!)
2. Causes you to send a blank e-mail! (That too!)
3. Causes you to send e-mail to the wrong person. (Yep!)
4. Causes you to send it back to the person who sent it to you. (Who me?)
5. Causes you to forget to attach the attachment. (Well darn!)
6. Causes you to hit 'send' before you've finished. (Oh no - not again!)
7. Causes you to hit 'delete' instead of 'send.' (And I just hate that!)
8. Causes you to hit 'send' when you should 'delete.' (Oh No!)
9. It is called the 'C-nile virus.'

CHAPTER 12

RULES FOR LIVING

Babies

The first lesson a new baby learns at his/her Mother's knee these days is to be careful of the pantyhose.

Today's father is really disappointed when his wife gives birth to a daughter instead of a son. He is hoping for someone to help him with the cooking and housework.

The new mother was having problems changing the baby's diaper. The father, looking on, says, *'No problem. Where's the manual that came with the kid?'*

Definitions for Parents:

- Amnesia: Condition that enables a woman who has gone through labour to have sex again.
- Impregnable: A woman whose memory of labour is still vivid.
- Dumbwaiter: One who asks if the kids would care to order desert.
- Family Planning: The art of spacing your children the proper distance apart to keep you on the brink of financial disaster.
- Feedback: The inevitable result when your baby doesn't appreciate strained carrots.
- Full name: What you call your child when you're angry with him/her.
- Grandparents: The people who think your children are wonderful even though they're sure you're not raising them right.
- Hearsay: What toddlers do when anyone mutters a dirty word.
- Independent: How we want our children to be as long as they do everything we say.
- *'Ow:'* The first word spoken by children with older siblings.
- Pre-natal: When your life was still somewhat your own.
- Puddle: A small body of water that draws other small bodies wearing dry shoes into it.
- Show-off: A child who is more talented than yours.
- Verbal: Able to whine in words.

- Whodunit: None of the kids that live in your home.
- Sterilise: What you do to your first baby's pacifier by boiling it and to your last baby's pacifier, by blowing on it.
- Top bunk: Where you should never put a child wearing Superman jammies.
- One-minute warning: When the baby's face turns red and she begins to make those familiar grunting noises.

Sixteen Year-old Logic

The following questions and answers were collated from British University entrance tests given to sixteen year-old students. Don't laugh too hard - one of them could become Prime Minister one day! You have to admit, some are very creative).

Q: Name the four seasons.
A: Salt, pepper, mustard and vinegar.

Q: Explain one of the processes by which water can be made safe to drink.
A: Flirtation makes water safe to drink because it removes large pollutants like grit, sand, dead sheep and canoeists.

Q: How is dew formed?
A: The sun shines down on the leaves and makes them perspire.

Q: What is a planet?
A: A body of earth surrounded by sky.

Q: What causes the tides in the ocean?
A: The tides are a fight between the Earth and the Moon. All water tends to flow toward the moon because there is no water on the moon and nature abhors a vacuum. I forgot where the sun joins in this fight.

Q: In a democratic society, how important are elections?
A: Very important. Sex can only happen when a male gets and election.

Q: What are steroids?
A: Things for keeping carpets on the stairs.

Q: What happens to your body as you age?
A: When you get old, so do your bowels and you get Intercontinental.

Q: What happens to a boy when he reaches puberty?

A: He says good-bye to his boyhood and looks forward to adultery.

Q: Name a major disease associated with cigarettes.
A: Premature death.

Q: How can you delay milk turning sour?
A: Keep it in the cow.

Q: How are the main parts of the body categorised? (e.g. abdomen).
A: The body consisted into three parts - the brainium, the borax and the abdominal cavity. The brainium contains the brain, the borax contains heart and lungs and the abdominal cavity contains the five bowels, A, E, I, O and U. (I love this one!)

Q: What is a Fibula?
A: A small lie.

Q: What does 'varicose' mean?
A: Nearby.

Q: What is the most common form of birth control?
A: Most people prevent contraption by wearing a condominium.

Q: Give the meaning of the term 'Caesarean Section.'
A: The caesarean section is a district in Rome.

Q: What is a seizure?
A: A Roman emperor.

Q: What is a terminal illness?
A: When you are sick at the airport.

Q: Give an example of a fungus. What is a characteristic feature?
A: Mushrooms. They always grow in damp places and so they look like umbrellas.

Q: What does the word 'benign' mean?
A: Benign is what you will be after you be eight.

Q: What is a turbine?
A: Something an Arab wears on his head.

And just think, one day our social security payments will depend on these kids!

Philosophy of life

One day I had lunch with some friends. Jim, a short, balding golfer type about 80 years old, came along with them - all in all - a pleasant bunch.

When the menus were presented, we ordered salads, sandwiches and soups except for Jim who said, *'Ice cream, please. Two scoops, chocolate.'*

I wasn't sure my ears heard right and the others were aghast.

'Along with heated apple pie,' Jim added, completely unabashed.

We tried to act quite nonchalant, as if people did this all the time. And when our orders were brought out, I didn't enjoy mine.

I couldn't take my eyes off Jim as his pie a-la-mode went down. The other guys couldn't believe it. They ate their lunches silently and grinned. The next time I went out to eat, I called and invited Jim. I lunched on white meat tuna. He ordered a parfait. I smiled. He asked if he amused me.

I answered, *'Yes, you do, but also you confuse me. How come you order rich desserts, while I feel I must be sensible?'*

He laughed and said *'I'm tasting all that is possible. I try to eat the food I need and do the things I should, but life's so short, my friend, I hate missing out on something good. This year I realised how old I was.'* (He grinned) *'I haven't been this old before ... so, before I die, I've got to try those things that for years I had ignored. I haven't smelled all the flowers yet. There are too many trout streams I haven't fished. There's more fudge sundaes to wolf down and kites to be flown overhead. There are too many golf courses I haven't played. I've not laughed at all the jokes. I've missed a lot of sporting events and potato chips and hot dogs. I want to wade again in water and feel ocean spray on my face. I want to sit in a country church once more and thank God for His grace.*

'I want peanut butter every day spread on my morning toast. I want un-timed long distance calls to the folks I love the most. I haven't cried at all the movies yet or walked in the morning rain. I need to feel wind on my face. I want to be in love again.

'So, if I choose to have dessert, instead of having dinner, then should I die before night fall, I'd say I died a winner,

because I missed out on nothing. I filled my heart's desire. I had that final chocolate mousse before my life expired ...'

With that, I called the waitress over. *'I've changed my mind,'* I said. *'I want what he is having, only add some more whipped cream!'*

A Few Facts:

- Coca-Cola was originally green.
- Every day, more money is printed for Monopoly than the US Treasury.
- It is possible to lead a cow upstairs, but not downstairs.
- Smartest dogs: 1) Scottish Border Collie; 2) Poodle; 3) Golden Retriever. Dumbest: Afghan Hound.
- Men can read smaller print than women; women can hear better.
- Amount American Airlines saved by eliminating one olive from each salad served first class: $40,000.
- City with the most Rolls Royce's per capita: Hong Kong.
- State with the highest percentage of people who walk to work: Alaska.
- Barbie's measurements if she were life size: 39-23-33.
- Percentage of Americans who have visited Disneyland / Disney World: 70%.
- Iceland consumes more Coca-Cola per capita than any other nation.
- The reason firehouses have circular stairways if from the days of yore when horses pulled the engines. The horses were stabled on the ground floor and figured out how to walk up straight staircases.
- Each king in a deck of playing cards represents a great king from history. Spades - King David; Clubs - Alexander the Great; Hearts – Charlemagne; and Diamonds - Julius Caesar.
- If a statue in the park of a person on a horse has both front legs in the air, the person died in battle. If the horse has one front leg in the air, the person died as a result of wounds received in battle. If the horse has all four legs on the ground - the person died of natural causes.
- Clans of long ago that wanted to get rid of their unwanted people without killing them would burn their houses down - hence the expression *'to get fired.'*

- Hershey's Kisses are called that because the machine that makes them looks like it's kissing the conveyor belt.
- The longest recorded flight of a chicken is thirteen seconds.
- The name Jeep came from the abbreviation used in the army for the 'General Purpose' Vehicle, G.P.
- Nutmeg is extremely poisonous if injected intravenously.
- The first toilet ever filmed on television was on *'Leave It To Beaver.'*
- The nursery rhyme *'Ring Around the Rosey'* is a rhyme about the plague. Infected people with the plague would get red circular sores *('Ring around the Rosey ...')* those sores would smell very badly so common folks would put flowers on their bodies somewhere (inconspicuously) so that it would cover the smell of sores *('...a pocket full of posies ...')*. People who died from the plague would be burned so as to reduce the possible spread of the disease *('ashes, ashes, we all fall down!')*

Nicknames:

If Gloria, Suzanne, Debra and Michelle go out for lunch, they will call each other - Gloria, Suzanne, Debra and Michelle. But if Mike, Phil, Rob and Jack go out for a brewsky, they will affectionately refer to each other as Fat Boy, Godzilla, Peanut-Head and Useless.

Eating Out:

When the cheque comes, Mike, Phil, Rob and Jack will each throw in a $20 bill, even though the total is only $22.50. None of them will have anything smaller and none will actually admit they want change back. When the girls get their cheque; out come the pocket calculators.

Bathrooms:

A man has five items in his bathroom - a toothbrush, shaving cream, razor, a bar of soap and a towel from the Holiday Inn. The average number of items in the typical woman's bathroom is 437. A man would not be able to identify most of these items.

Money:

A man will pay $2 for a $1 item he wants. A woman will pay $1 for a $2 item she doesn't want.

Arguments:

A woman has the last word in any argument. Anything a man says after that is the beginning of a new argument.

Note to married men: Forget your mistakes. There's no sense in two people remembering the same things.

Groceries:

A woman makes a list of things she needs and then goes out to the store and buys these things. A man waits till the only items left in his fridge are a funny green colour. Then he goes grocery shopping. He buys everything that looks good. By the time a man reaches the checkout counter, his cart is packed tighter than the Clampett's car on Beverly Hillbillies. Of course, this will not stop him from going to the 10-items-or-less lane.

Shoes:

When preparing for work, a woman will put on a Mondi wool suit and then slip on Reebok sneakers. She will carry her dress shoes in a plastic bag from Saks. When a woman gets to work, she will put on her dress shoes. Five minutes later, she will kick them off because her feet are under the desk. A man will wear the same pair of shoes all week.

Cats:

Women love cats. Men say they love cats, but when women aren't looking men kick cats.

Future:

A woman worries about the future until she gets a husband. A man never worries about the future until he gets a wife.

Natural:

Men wake up as good-looking as they went to bed. Women somehow deteriorate during the night.

Dressing Up:

A woman will dress up to: go shopping, water the plants, empty the garbage, answer the phone, read a book, get the mail. A man will dress up for: weddings, funerals.

Laundry:

Women do laundry every couple of days. A man will wear every article of clothing he owns, before he will do his laundry. When he is finally out of clothes, he will wear a dirty sweatshirt inside out, rent a U-Haul and take his mountain of clothes to the Laundromat. Men always expect to meet beautiful women at the Laundromat.

Offspring:

Ah, children. A woman knows all about her children. She knows about dentist appointments and soccer games and romances and best friends and favourite foods and secret fears and hopes and dreams. A man is vaguely aware of some short people living in his house and never raises his hands to his kids - it leaves his groin unprotected.

CHAPTER 13

ON THE SERIOUS SIDE

Time management

One day, an expert in time management was speaking to a group of business students and, to drive home a point, used an illustration those students will never forget.

As he stood in front of the group of high-powered overachievers he said, *'Okay, time for a quiz,'* and he pulled out a large, wide-mouth jar and set it on the table in front of him. He also produced about a dozen fist-sized rocks and carefully placed them, one at a time, into the jar. When the jar was filled to the top and no more rocks would fit inside, he asked, *'Is this jar full?'*

'Yes' everyone in the class yelled.

The time management expert replied, *'Really?'* He then reached under the table and pulled out a bucket of gravel. He dumped some gravel in and shook the jar causing pieces of gravel to work themselves down into the spaces between the big rocks. He then asked the group once more, *'Is the jar full?'*

By this time the class was on to him. *'Probably not,'* one of them answered.

'Good!' he replied. He reached under the table and brought out a bucket of sand. He started dumping the sand in the jar and it went into all of the spaces left between the rocks and gravel. Once more, he asked the question, *'Is this jar full?'*

'No?!' the class shouted.

Once again he said, *'Good.'* Then he grabbed a pitcher of water and began to pour it in until the jar was filled to the brim. Then he looked at the class and asked, *'What is the point of this illustration?'*

One eager beaver raised his hand and said, *'The point is, no matter how full your schedule is, if you try really hard you can always fit some more things in it!'*

'No,' the speaker replied, *'That's not the point. The truth this illustration teaches us is: if you don't put the big rocks in first, you'll never get them in at all. What are the 'big rocks' in your life - time with your loved ones, your faith, your education,*

your dreams, a worthy cause, teaching or mentoring others? Remember to put these big rocks in first or you'll never get them in at all.'

'So tonight or in the morning when you're reflecting on this short story, ask yourself this question: What are the 'big rocks' in my life? Then put those into your jar first.'

Saving for a Special Occasion:

My brother-in-law opened the bottom drawer of my sister's bureau and lifted out a tissue-wrapped package. 'This,' he said, 'is not a slip. This is lingerie.'

He discarded the tissue and handed me the slip. It was exquisite; silk, handmade and trimmed with a cobweb of lace. The price tag with the astronomical figure on it was still attached. 'Jan bought this the first time we went to New York, at least eight or nine years ago. She never wore it. She was saving it for a special occasion. Well, I guess this is that occasion.'

He took the slip from me and put it on the bed with the other clothes we were taking to the mortician. His hands lingered on the soft material for a moment and then he slammed the drawer shut and turned to me. 'Don't ever save anything for a special occasion. Every day you're alive is a special occasion.'

I remembered those words through the funeral and the days that followed when I helped him and my niece attend to all the sad chores that follow an unexpected death.

I thought about them on the plane returning home from the town where my sister's family lives. I thought about all the things that she hadn't seen or heard or done. I thought about the things that she had done without realising that they were special. I'm still thinking about his words and they've changed my life.

I'm reading more and dusting less. I'm sitting on the deck and admiring the view without fussing about the weeds in the garden. I'm spending more time with my family and friends and less time in committee meetings. Whenever possible, life should be a pattern of experience to savour, not endure. I'm trying to recognise these moments now and cherish them. I'm not 'saving' anything. We use our good china and crystal for every special event such as losing a pound, getting the sink unstopped, the first camellia in blossom.

I wear my good blazer to the market if I like it. My theory is if I look prosperous, I can shell out $28.49 for one small bag of groceries without wincing. I'm not saving my good perfume for special parties; clerks in hardware stores and tellers in banks have noses that function as well as my party-going friends.

'Someday' and *'one of these days'* are losing their grip on my vocabulary. If it's worth seeing or hearing or doing, I want to see and hear and do it now.

I'm not sure what my sister wouldn't have done had she known that she wouldn't be here for the tomorrow we all take for granted. I think she would have called family members and a few close friends. She might have called a few former friends to apologise and mend fences or past squabbles. I like to think she would have gone out for Chinese dinner, her favourite food. I'm guessing - I'll never know.

It's those little things left undone that would make me angry if I knew that my hours were limited. Angry because I put off seeing good friends whom I was going to get in touch with - someday. Angry because I hadn't written certain letters that I intended to write - one of these days. Angry and sorry that I didn't tell my husband and daughter often enough how much I truly love them. I'm trying very hard not to put off, hold back or save anything that would add laughter and lustre to our lives. And every morning when I open my eyes, I tell myself that it is special. Every day, every minute, every breath truly is a gift to take advantage of.

Three Yellow Roses:

I walked into the grocery store not particularly interested in buying groceries. I wasn't hungry. The pain of losing my husband of thirty-seven years was still too raw. And this grocery store held so many sweet memories. Rudy often came with me and almost every time he'd pretend to go off and look for something special. I knew what he was going to do.

I'd always spot him walking down the aisle with the three yellow roses in his hands. Rudy knew I loved yellow roses. With a heart filled with grief, I only wanted to buy my few items and leave, but even grocery shopping was different since Rudy had passed on. Shopping for one took time, a little more thought than it had for two. Standing by the meat, I searched for the perfect small steak and remembered how Rudy had loved his steak.

Suddenly a woman came beside me. She was blonde, slim and lovely in a soft green pantsuit. I watched as she picked up a pack of T-bone steaks, dropped them in her basket, hesitated and then put them back. She turned to go and once again reached for the pack of steaks. She saw me watching her and she smiled. *'My husband loves T-bones, but honestly, at these prices, I don't know.'* I swallowed the emotion down my throat and met her pale blue eyes.

'My husband passed away eight days ago,' I told her. Glancing at the package in her hands, I fought to control the tremble in my voice. *'Buy him the steaks. And cherish every moment you're together.'*

She shook her head and I saw the emotion in her eyes as she placed the package in her basket and wheeled it away. I turned and pushed my cart across the length of the store to the dairy products. There I stood; trying to decide which size milk I should buy. A litre, I finally decide and moved on to the ice cream section near the front of the store. If nothing else, I could always fix myself an ice cream cone.

I placed the ice cream in my cart and looked down the aisle toward the front. I saw first the green suit and then recognised the pretty lady coming towards me. In her arms she carried a package. On her face was the brightest smile I had ever seen. I would swear a soft halo encircled her blonde hair as she kept walking towards me, her eyes holding mine. As she came closer, I saw what she held and tears began misting in my eyes. *'These are for you,'* she said and placed three beautiful long-stemmed yellow roses in my arms. *'When you go through the line, they will know these are paid for.'*

She leaned over and placed a gentle kiss on my cheek, then smiled again. I wanted to tell her what she'd done, what the roses meant, but still unable to speak, I watched as she walked away as tears clouded my vision. I looked down at the beautiful roses nestled in the green tissue wrapping and found it almost unreal. How did she know? Suddenly the answer seemed so clear. I wasn't alone. *'Oh Rudy. You haven't forgotten me, have you?'* I whispered, with tears in my eyes. He was still with me and she was his angel.

The Whale

If you read the front page story of the SF Chronicle, you would have read about a female humpback whale that had become entangled in a spider web of crab traps and lines. She was weighted down by hundreds of pounds of traps that caused her to struggle to stay afloat. She also had hundreds of yards of line rope wrapped around her body, her tail, her torso and a line tugging in her mouth.

A fisherman spotted her just east of the Golden Gate and radioed an environmental group for help. Within a few hours, the rescue team arrived and determined that she was so bad off, the only way to save her was to dive in and untangle her - a very dangerous proposition. One slap of her tail could kill a rescuer. They worked for hours with curved knives and eventually freed her.

When she was free, the divers say she swam in what seemed like joyous circles. She then came back to each and every diver, one at a time and nudged them, pushed gently around - she thanked them. Some said it was the most incredibly beautiful experience of their lives. The man who cut the rope out of her mouth says her eye was following him the whole time and he will never be the same.

Lifestyles:

An American businessman was at a pier in a small coastal Mexican village when a small boat with just one fisherman docked. Inside the small boat were several large yellow-fin tuna. The American complimented the Mexican on the quality of his fish and asked how long it took to catch them.

The Mexican replied, *'Only a little while.'*

The American then asked, *'Why don't you stay out longer and catch more fish?'*

The Mexican said, *'I have enough to support my family's immediate needs.'*

The American then asked, *'How do you spend the rest of your time?'*

The Mexican fisherman said, *'I sleep late, fish a little, play with my children, take siesta with my wife Maria, stroll into the village each evening where I sip wine and play guitar with my amigos. I have a full and busy life senor.'*

The American scoffed, *'I am a Harvard MBA and could help you. You could spend more time fishing and, with the proceeds, buy a bigger boat. With the proceeds from the bigger boat, you could buy several boats. Eventually you would have a fleet of fishing boats. Instead of selling your catch to a middleman, you would sell directly to the processor, eventually opening your own cannery. You would control the product, processing and distribution.*

'You would need to leave this small coastal fishing village and move to Mexico City, then Los Angeles and eventually New York City where you will run your expanding enterprise.'

The Mexican fisherman asked, *'But senor, how long will this all take?'*

To which the American replied, *'Fifteen to twenty years.'*

'But what then, senor?' asked the Mexican.

The American laughed and said, *'That's the best part! When the time is right, you could sell your company stock to the public. You'll become very rich, you will make millions!'*

'Millions, senor?' replied the Mexican. *'Then what?'*

The American said, *'Then you could retire. Move to a small coastal fishing village where you would sleep late, fish a little, play with your kids, take a siesta with your wife, stroll to the village in the evenings where you could sip wine and play your guitar with your amigos.'*

Who Packs Your Parachute?

Charles Plumb was a US Navy jet pilot in Vietnam. After 75 combat missions, his plane was destroyed by a surface-to-air missile. Plumb ejected and parachuted into enemy hands. He was captured and spent six years in a communist Vietnamese prison. He survived the ordeal and then conducted lectures on lessons learned from that experience.

One day, when Plumb and his wife were sitting in a restaurant, a man at another table came up and said, *'You're Plumb! You flew jet fighters in Vietnam from the aircraft carrier Kitty Hawk. You were shot down!'*

'How in the world did you know that?' asked Plumb.

'I packed your parachute,' the man replied. Plumb gasped in surprise and gratitude. The man pumped his hand and said, *'I guess it worked!'*

Plumb assured him, *'It sure did. If your chute hadn't worked, I wouldn't be here today.'*

Plumb couldn't sleep that night, thinking about that man.

Plumb said, *'I kept wondering what he had looked like in a Navy uniform: a white hat; a bib in the back; and bell-bottom trousers. I wonder how many times I might have seen him and not even said 'Good morning, how are you?' or anything because, you see, I was a fighter pilot and he was just a sailor.'*

Plumb thought of the many hours the sailor had spent at a long wooden table in the bowels of the ship, carefully weaving the shrouds and folding the silks of each chute, holding in his hands each time the fate of someone he didn't know.

Then Plumb asked his audience, *'Who's packing your parachute?'*

Everyone has someone who provides what s/he needs to make it through the day. He also pointed out that he needed many kinds of parachutes when his plane was shot down over enemy territory - he needed his physical parachute, his mental parachute, his emotional parachute and his spiritual parachute. He called on all these supports before reaching safety.

Sometimes in the daily challenges that life gives us, we miss what is really important. We may fail to say, *'Hello, please or thank you,'* congratulate someone on something wonderful that has happened to them, give a compliment or just do something nice for no reason. As you go through this week, this month, this year, recognise people who pack your parachutes.

I am sending you this as my way of thanking you for your part in packing my parachute. And I hope you will send it on to those who have helped pack yours! Sometimes, we wonder why friends keep forwarding jokes to us without writing a word. Maybe this could explain it: When you are very busy, but still want to keep in touch, guess what you do – you forward jokes. And to let you know that you are still remembered, you are still important, you are still loved, you are still cared for, guess what you get? A forwarded joke.

So my friend, next time when you get a joke, don't think that you've been sent just another forwarded joke, but that you've been thought of today and your friend on the other end of your computer wanted to send you a smile, just helping you pack your parachute. Have a great day and stay in touch ...

CONCLUSION

I hope you have enjoyed these jokes enough to obtain Volumes 1, 3 and 4 that cover humour in different areas, so there's no repetition.

Laughter is an essential ingredient to everyday living. If you haven't had a laugh today - you're depriving yourself enjoyment in life. Bring them out when you're having a bad day - that's what I do. You'll find that things just get better.

If you wish to read books on more serious topics, please go to our web page: www.dealingwithdifficultpeople.info

www.ingramcontent.com/pod-product-compliance
Lightning Source LLC
LaVergne TN
LVHW051550070426
835507LV00021B/2504